Dear Faranke & Jorg

This is the second [...]
from me (about me!) [...] your enjoyment. It's
such a great pleasure meeting you and being able to
call good new friends in our new chapter of
life here in Abbotsford. This helps to explain
me a little more to help understand...
When I find a copy of my FIRST novel,
"Maynard & Zeke - A
Liar's Playground"
- I'll get that to you,
too!

Akimbo:

A SOW BUG'S LIFE
(AUTOBIOGRAPHY-
...or part of one)...

Meanwhile.. enjoy
this au gratin
gratis!

by
Kim Parrish

hugs, KP.
Kim Parrish
xoxo.

Strategic Book Publishing and Rights Co.

Strategic Book Publishing and Rights Co.
12620 FM 1960, Suite A4-507
Houston, TX 77065
www.sbpra.com

For information about special discounts for bulk purchases, please
contact Strategic Book Publishing and Rights Co. Special Sales, at
bookorder@sbpra.net.

ISBN: 978-1-62857-430-2

O.K., I'm a cross-dresser-what can I tell you? Me, 'Mr. P', in my scarecrow get-up at school for Hallowe'en!

During my teaching stint which spanned just over a decade at Sir Winston Churchill Secondary in Vancouver,B.C.-all through the 90's until June, 2003

> "In the activities of the school, English language holds a position different from that of any other subject. Not only is it the ordinary medium used for communication, but it is also the chief instrument needed to gain knowledge in other subjects and is, moreover, an important object of study in and for itself." (–excerpted from an 1930's Ontario Teachers' manual on Composition and Spelling.)A Gift for the Obvious (and that would be what we call a 'sentence fragment'-(' Clap that man in irons!')"

"Tom's letter to Kim!"

Ah.. Yes..! I was quite fortunate as a Churchill 'bulldog'-blessed really! - to have taught so many wonderful young people, and to have worked shoulder-to-shoulder with so many other remarkable people, master- administrators and fellow- teachers alike, who mentored me and fanned the flames of my younger and still eager teaching fires, several

1

of whom would become dear friends as well as colleagues. I had many days in all honesty, while driving to work in the mornings when I would feel... just so lucky to be a teacher, and lucky to have the job and school I did. One of those mentioned was Tom ("Hendy") Henderson who –sadly- is no longer with us. Tom was a fellow- English teacher, a musician (trumpet) cold beer-drinker, rugger, a writing soul-mate and confidante. Truly an extraordinary man, he was a genuine treasure, some of a 'renaissance- man', really, who forever changed the lives of all who knew him and made them all the better for it. Well, over our years together at Churchill, we shared more than a few cold beer... and much of our writing with each other-he writing dark, twisted murder-horror/fiction novels(a la 'Silence of the Lambs'); he had both his playful and dark side, like us all...) and me, writing humorous fiction and poetry...The two of us and a third teaching comrade, R. B, loosely formed a triumvirate that would eventually be dubbed "The Winston Trio" whereby the three of us would stand front- and- centre at staff parties, holidays and retirement send-offs and present some light verse in honour of the occasion; Our little group performed often over all those years of my tenure there and, I daresay, gained some notoriety... After reading two, perhaps three of his neck-hair tingling manuscripts - he adored Thomas Harris(as do I) and that writer's lambs' trilogy with' Clarice Starling & Hannibal Lector'- for giving us one of the richest, most intelligent, charming serial killers in history. \Well, it was then, only after reading his excellent, darker manuscripts when I found the courage to share my first novel with him(written twenty-five years earlier as a young man, before I even embarked on my teaching career...)- this, after he had read and was already familiar with some of my poetry('that's what friends are for..' -thanx ,W. H.); I only rediscovered his rather glowing letter of encouragement, again, in 2009 when my wife and I re-settled in Vancouver from China for three years, and it was enough to edge me to the publishing "start" line! When he first returned my manuscript to me way back in those original days, he included the following handwritten note which I have re-copied , here:

 ### March 18, 1999—Tom's Letter

"-(K. P.) -O.K., Kim- enough fooling around,! It's time to submit your stuff, 'Boyo', and I mean everything- poetry and prose. Maynard and Zeke is good stuff! I groaned, I winced, I chuckled, and I laughed out loud. Even got a forbidden tingle now and then, too. It's got everything-originality(!) Timing. Word-play. Romance? Freeze- Frames! And ,then, there are those pterodactyls! After also reading my own self-mocking reviews (some of which I know will come back to haunt me!), included at the end of that first book, he continued on with some review of his own,

I heartily second the reviews from Some People Mag., The Toronto Starr, the Toronto Sun-Up, and the Provence. Here's one more to add to the list..:"

"There was a stout wordsmith, Kim Parrish,
Whose view of the world was (?) nightmarish?
He wrote about Maynard, the geek,
And his pet zebra named , Zeke,
In a word, it's superb-one to cherish!
Yours (Un) Truly (kiddin'), Tom…
P.S.. ("Can you set me up with the Chicago cheer-
    leader..?")

* * *

When my wife and I moved back to Canada in 2009(and lived for 3 years in Vancouver!), it was only after finding and re-reading Tom's letter, hidden away in one of several of my own poetry booklets for safe-keeping that I felt his swift kick in the ass and finally determined to hunt for an agent and publisher for my manuscript which had sat dormant for some time. After another two years or so of publishing in's and out's(two steps forward, one back sort of thing..), my 'dormant –thing' erupted and spilled out onto the mountainside(or printed page, if you will..) when first released in May, 2012- perhaps "bubbled up" is more accurate; it remains a slow-moving yet still-steaming lava-puddle six months later. So, to him, now, I doff my hat and raise a glass of ice-cold beer! 'Cheers, 'Boyo!' "Boyo" was a nickname of a police detective in one of his novels (And, yes, used by Sean Connery's Malloy character in the good film, The Untouchables ..and found in a host of others.including,The Titanic. It is simply an archaic Irish term meaning 'buddy' or friend! Whereas 'Hendy' had been his long-serving nickname among his 'Loma rugby circle' of which I was not a part, the two of us had taken to calling each other simply 'Boyo' in those last few years before I moved away to China. He was a theatrical presence of a man- a real showman- and anyone who knew him knew how painstaking he was in his preparations for most everything, "Rehearse! Rehearse! Rehearse!" he would always say with that irascible, impish grin of his, and also, growling on the side to me, "Always leave them.. wanting more...- and he did exactly that to us all- by leaving us all so early, Boyo!

-DEDICATION-

To my dear mother for telling me repeatedly, about words I did not understand or know how to spell, "Go and look it up, dear!" which always led to at least half-hour sessions with the dictionary for me("Don't you be obdurate or impertinent with me, young man!")" Ob-what?Im-per-what?)- and to my father for pressing me, his once fourteen year old, grunting, stuttering Neanderthal-son to use words to describe stuff, resolve disputes, and explain things in the world, - and for forcing me to try something other than "hamburger, French fries and Coke" while dining out at restaurants -and,finally,for unlocking and revealing to me- my own powers of observation-with his constant dinner-table badgering, "What did you SEE, today? What do you mean, 'nothing?-no People(!), no Cars(!), no Buildings(?*?*!)."And…then to my always adorable, adoring wife, Hairong, who brought me back from the brink, breathed new life and love into me with every step, making this dream-endeavor even possible. And then to her gracious family for shaping her in every way possible! And then! And then..,and then… we sound like we're in grade 5!

In my academic "career" - brief as it was ..(4 yr.B. A.+2 yr.teacher's certificate) - I spent much of my time with poetry and poetics-my first love- and came to admire many different poets and writers through the ages. Alexander Pope was one of them- and one of his signature pieces for me was his "Essay on Man" So- also by way of introduction- I have included my light 'homage' to Mr. Pope, here at the start…soon. As his forebear the Bard, was- Pope was a master of "iambic pentameter" (light stress followed by stressed syllable-'heroic verse' if rhymed, and-'blank verse' if not) and then the even..better: "Discordia-Concors"- the striking of balance/harmony of opposing thoughts and phrases- often within the same line; much more cerebral. 'Methinks,' a rather perfect and ultimate evolution for Shakespeare's"bittersweet"sassy oxymorons and double entendres! All in an effort to condense, juxtapose and harmonize our and life's inherent, myriad contrasts in as little space as possible: five poetic meters- ten syllables to be exact! The world in a grain of sand….

 "Kindling-Preface"

We've known for quite some time now that it was not lead in the aqueducts at all that killed off the Romans. When I look around me at the world today- all around us, everywhere we look the world seems to be oozing with sex and sexuality;

yes that 'good ole Internet' and its slow-witted, slower-moving cousin, conventional/traditional media- that keeps promoting the web to have many of us drooling bipeds moping around, heads bowed in idle-worship over e-gadgets and saying important-sounding, next-to-meaningless stuff like:

"We're connected more today than ever before" -true- but to just what(?); just the other day, in fact, the Internet had a feature in which some of the world's best-known women were judged simply according to how "hot" their bods, arms or legs were; I'm curious then who is reading that stuff(besides me), or even wants to(now I know)?.The original vivisectionists?Butchers?I suppose, in a manner of speaking…. Not long ago(2011/12), in that ah-so honorable place called Japan where some men regularly scan porn-mags on the subway on their way to work in the mornings-after kissing their wives goodbye- all with young uniformed schoolgirls standing next to them, they have just recently opened the first of several new "Cuddle-Shops" (now, with a toehold in our Pacific NorthWest!) where men can get naked and lay next to a naked young woman(she perhaps in a sheer nightie.?.) in bed for gentle touching, ONLY, of course! Here then, are we not pushing the boundaries of taste, morality and ethics further to the periphery once more yet trying to keep an honorable (?), smiling happy- face on as we do…. Do I hear 'one thrust-only shops' or' Leave-the-Touching-To Us shops' on the way? Sorry-we already have those, don't we?Gee-Whillickers, Caligula would have enjoyed our times, I think…. Come on; go tell it on the mountain!

In an age when our latest modern-day princess(Ms. Kate) is often solely judged in media circles on how snugly her latest designer-gown clings to and reveals her admired rear end! Funny, too- how both men and women admire that same Gluteus Maximus-obviously, of course, for very different reasons. That's deep! So deep, shall we say 'skin-deep' (?) O.K. fine, so what if the woman has a cute behind-let's move along shall we? I appreciate a nice rump as much as the next guy as you'll see soon enough, but let's not dwell on it, shall we? Leave that to me. As a society, Let's not fix-ate. No, I'll do that later, thanks. I'm just saying comments or accusations toward me of being sexually-obsessed from earlier writing(one talking penis!) just seem so specious and out of left field..Soo what? Ludicrous! Who isn't? Just look around you!?? Advertising? T.V.?Music?

Whereas a generation ago, the rage among some women was breast implantation thanks to one of our Canadian own and her twins' mountainous success on the Hollywood land-scape. All of that 3-D"cutting and pasting" was intended to give a fuller, rounder, more 'voluptuous' look to things. To-day, however, thanks to an empire built mostly on an ass from what I can tell, "bum augmentation" has been the next popular wave of desperate self-mutilation to sweep New York and L.A... to try to please the always leering eyes of the Patriarchy(of which my parents made me a part,yes..) -while all still searching for those fuller, rounder, more 'Ru-benesque' lines more common and preferred in the 1950's and 60's(before 'Twiggy') or, luv-a-duck, the Middle Ages..! Always "buxom wenches" serving in those taverns, ever notice? The 'Boobers' Franchise would have thrived back then. One of the most-watched and thus sought after air times in our still most powerful medium of the day, tele-vision (sorry, Internet..)might as well be renamed "Who's-Zooming- Who? "and its even worse clones/ spin-off's!-or incestuous progeny. That is, of course, with their focus clearly on the rich &famous, well-bodied crowd of Holly-wood- celebrity for which we have such a morbid and absurd envy-fascination!Ah , the power! Ah the bodies!,Ah, the money! Ah, the power! Ah the bodies!- Amen. Thou shalt worship no other god but me...? A beautiful, young woman from South America auctions off her virginity for about half a million dollars in the virtual-world! The would-be-groom, of course, was first enticed by pictures of her frolicking on the beach in her thong bikini-surprise, surprise! Rumor has it one of America's biggest movie-stars, Rocky, mar-ried one of his wives after she sent him a full frontal nude

picture…? Dental Floss for the bum ('Gluteal Floss'?); you
might as well just draw it on. Such visual creatures, we men!
This, at least if we choose to believe what we read about in
Cyberspace. and many do, including even me at times, it's
true!(One eye for curiosity, one eye for ridicule!) And the
'King of Swing', himself, is there once again proving his
virility at eighty-? by marrying yet another young, pretty,
'Middle Ages'- buxom wench again; I can only hope he's
got it right this time-or else he will need a good- talking-
to from 'Dr. Phil' about that sexual- addiction thing(like to
see that 'pre-nup', huh?) What pretty, taught-skinned young
actress will be the next Mrs. Cruise? Excuse my diction, but
how titillating!(I just can't wait!) What do wealthy, powerful men want, you ask? Like most men, probably, they want
to be 'reconciled' as much as possible! Simply put? They
don't want the sexual- love stage to end. Shock! And, with
facing too many head-ache filled nights in the marriage bed,
many simply turn their attention elsewhere to more recep-
tive less encumbered possibilities… From actors to politicians to golfers, it's all just the same old song and dance.
What does a prowling penis look for? Who are the potential
candidates for Mrs. C.? Who really cares? Is that on par with
discovering life on Mars? On a child's first steps? Melting
icecaps? Two free cocktails at Bananabee's with each en-
trée purchased?IS IT WORTHY OF OUR ATTENTION?
And who among us are making those decisions every day on
what is net or trad-newsworthy? Our media will be only too
happy to pre-screen them, do background-checks(religious
and otherwise..) and find bikini photos of said starlets- So,
there then, with all that in mind, I have included my parody
of Mr. Pope's "Essay on Man" with a certain, modern-per-
sonal touch, "je ne sais quoi."

(The Original): Know then thyself
Presume not God to scan.
The proper study of mankind is man
Placed on this isthmus of a middle state,

A being darkly wise, and rudely great:
Great lord off all things, yet a prey to all;
Sole judge of truth, in endless error hurl'd;
The glory, jest and riddle of the world!"
(Pope:1688-1744)

"Essay on Dan" (mine!)

Come, now, look around you- at this forest of thighs,
Everywhere are buttocks, bosoms, and those... teasing bedroom eyes;
When offered an apple now, Dan just shakes his head in disgust-
That small, one-track mind of his is thinking-if at all- just of lust.
Back in that day, they started with maybe- twins, Cain and Abel,
And before very long, Jealousy and Murder, too, came to the table:
Cain and Abel, even then- strong symbols for the pairing
Some pair, those two, destined to symbolize the evil and the good,
And so brother killed brother-knew he shouldn't, but did... 'cause he could

* * *

Many writers try to do it
So then, why shouldn't I?
And to those who say, "Phooey!", I can only say, "Fie!"

* * *

They all attempt, at least at one point, in their way
To do the 'big' "examine mankind" with dismay:
Ascent, First through his Rise,

Then, of course, through the Fall
And a snake, and a modest apple
Are to blame for it all? (Snicker, Snicker...)
True, some apples have worms,
But a slithering snake?
Both of us, man and woman, from Eden, he'd banish;
Yes, both he'd forsake. (; Yeah, right!' From the back rows!)
He gave us each a larynx,
Some brains and a voice…
And aside from the ruffage, (sic)
He gave us both choice.
So, when 'Dan' glanced around some, there was only one other near
And, standing behind her, he had a good look at the rear.
Strange beauty in all directions, yes- this is what he would see
Yet surrounded by that, his first thought.was.. .to pee
If the Garden had books, he could sit down and read one,
But, instead, he looked for a third party, and thought already a threesome?
Once more back to Eve then, to hell with the apple –and the ruffage can wait;
His nose was now shouting, 'she's ready to mate!'
And, so, first conceived, our long line of bipeds,
With big brains, of course-and those handy, opposable thumbs
Some of us had tiny, while others… huge bums
With Dan, he can't help it- dithering idiot, ignorant man
When his member grows enormous he'll show it off-if he can;

* * *

Clearly, too early for that key lesson:' Pride goeth before falls!'

No, for him the world started with penis, and ended at balls…

Like the NBA 'trash-talker' who shouts "Look at ME, I'm so good!

I got this big 'pecker' –Me? Biggest trunk in the woods!(People actually scream and applaud, here!)

(Footnote/sidebar: 'pecker and wood' in some realms are both slang terms for erection!)

He jumps around court, pointing finger at self,

Maybe, too, slamming his hand into his chest

To say the others are worthless,(In that 'silverback' way so common among mountain gorillas..)

Right here, it's me only, yes ,I 'm the 'Alpha'- I am the best!

- So, our Dan he's no different, not enough hugs as a child-

The father neglected him blah, blah,blah, so….he grew desperate and wild!

Oh-so cerebral that when he's engorged, he can't talk….

No, not until he takes that thing for a walk!

His brain it stops working,

Eyes glaze over like a troll

And stay that way, I'm afraid

Until donkey's had his soft-meadow stroll…

Dan, in his infantile-wisdom

Yes. We, His 'Infinite Jest'-

Saw fit-even then… to point fingers-

Straight at Eve's double-breast

Poor Eve, that poor woman.., just sharing is all

Yet that feminine instinct.., if you will

Brought about our Great Fall!?(Chorus: Hiss..Yeah, Right!!? Can you spell misogyny?)

I mean really, though:

To examine "mankind"?

 For our purpose –to know the who's,

The how's, the why's, or the glory…?

Is- apple aside- kind of empty,

A 'fruitless' exercise, sorry..

* * *

But for a spell , let us rethink that poor, slighted apple;
After all, it does represent our whole, bloody planet;
Some say it was innocent, and the real 'perp', pomegran-
ate!
So now, I say to you all…,
In weak defence of the apple, and so, too, then of Eve
Our world, it keeps spinning,
No matter what you believe-(Peanut Gallery: Preachy,
but O.K.)
In Jupiter, in Jove, in Zeus, God, or in Allah
In truth, really-just all one and the same:
Good Stratford Bill said it best with, "a rose, still a rose
by….." (You finish that one..):
Peace and Tolerance, Respect and Love,
To help each other abide; After all, we're all merely flot-
sam
On this one global tide!
To forgive, and to share; she's shown "Dan" all along;
Yet still so misjudged, for a questionable wrong;
No, it wasn't HER pride that got in our way;
She taught men," I love you," even stepped out of his way
But he didn't listen- muttonhead- from his place,
at the back of the class:
A real slow-learner, that Dan-
in truth, a DUMBASS!
Don't believe me?-
Ask any woman-she's bound to agree,
When she sees her thoughtful lover there, glued to T.V.
When the dishes are dirty;the lawn, too, needs a cut..?
The children are restless,Another day dawns-oh! talk
about your "rut!"

* * *

-So, guilt and persecution could begin there and then, there and then

But Eve would forgive- another of Womyn's weak charms
And not only begat lots more men,
But would shield them from harms;
Ah- the pains, and the labour-all this she endured
And innumerable sacrifices,
of this, we are sure!

* * *

Oh- the many faces then of Eve, and of Dan...

Yet, still the poor woman, Eve, given weaker voice, don't you see?

It grew stronger- albeit slightly- when we turned on our T.V.(not sports!)

Even then, first as 'sidekicks', as "Weather or Bat-Girl" if you please, but- suddenly... then-

'Wonder woman' bounded in to please we visual men.

In a suit that was sprayed on, to stick to her lovely taught skin,

To conceal nooks and crannies some, and hold everything in.

There she was in her glory, no belts, buckles, garter-

The beautiful, the voluptuous, the all- Linda Carter (!);

Then along came "She-Ra," , too, of course, though- she was merely cartoon

Yet even animated, she could make young men swoon

And, there, in the backrooms, the movers, makers and shakers.

"Quelle surprise!" , mostly men, putting forth their designs

Who with a short break, then brought forth "Xena" to show off her lines

Yes, the "warrior-princess" leapt in, and she, too, in fine form -

To redefine beauty yet again, in the lovely Lucy Lawless,

Wearing "S&M" black leather,
to show girls everywhere, chested-women could go bra-
less
(So Many Before...)
Try as he might, valiant, yes- but needless to say, all in
vain...
Poor Milton tried his best at Man's nature, to try to ex-
plain
Houseman,(A.E.), with 'Terrence', just laughed at his
turn
While poor Dante's 'Inferno' continued to burn
'The Shropshire Lad', said more or less- I misquote:
Forget about it there, don't worry- Have a beer, it's a
Joke!
Let's not waste our time here, trying to answer" the Great
Why?"
We live some, love and laugh some, then in our time, we
die.
Relax- and enjoy, just use all of our senses
And whilst here, don't burn any bridges, and try to mend
broken fences...
Your first love must be "self", before "other" appears..
(Caritas/Cupiditas)
To walk path as companion
And allay those "lone" fears. (Fall, Beijing, 2012)

 "PRE-BLURB- Introduction"

Just for the record, let it be known that after a heart- attack
/angioplasty in 2000, I have had a stroke also (2006,while
stationed in Beijing)which left me paralyzed on the left side
of my body. Most all of "Sow-Bug" was written post-stroke.
Whoopdeedo..,so? (So, I have that to fall back on...)
But this now, what follows here- is not a story about stroke,
or surviving it, or even living with paralysis. It happened,

yes; it is part of my story, but it is hardly the whole story - in fact far from it.

The current politically- correct jargon to describe me is as a "stroke survivor", not a 'stroke victim or sufferer'-though, admittedly, having lost the function of my left arm and leg and much of my former physical ability has led to much suffering- of the mental and emotional anguish- variety. Call it what you will; like so much of what it has done to me, forever changing my life- I continue to try and not dwell on the negative aspects…and there are a few, I give you that. My paralysis is there waiting for me every morning when I rise. From the best I can tell about myself, however, my poor brain is still in reasonably good working order(?) and I think in much the same way I did before. No miracle improvement there, darn it! Of course, the 'what' I think about is different. Has to be, if every time I go to the john in a new place, it's a bit of an ordeal/challenge. When I don't always think of how delightful the meal might be at the new restaurant, but if its washrooms are-first and foremost- wheelchair accessible! That does add a new twist to things, a new dampening dimension alright.

Now- by way of foreword, I have chosen instead to enlist/draft the aid of several dear friends to jot down a few thoughts about me, and these I will sprinkle throughout as "midewords"in order to fill in more of my "writer's profile." for those curious-minded of readers? Of course you did get the book to begin with, so it's probably safe to assume there was some curiosity, right?… The first that follows here is by Gary. Gary was one of those aforementioned master-teachers and, in his case, administrators (Principal) who helped guide me and mentor me early on down my teaching path. and along the way became a treasured friend. None of them, by the way, were paid to do this writing- favour for me-although after reading a few, I've started to think they should be:

"Kim Parrish, teacher, story-teller, old-school friend, the kind of guy whose hand you shake and you instantly know that no more need be done. No legal contracts. No questioning of motives. No doubts. None. Kim is one of those larger-than-life figures whose passion for literature is exceeded only by his passion for life. His writing betrays the twinkle in his eyes and the joy he has for those little things in our petty day-to-day existences that we typically overlook: the irony inherent in each and every one of us, the idiosyncracies that others see so clearly in us and that we, ourselves are blind to. He is a fascinating man with a gift for the written word. I am honoured to know Kim as a teacher, story-teller and friend; I know you will be as well."

—Mr. Gary Little, former Principal, Associate Superintendent at Vancouver School Board(ret.),&now acting Education-consultant, musician, and friend!

A Sow bug's Life (A*k*imbo..)

-CLUSTER ONE-

Maybe hard to believe- now:

> "Kim Parrish is not a man who promotes himself. He is truly an unassuming, gentle man. Only gradually does one come to know Mr. Parrish-and only over time does one realize just how good he is." -excerpted from an early letter of reference by Vice-Principal, C.E-T., 1990. Got a minute?? Obviously, something happened along the way to turn me into a shameless self-promoter!

 "Dark Mornings"

It wasn't as if I woke up one day, early in the dark morning to find myself sitting on the edge of a strange bed in northeastern China. Well, It was and it wasn't, No, not really; it had been thirteen years –and no, I'm not superstitious- in the making when I pulled the plug on my way-too-comfortable life as a high school English teacher in Vancouver, B.C. did some research, and accepted a teaching position at a Sino-Canadian international high school in mainland China's northeast region (known there as "DongBei"..). It was an abrupt turn-about alright, leaving a school and staff which I had called home for those first fifteen fulltime years of my teaching career. I knew I had to change my life in a big way, if it was to continue much longer, and there was still so much of the world I had not seen. No, there were no terminal illnesses-just a lifestyle that was increasingly dictated to by my addictive personality, namely alcohol and tobacco. I had travelled extensively, by that time, both in Europe and the

Mediterranean, including even a brief sojourn in Morocco -but had not, before then, set foot upon the Asian continent. So, indeed, there would be a few of those dark, early mornings with me sitting on the edge of a bed there in China, shaking my head and wondering where my life was and where I was? At least I knew where I was from! And that's where we're going to now…

"I shot an arrow into the air, It fell to earth, I knew not where…." (H.W. Longfellow)

Just to let you know.., I will flip-flop back and forth in time and place often because that's what our brains do (we are so not linear), I think, and maybe I'm lazy (?), but suffice it to say, because of my fellow Canadian teaching staff and my predominantly Chinese students that first year on Chinese soil was a simply marvelous experience! It did not end quite so well, however, when I was unceremoniously informed that due to philosophical/ideological differences (I was a bit of a "no" man I suppose, he says with a perverse, pyrrhic pride. ha!), I would not be asked to return for another, cushy, fun-filled second year at the same school. Aside from a bumbling Canadian-born and trained administration and a Gordon Gecko ("Greed is Good!") ownership mentality, my colleagues and charges were terrific and a lot of fun to be around! It was full circle, I guess, from being held up as model-teacher and moderately hard- marker to colleagues one day in the ever-beleaguered English Department of which I was 'appointed' head early on(by October) for having some of the lowest(and more realistic) grades in the grade 12 level to then being informed come April/ May that I would not be asked to return for year two-after declining to support an out-of-the-blue, silly administrative edict (of which most of them were)which called for increased weekly teaching hours –and more focused teaching to the exam(a practice highly valued here), contrary to our agreed- upon contract, and all this only done in a typically last- minute effort to improve exam grades and placate restless parents,(the latter being an all-too common tail-wagging the dog exercise here in China-read: 'cultural gap';if you're paying for it , you should be allowed to tell the surgeon where to make the incisions!); maybe the owner's secretary had a brainstorm about it one day -who knows? I would not partake in their hair-brained plans and was curtly told, 'if I would not abide by their rules, I would not be welcomed back.' Hmm..Tough one! But don't be putting me up on a pedestal just yet…

 ## "A Fork in the Road"

So, after a few months of 'camping' inside with all of my worldly possessions boxed- up and ready to move some-where else for a new job –all at a dear friend and family's apartment, I was able to latch onto a lucrative and fantas-tic job in Beijing as English Trainer for a huge computer-maker, and my life would never be the same (aaghh! –for the second time!). My boxes were all trucked down there to the capital (in one of those ubiquitous, blue, open-air flat-bed trucks so common during the Cultural Revolution!)) and dropped off in what would soon become my new three-bed-room, two bathroom/ one Jacuzzi apartment-home on a fifth floor walk-up in a Beijing suburb, about an hour from down-town and the 'Forbidden City'! The former -friend who first helped me land this new job and apartment was there with the landlords as I lay down on the bed for a trial-it was a child's bed we immediately discovered- and my feet hung sadly over the end (I have sad feet.!.), but they would have the issue resolved with a newer, bigger bed in a matter of hours! There had been too much tobacco and alcohol in my life for some time by that point and those addictions made their way to Beijing with me along with my smaller, accu-mulated material chain. It wasn't long before I had settled into yet another rather comfortable lifestyle (do you see a pattern here? I do.), again, in which I was fueling all of my addictions and now more cheaply than ever before. No pity, no applause. Maybe I'm just a restless spirit who doesn't like being too comfortable in any place I exist? However, I'm kind of a 'nester', too –go figure! Just a 'mess of contradictions', emphasis on the 'mess'. Of course, I believe some and have promoted just that sort of thinking around myself, too in a weird' defensive strategy', I suppose, leaving many people uncertain just how to take me: Neanderthal beer-swilling linebacker(?) or gentle-spoken tender-hearted writer..? If I had my way, I'd leave 'em all guessing…and be some of each! Just a polysemical guy, I guess.

 "A Red-Hot Coat Hanger"

I do have a distinct memory of a double-dream that occurred, I'm sure, when I was still comatose(if possible..), a state in which I lasted for almost a week, apparently, after suffering my stroke. I had lapsed into that state after the stroke and the life-saving brain surgery which accompanied it to relieve the massive pressure building up inside my head. Part One: It was as if someone with a red-hot coat hanger had plunged it directly into my brain; I could feel it melting the surrounding area. I swear I could hear the sizzle of burning neurons. Hell, on occasion, I could even SMELL that burning part of me…not pleasant at all! It was as real to me, as the smell of fresh muffins being removed from the oven just nowhere near as appealing…. PART Two: Accompanying that high-definition dream, or' body-memory' or whatever you wish to call it, was another equally clear dream(or second installment?) in which my partner magically delivered healthy beautiful twins –by herself- in a cavernous, underground skating rink-arena(I've often wondered why they don't build those things sub-surface; It was so vivid to me-all brightly lit with glowing hot-neon pinks and greens and oranges. She walked out toward the rink from the recessed dressing room area and then gingerly set the newborn pair down, the two of them beautifully swaddled in their cozy white blankets, on a mound of snow next to the rink's boards. One of the first things I remember having uttered, or so I thought, was the word "two." The thinking was that at least some of me was ready to parent two children (I know you can't be in that 'halfway!'). The other word which soon followed, my wife later explained was "both". Or, more accurately, what followed was my version of it which came out as "bo"-at the time having a feeding tube in my nose, and an inhalator in my mouth. In those early days my face was a busy place. There was some relief in hearing me say, or attempt to say those words as it seemed to indicate to me and those around me that I had retained some or perhaps even all of my speech..? I'm happy to report that five years later I retained enough of my speech through it all to prompt some people in my current circle to even urge me, on occasion, to "shut up!" My first understandable physiotherapist back on English-speaking, Canadian soil (this, five years after the stroke occurred), a pretty, young Chinese-Canadian mom would simply give one command as I chatted away incessantly from between the parallel walking- bars (and this, much more recently! Nodding and smiling, she would simply tell me in gentle yet unmistakable terms, "Shut up and walk, Kim." I thank her for indulging me now and then.

My next substantial exchange, of course, after blurting out "Bo" would drive home the reality of the life-altering, soul-bending experience of having survived a stroke and the brain surgery it necessitated. The first would leave me paralyzed on my left side (both arm and leg), and the latter (apparently?) would leave me an epileptic, prone to occasional seizures which rather plagued us for three years. Happily, it's going on almost four years, now, since my last seizure! My then live-in girlfriend (common-law, if you will...) looked me in the face and quietly explained I would not be able to move my leg, or my arm, as it turned out. I have since often reflected on that moment and the courage it must have taken for her, this young thirty-something woman, to tell me that with some dreams of the future 'us' doubtlessly crumbling before her eyes. Fortitude.

"No Laughing Matter"

"Whaddya mean? What?" I choked out, having heard her words very clearly- and secretly, desperately, already at that instant trying in my prone position on the bed now to move any part of my arm or leg to prove her wrong so we could start giggling at the bad joke. But it was no joke at all, just bad. The realization set in but because I was in a grungy, always dimly-lit Chinese hospital, no one had adequate-enough English to fully explain to me what was happening. All of that was left to my girlfriend- my angel- and now my adorable, adoring wife. Oh yeah, by the way- I will pile that kind of stuff on at every chance-so you've been fore-warned. Stuff? The overly-sentimental, sickly-sweet, sappy stuff that is... Some of us like it, some of us don't-I hope you do(?); Some of us used to like watching "Three's Company", too!(not me, unless Chrissie was wearing her bikini!) There's no really explaining taste is there? Some still enjoy watching live-police shows and the hilarity of backyard pool- parties with Dads being hit in the groin with a volley ball, too! Not one thing that has always fascinated me (And that's one of them!), always drawn my curiosity close is life's continuous and myriad dualities, the omnipresent jux-taposition of contrasts, life's dichotomies and the knife-edge which so often only separates many of them: love/hate; old/new; serenity/chaos; spiritual/physical; politicians/soldiers or Diplomacy/War(bear with me)-as Maximus tells Quintus in Gladiator, 'Dirt is much easier to wash away than blood-and then one of my all-time favorites- laughter and tears, occasionally together for a reason or- happiness-anger/sad-ness- which are more intertwined than many of us think, I feel. Ever shed happy-tears? It was partly that, and a quasi-debate on the proper pronunciation of little-used colours with an American acquaintance once at a teachers' confer-ence in the States that prompted the following verse from me years back

"I Only Wear Mauve"

When the sun sets so sadly in that cinnamon sky,
When there's so much to live for, and you just want to
    die;
When the shy coyote howls beneath a pale, summer
    moon,
When time moves infant-slowly, and slowly's too soon,
When miles of tufted sagebrush is a welcoming sight,
When there's twin rainbows shimmering in the late after-
    noon light,
When the wind blows steady through that Ponderosa
    Pine;
When I know you're his, but still wish you were mine,
When magenta-edged clouds shift lazily through the
    night,
And burnt sienna grasses sway in darkened fright,
When where you are coming from ..is all just where you
    are..,
When the sunset saddens you- but then there's a shooting
    star!
When spruce and cedar scents waft through those ever-
    green woods,
When you're filled with "I can't's, and maybe some
    "should's;
When the people around you , all start to look the same..,
When the rose is still a rose, but then only in name;
When there's six shades of purple and they all seem to
    fuse,
When there's jazz in your head- but your heart's got the
    blues,
When that smooth adobe red helps paint that cinnamon
    shade,
When the last vestige of sun sets on dusty-green sage;
When the moon's pale face glows , sitting still and high
    in the sky,

When you're laughing so hard, a tear comes to your eye:
Just certain times they surround me, with those dry,
    white-hot truths
-For instance, I only wear mauve,
When the sky is chartreuse. (July 26/98, Montezuma,
    New Mexico-By the way, there was no "you're. no
    other! K.P.)

She was right, of course. Nothing was happening. I was
sending signals to the brain like I had done most of my life, or
so I thought. The realization set in, but again, because I was
in a Chinese hospital, no one had adequate- enough English
to fully or directly explain what had happened or the process
I was then embarking on. All of that was left to my then- girl-
friend-and angel-and now my wife. I have since reflected often on that moment and to the strength and courage it must
have taken her to tell me such news; little could I have imagined the remarkable strength and maturity deep in the heart
of this beautiful young woman. The first of many of my tears
made their way to the external world and clouded my eyes.
"For how long?" I whispered almost breathlessly, already
suspecting the answer but not wanting to hear it verbalized.
Her confirmation came in the shape of a shoulder shrug and a
nod. "They don't know, she said quietly, tears welling in her
eyes also, in response to seeing my own.

 ## " Vertical Fair Game"

Peeing was so quick and easy before, it was almost fun! As
a man, any pole, tree, fire hydrant, fence or wall had been
fair game. Now, of course, accessibility issues dramatically
limit the when and where I can relieve myself in such a fashion…as I continue to learn daily after too much coffee.
    I miss a lot of things, sure. Funny, but I miss skating and
ice- hockey dearly, the smell and feel of the ice and just
the rink itself and, yes, even my old, stupid, smelly hockey
equipment….But, you know, I think I've come to realize it's

more about sitting in that change room and laughing with the other guys as we donned our armor for another week's chapter of the great Canadian ice-joust, once more, in the trenches..

 "40 Days and 40 Nights…"

I did spend the first forty days after my operation in the I.C. U. ward because I had contracted influenza somewhere along the way, a not unusual occurrence for many of us who suffer strokes and undergo the brain surgery that often accompanies them. I remember twenty, perhaps more of us on our beds or cots in this one large greyish-green drab, dreary room It was very hot then(by early summer-that's Beijing!) and they brought in 2-3 stand-up fans to help cool us all down some. In fact, apparently, so I've learned, one in five of us will die due to post-op complications and infections- a staggering number of lives lost each year; Also, from what I gather, most of those will be women! Never being much of a gambler (addictions aside), really, I started to examine those odds more and more and began recognizing my severely limited physical state-and the fact that-even after being clobbered in such a way - I was one of the lucky ones and yet still being blessed with more time on this planet, another kick at the cat so to speak(although I love cats!), more sunrises and- graciously- more time in the company of this beautiful young woman, at the time my girlfriend and now my wife.(You see, even today, I will sometimes call her my 'best girlfriend ever!' I was being given a second chance to maybe take evening strolls with her, to hold her hand and possibly one day walk along the shoreline while gazing into her soulful brown eyes and falling in love with her radiant smile over and over again. Really!

The fact that I was an alien- a Canadian, an outsider, a foreigner, a "lao wai," or "waigoren" helped my cause immeasurably, I think. My normally gracious Chinese hosts (you'd be hard-pressed to find any better hosts the world over!)

raised the bar some. Here, now, with this medical-recovery backdrop of mine, it seemed there was an even greater urgency to impress and give me superior care and attention. Probably can't be good press either, if a foreigner dies on your shift!

After release from the I.C.U., we (I will often speak of myself in the plural, the 'royal we', silly wave...) relocated to a huge, red brick, stroke and head-trauma rehabilitation center in the heart of Beijing where I would stay seven or eight months and begin the physical rehab. in earnest; I would also be awarded a little fuzzy ball for winning the karaoke competition of our ward with my rendering of a fave, "Moon River"! I was as big as three of the young male Chinese doctors-physios who were assigned to me and whose principal job, it seemed, was to pin me belly- down to the low, hard exercise-bed as two others tried to bend my" affected" leg at the knee to touch my foot to my rear end in an effort I imagine to get the knee-joint working some again. Although- it's hardly an action any of us make normally during waking hours in the real world? It hurt terribly, so I struggled like a fiend every time. Most often, two of them would end up sitting on top of me or stretched out over top of my back in a fruitless effort to stop my painful squirming. The pain-any pain at that point they'll tell you is good because it indicates some nerves are still hooked into the system and trying to alert you to danger...Sure. Keep your "no pain- no gain" platitudes to yourself; Go tell it on the mountain!

Of course there was a phase-early on- in which, emotionally, I was angry at the world, God, and mostly myself But after much earlier therapy in my life I had long-since learned about "anger" and its lesser-known twin, "sadness". Anger was simply the knee-jerk response to the much more profound, contemplative sadness that many of us dread facing, and often try to avoid!. You are initially overwhelmed by sadness...at the loss of movement, or the game, or relationship, sure, but more at the immense loss of a former, familiar life-isn't everybody? Like a vacuum, there is suddenly a hollow

part. I just did my best to swallow that anger and try not to
vent it outwardly (though I certainly had my moments!) at
those around me, especially my angelic wife who has so self-
lessly devoted herself to me, hour after hour, day after day.

"Yibu, Yibu" (One Step, One step, or 'One Step at a Time')

Each step there was a labor,
A labor of new-found love beginning to climb-
A puzzle, a puzzling thing,
A mystery…
Of what lay ahead in those
Fragrant mountain sides of yours.
Such a climb.
Each step before me-
And there was your beauty-always,
Always, your smile. Not shrouded at all in fog, and more
    dazzling
Than the hidden sun..
And, I wondered, and I wondered…
Again and again
What of your beauty would open to me.
Then, you took my hand coming down-
And I could see, suddenly, and feel
Whole unexplored vistas opening to me , to us
And I felt more alive.. than ever before.
And all of your innocent beauty, in the nakedness of an
    approaching new winter
And all that you are and all you could become
Was there, your hand in mine, step by step…
Yibu,Yibu, up or down.
I wanted so much to be with you then, and my heart be-
    gan its ache because
I was dazzled, mesmerized by your smile- a mountain,
    too, I want to climb, so

That one day I may touch the pinnacle of your soul and
  perhaps hold more than just your hand in my hand;
  step by step. Yibu, yibu.

(one of my first poems to Miranda;2004-before we
tied the knot; It was an early 'date' where she asked
me to join her in climbing a "hill" which turned out to
be a large, famous mountain in Beijing!) I did wonder for a moment, right then with every step, at her
English proficiency...which is just fine!

Next to air, she was (and remains...) my life-force, the
sparkle in my eyes that greets most mornings and makes me
grateful for every extra day above ground!(Sorry, too bad
if you don't like the 'sappy' stuff!) She helped me better
comprehend Kundera's "The Incredible Lightness of Being"
because my love for her feels boundless (maybe every new
husband feels the same..?) and I do- truly- feel lighter just
being in her presence! Hokey, maybe, but feelings often are;
it is what it is. I should hope all husbands feel the same way-
or do I overly romanticize the practical?

  Was God a vengeful Jehovah (Yahweh) and punishing me
for my childhood transgressions, poor decisions and lifestyle
choices(?): for helping to put a plastic bag full of dog poop
inside a mail box one summer? For being one of five who
ambushed a city bus late one winter night by running out
from our hiding spot in the dark, deep,' Robert Frost woods'
to pepper it with fifteen or so hard-packed snowballs? That
is until the driver stopped, got out and started chasing after us? For helping do the now almost- cliché flaming paper
bag of dog shit on somebody's porch a few times? Not an
urban-legend, by the way! There were a lot of dogs in the
area, I guess. For sneaking a peek between the legs of Natasha Gurnlistadel (yes, that's made up!)only to see butterfly
panties? (the panties are not made up!) For putting our beautiful, loving white Persian cat inside the clothes-dryer one
day and watching his panicked face through the porthole-
like window? Geez, and no, I did NOT turn the dryer on....

really! For making false birth certificates at the library with a friend when we were what (?), fourteen, to better facilitate our underage drinking exploits? For accidentally lighting an overturned car on fire (oops!)? For telling lies to some women for the sake of fornication? Yeah- and I would be the first in history to be guilty of that one, I'm sure…. It's a long queue….

 "Sermons and Catfish!"

Being raised a Protestant (by which I clearly took the meaning too literally.) would eventually for me morph comfortably into its more visible and disagreeable cousin, the lesser-known 'Contrarian'..) Having weekly attended a Presbyterian church when little- as a youngster- I always managed rather easily to rationalize any immoral and occasionally illegal activities I partook of. There were always people doing far worse things somewhere in the world, including my own little neighborhood. Sure, I might have killed dozens of catfish at the local pond by whipping them repeatedly against the road until they fell off the hook because of their 'poisonous stingers', of course; ok, guilty as charged. Uganda, on the other hand, was dealing with Idi Amin taking his small-brained, dictatorial, murderous wrath out on his brethren, in ordering the killing of thousands of sentient beings…, so what were a few dead catfish, after all? As George Carlin so wonderfully proclaimed to the world in his seminal album Class Clown, which I knew by heart! (Remember the 'seven Words'!?) the Catholic boys could do their weekly church visit, confess all their sins-and be given a clean slate.Ah, yes! There's an idea; Ah-those Catholics! We Protestant boys, on the other hand - especially Presbyterians it seemed to me -would have to live with our shame and guilt until we died –and would, even then, burn in the everlasting, guilt-ridden fire pits of 'Ole Horny's Hell' ! Come on, really? For a bag of dog shit? Not possible!

Whenever our minister scanned the pews from the traditionally- elevated pulpit in front of the organ during all those "fire and brimstone" sermons on Sunday mornings, I don't know how, but it always seemed to me that he was directing most of his focus solely at me, and me alone. It was as if he knew exactly what I had been up to with my friends that week. Of course, there was always hope he would not relay that knowledge to God, or… even Santa Claus, for that matter. Only much later would it finally dawn on me that this magic, sensing, divining-rod of his was nothing more than my own guilt, pure and simple! I had stockpiles of the stuff. Enough to go around.

"Clouds and Rain"

When storms hit, it's awful to see
Tornadoes come and knock posts down
And sometimes trees
But when it goes away,
it leaves awful mess that some people don't like and they
    start to cry.
I can't help it because it is stormy weather-
I have to do this and I am –
I'm going away and find a new country and a better
    house.
"Amen", my mother added, at the end.. (Written
Aug 12, 1965(to help some, I was seven).

No, I did not run away from home-we were probably all out of cookies! It's a long way to Tiperary!(or in the making of a writer) At this time, Mom had spent 10 days in hospital for a (partial colonectomy. It was one of many young writing pieces of mine she collected and saved in, of all things, a shoebox for years and she presented this treasure to me in 2001! (two years before she died, and I moved away to China); I will forever remember standing at her hospital bedside back then and crying(but of course), with my father holding my hand in that recovery ward, 'What was happening to my mother?!' Home was neither peaceful nor happy without Mom in those days though Dad always put on his brave face when we visited. He had to model for me, of course.

> J. Michener is quoted as saying, "I love the swirl and swing of words as they tangle with each other and human emotions!."

I concur and for me, the whole writing process consists of two parallel streams, the first being the cognitive- creative generation of thoughts and the second more 'mechanical' side of condensing those thoughts to paper, and then wrestling endlessly with diction, syntax and punctuation. All of that was enthralling to me, not to mention just the feeling of the pen gliding across the page and leaving its ink trail behind! For me, it was a twin process: the cognitive/ephemeral aspect of the ideas themselves and then the mechanical-as I like to describe it, very tangible part of capturing them just-so on paper!

 ### "Ingrates and Toe Jam."

Skip ahead some time now to after our (my wife and me) move back to Canada and our settling into an apartment in S. Vancouver just about three years ago or so now. I would go to a nearby park every day, leave my wheelchair at one end and walk beside this strong, wooden fence for fifty-sixty yards or so, rain, snow or shine, as part of my exercise-recovery. All on my own- leaving 'sleeping–Did I mention just how beautiful my wife is?!–beauty' at home, sleeping. I would meet many people on those morning- walks as they came through the park on their way to work, or to the bus stop, or local coffee shop. Two men I met-I'll nickname the "Double - J's".

J &J were born-again-Christians- whom I've never much cared for (sorry..)- but only because of their urgent, hard-pressing salesman-like demeanor(I'm the same with car or shoe-salespeople!), their in-your-face recruiting zealousness;

don't get me wrong here-those types have every right to believe in Jesus Christ as our lord and savior(as do I), but what
I feel they don't have a right to do is to so adamantly try
to recruit new believers all the time and preach to others.(
I'm sure I would have been killed very early on in the cru-
sades…?) By my way of thinking, they were clustered way
down low with Jehovah's Witnesses, toe jam, and Amway
dealers(sorry, no offense to the toe jam.); yep, they all sink
to the bottom of the glass for me, I'm afraid-and that's one
drink you don't want to imbibe! Minus the toe jam, all can
start off so nice, all things peachy and oh-so-friendly; now,
of course, I can recognize that all-too-friendly-for- strangers
façade at a quarter mile or more. Then, needless to say, it is
just one-two minutes before they introduce 'God' into the
conversation and the segue is often ham-handed. "Beautiful sunrise..," I say. "Yes", says one of the J's,God gives us
these small blessings every day, doesn't he?"" Ah, look at
those poor drowned worms-didn't get through the rain last
night." I might have said. "Everything has its purpose under God" one of the J-Men respond, shaking his head sadly,
as if the worms were kittens. That, in itself, triggers in me
a quasi-knee-jerk reaction to engage them in a somewhat
mocking, taunting stance (Do you think Christ and Bud-
dha ever met on the road (chronology aside..) and shared
a pint at the local tavern? That would have been one-hell
of a conversation, don't you think? You know, chewed the
fat some?).When they do ask, I explain one day that I had a
stroke while living and teaching in China, and was left paralyzed on my left side….

"If you would just open your heart to Jesus Christ," one
of the J's told me one morning in the park, "I'm sure you
might be healed. Quickly, he corrected himself and looked
skyward," I know you would be healed. "Put right, I could
maybe accept; 'heal' still makes it all sound like some sort
of disease! And that sort of ignorance, I'm afraid borders on
stupidity, so I instantly get itchy foot.

I nodded and smiled, not wanting to offend too early in our chat; that could wait a while. I called on all the patience I could muster in the moment- a smidgeon, perhaps. "We find you inspirational, doing your walk every day. We will pray for you, "he continued.

"Thanks," I muttered not very sincerely, "That's great, very kind." (How do you insult someone who is praying for you??)Before he left me, he turned back and added," If you only open your heart to Christ... 'Open my heart to Jesus Christ?' I wanted to repeat mockingly because I'm a petty, cruel, mean-spirited son-of-a-gun. Look friend, Jesus Christ has been in my heart for a long time; I daresay, he's been in my heart longer than in yours, you superficial knat!. In fact, he was there when I suffered my stroke and has been watching my painfully slow progress in recovery ever since; He knows what's going on, got it!? My Pulpit Master was whispering to me right then, 'Careful, Kim, careful.. .'.

Oh yes, and, if you could lean in just a little closer toward me, then I would be able to deliver a devastating right hook directly into your face, breaking your nose, ok..? Then, we could both see if he's in your corner to strike me down or at least wipe away the blood and apply some ice. 'Careful!' My P- Master cautions me. Personally, I have no doubt that Jesus had a good sense of humour, and I need look no further than the creation of men and women(and their respective genitalia to know that the Father does, too(careful Kim, says my P.Master): all were not created equally to play that same game. When we were just barely teens, a few of us boys would play a special game of "dare" down on the beach It consisted of just one popsicle stick and several unwitting teenage(or pre-teen) girls in bikinis, face down on their towels.; the 'loser' of this challenge would then have to sneak up on one of these girls in a 'walk-by', swoop down quickly, and pull loose the knot of her top. Only the small-breasted, stupid ones, it seemed, would ever stand up to look around! Not to suggest there's any correlation there at all; no, I've come to know a few vacuous, buxom types, too.

"Every Time"

Swirling whirls of colours, girls...
Confuse the grey and scare me,
Like on the beach, and within reach, bikini straps to dare
   me
Like starry skies, their sparkling eyes
Tickle me with wonder
For as in Spring, I hear a thing
Like eerie summer thunder;
If I allow my eyes to speak,
The look falls into rhyme-
But my tongue must enter in
And I lose it every time!

(-1972/3 early experimenting, I guess, with internal and feminine rhymes. And... probably trying to purge residual feelings about my early speech impediments/therapy!(No young girls in their first bikinis were ever truly harmed in the writing of this piece... though many popsicles did bite the dust, and some egos were doubtlessly somewhat bruised, by our bullish, idiotic pranks.)

Don't blaspheme!! Another, quieter voice chimes in; it is probably my other pulpit master (did I mention there's two?), sermonizing with not-so gentle reminders of the command-ments from Sunday School days. I rationalize some, thinking my transgression could not be any worse than that soul-less few who pray to God, when asking for raises, promotions, winning lottery tickets, etc. Clearly, so says my Bench-Voice(more on him later aka, 'Mr Facetious/Snide'..), "These are deeply spiritual believers – who have somehow in their ut-ter shallowness completely missed any and all understanding of what core- religious faith is all about." Like a bad smell, this phenomenon permeates our current society, in my opin-ion (excuse the rant..). Look around. We all know someone (maybe ourselves..?) who "prays" every week to win the jack-pot million dollar lottery prize. That's Deep, really deep! Then there are those professional sports teams who will all go down on one knee in the locker room just before game-time extolling the Almighty for a win, or at least to allow for individual players to play 'lights out'. Here's an idea: why don't we solve world hunger, child poverty, domestic abuse, child-trafficking and prostitution, addiction, gun violence and homelessness first and then perhaps think of personal lottery- wins a distant two hundred and ninety-seventh, OK.? My Lord-and worse still, how so many people can tell you exactly how they would divvy up their winnings and spend the six million- dollar jackpot! I'll always remember an oldie- but- goodie cartoon showing two enemy warriors on the night before battle, each down on one knee, presumably praying for victory in the next day's battle: One is on one side of the mountain, the second on the other side of that same mountain-and both are looking upward to the summit where a very confused and beleaguered 'Lord' sits, unsure how to mark his ballot. Winners and Losers are determined at the same instant in time always, aren't they? Or they used to be…

 ## " A Bad Case of Crabs"

While on a terrific family holiday once to Jamaica, I guess I sort of sealed my twisted fate with the alcohol bottle, just as the Carpenters were singing their number one hit," I'm on the top of the world" (you can figure the rest out if you really want to; circa 1974 or so)

First off, they had one of those fairly typical (as I now understand things..) cabana-bars in the centre of the pool. How ingenious! Drinking and swimming put together like that- to keep 'Jack and Jill Tourist' happy, when they weren't dining out at the local town's McDonald's To me, that was just "crazy" …and more than a little enticing for a sixteen year old. I'd never seen anything like it; hell, I'd rarely seen the inside of a real, 'land' bar at that point(maybe a couple of exceptions in dingy hotel bars). They also had a mini liquor store in the lobby and a cigarette- vending machine. So, I was on my way…that is if you're into that sort of thing.

 ## "Thank You!"

Then, there's the refuge offered to folks like me (stroke survivors) these days by mostly volunteer-run rehabilitation and stroke-recovery groups in nearly every region and city around the world. They offer a pure-place devoid of judgment because they are comprised predominantly of stroke survivors and other Acquired Brain Injury(ABI) folk. Some of us because of paralysis are still in wheelchairs or scooters, some use walkers, others perhaps just canes while still others who remain in the grip of aphasia have much difficulty articulating their thoughts in clear speech.

 ## Balloon Volleyball" (no beach in sight)

Before she died, my mother suffered a stroke as well and lived the last few years of her life between the hospital's acute care ward and a geriatric nursing home on her back in bed. She was unable to join in most all of the activities and reindeer games there, including "balloon- volleyball" which the first time I saw it, I thought was absurd and demeaning; Now, admittedly, with the shoe on the other paralyzed foot, I look forward to seeing other people hit in the face by a balloon every week! I'll even go out of my way to ensure it happens! Funny, isn't, how it's always those small things in life that often give us the greatest pleasure? Balloon-Bully, that's me. Tiny pleasures- tiny minds. You know, I simply did not fully appreciate at the time how difficult it must have been for my Mom because she was such an intelligent, vibrant woman whose life, minus weekly outings with me by then, had suddenly been reduced to a world that consisted mostly of bed, wheelchair and toilet-something her father had known, too, in his many years struggling with consumption when she was a young girl. Today, many of my stroke-survivor peers also suffer from the aforementioned aphasia, the inability to speak, to articulate, to verbally communicate their many, continuous thoughts. The remaining brain continues apace, even in its weakened state, to churn out the ideas, but they have no real, clear release so all attempts at communication are impaired and doubtless terribly frustrating- the 'marble-mouth' condition. Her paralysis and frustration at her condition I have had the chance to revisit in my mind many times since. It was another of her marvellous gifts to me, I suppose, seeing close-up where I, myself, would be all these years later- Back then, of course, I did not possess the wisdom enough to see it for what it was. Perhaps a warning. She was a truly remarkable woman and a wonderful mom with a loving heart and overflowing creative spirit! I miss her dearly-Is that alright for a man in his fifties to say? Don't care. I feel it, I said it.

She was a fighter alright and did not go gently into that good night (to borrow loosely from D. Thomas). Come to think of it, she did not go gently into most everything-there was always a passion/zest: high emotion, sadness, joy, anger and a whole-hearted commitment! When her time did come and she was down to mere minutes on her life-meter, I was at her bedside holding her hand and there the very instant I saw the divine spark burnout from her eyes. I don't doubt for a moment that she was ready to leave the world, to 'checkout'-it was hardly the express lane after a solid eighty-two years! I was able to reassure her some that her children were ok, her grandchildren were ok and we both knew that her lover and best friend, my father, had long since left her side, leaving her to fend for herself in the world(a decade, really), and to revisit her earlier life as an only- child in a funeral-director's home. I'm sure she found considerably less joy in the world given her age and state. I had been out of town at the time, but she waited it seemed, had hung on for me to return from my camping- sojourn to the Kootneys to visit friends; I was gone for four days and she died within half an hour of me arriving back at the hospital and to her bedside, Coincidence? Don't think so. Remarkable is what it was. Other than giving me the gift of life, this-being with her at the exact moment her spirit left her body was perhaps the greatest, most profound gift of all. Full circle.

To say goodbye, a final farewell and wish them well on their way. That is what so many of us ,stereotypically, are conditioned to hope for and expect in this funny, so often unrealistic world of ours and when it doesn't happen why so many people can feel "cheated" by the sudden(!) loss of a loved one, especially a family member. We just didn't see it coming, you know? How old was your uncle, anyways? Oh, eighty-eight. Me? I had been given that chance to say goodbye by this determined, strong-willed woman, my Mom, the woman who had conceived me and gone on to tie-up my skates on countless frosty early mornings when I was a young hockey player. The hand of God and Grace was most certainly in the room with the two of us on that gloriously sunny, early summer afternoon. When I finally did gather the strength to leave and drive home, I did think just that: I had left her safe and in very good, loving hands. There was nothing but clear, blue skies and a gentle breeze as I drove home, and that I shall remember; like the one 'little piggy' in the nursery rhyme, however, I cried all the way- my mother was dead. She would never again say her prayers with me, soothe my boo-boos, or be there so I could gently kiss her forehead or cheek. I will forever miss her, her inimitable way and laugh, our chats, and seeing her stooped over in one of the gardens she so adored come springtime. That same feistiness and creativity would inevitably be warped some over time into an orneriness with a pinch of bitterness that did chafe some people toward the end - though , to her credit, she did remain remarkably positive into her early eighties.

"Mommy's Boy?"

So what? Wanna make something of it…!? Years earlier before we sold her turn-of-the-century childhood/family home back in "Ontar- ee-air-ee-oh," our family spent innumerable hours cleaning, painting and reconditioning it for prospective buyers. She and I spent many joyful hours in that old kitchen and pantry, the same she knew as a child, just chatting, being together, and often starting the day off with a delicious fry-in-your-cholesterol –face breaky; you know the kind: soft, dripping- greasy bacon, fried eggs and washed down with endless sweetened coffee. She gifted me, too, in those special mother-son moments back then with the knowledge of how her children had entered the world: my older sister was easily conceived and popped out into the world within two years of their nuptials. I, on the other hand, would take considerably more effort and planning, including charting temperatures and incorporating every position imaginable ("You did WHAT?! Upside-Down?!") and then some, thanks, Mom! All modesty aside, I've always thought I was worth the effort. It was nice to know I was such a labour of love!

   She regaled me with such stories day after day and-even then-at fourteen or fifteen, I knew they were precious times,

(115 Fleming St., where Mom grew up, and much later.. I would toil..)

1968(Mom in a rare relaxed yuletide moment by the tree!)

a gift from her to me. After our coffee-break chats, I would don my painter's mask and return to the dungeon –basement, to my workspace and to my task of cleaning out the nearly three tons of residual coal stores(left behind after the war)and all while listening to Elton John and the Captain &Tennille on a small, scratchy transistor. One bushel-full of coal after another from the coal bin-room. Each of them had to be walked out to the massive rental dumpster sitting in the backyard beside the garage that still housed the '41 deSoto!

 "Winning Teams!"

I was lucky enough to be on both a championship (junior) high school football team and a championship double-AA midget hockey team that same year- a real watershed year for a teenage boy who much later now, in almost modesty, might suggest he contributed some to each. This was also the era that I came across my first "man-boy." What's a "man-boy", you ask? …

"The Man-Boy!"

There's always one in the showers,
Each male team must have its member..
With a very low, gravelly voice and stubble on the chin
And oh! Some dink there to remember!
The 'Man-Boy', yes, we'll call him...
We were most, left sore afraid
Because, if that's what it was supposed to look like,
The rest of us needed aid...!
A satyr, really, who'd somehow sprung to life,
And much later as we tittered, we would all pity the wife!
We'd seen it all before, we all had one down there , of course-of course!
Still, there was always one among us who stood out far from the rest
Why? Because He was hung like a Clydesdale horse!
Why, even the coach knew the legend-
Or, perhaps, by the sound of his voice?
Maybe he'd peaked 'round the corner one day
To glimpse at we showering boys?
So, to hear the phooey- those words much later(no offense intended..)
From the American constitution was..
All men are created equal,
Hah! Even then, we knew they were lies…,
When a few of us had penises
As big as other men's thighs!
It weren't just a picture, too, this sideshow
This thing, between the groins there, hanging...
No, the 'Man-Boy' was already busy-no lie-
By grade 8(yes, sadly!), with the 'banging'...
He had a man's body,
And, no, not just there in the crotch...
He was shaving twice a day.at least.

While the rest of us just watched!
He treated the girls, like they were collectibles, really no
more than mere chattel
But even then before too long, you know
He had a bevy- herd of these willing cattle...
We even imagined a few of his girls,
Saying what, "You want to put that thing WHERE?!"
When a couple of them, themselves, were barely started
on their own pubic hair!
He became a porn-star, this fellow,
A porn-actor, though there, with 'acting' there's actually
none-
But the A.I.D.S., I'm afraid, it's a badee and something
he just couldn't outrun.
Oh- to make the folks proud, huh?!
There was their little boy-
They sure liked their new house though-all smiles that
Janice and Dick,
And all because their one little boy was born with a
mammoth-sized prick.
For the rest of us boys,
Catholic, Protestant, the 'odd' Buddhist and Jew
We nodded our heads, knowing, yes, we could all tell...
That the little among us would find peace in heaven
While the big pricks, went straight down to hell....
(Oct/Nov.2012, Beijing.)

 "Stupid People"

I am acutely aware of much of the prejudice and bigotry that
exists out there in the world; for the most part, I am now
simply intolerant of it, myself, and I guess that makes me a
bigot,too.Seriously,I cannot stand the people who exhibit it,
racism and sexism in particular. If I ever hurt them by telling
them directly how offensive they are, then too freakin' bad!

Having said that and, no, I'm no angel; I have a few of
my own.

Racists and sexists you know about, but I am also quite
intolerant of stupid people(stupidism?). Young or old, male
or female, gay or straight, it really never matters. I Just

don't like being around them-first I get jittery then I'll leave quickly. It's also harder to spot them in a crowd because it usually requires an even brief conversation. Now, that's quite something for me, as a high school English teacher to admit to. Maybe it's just the 'Archie Bunker-Sue Sylvester' in me, I guess?. Maybe that's why some of me can identify so strongly with that last nasty character on the hit show, Glee. No, I have little time or patience for those among us who lack much common sense and most all logical reasoning which in old world terms might have been labelled dim or slow-witted- in short, those who don't think like me; yes, it's a small world, indeed. Now, There's a presumptuous, pompous-ass thing to admit to.? That's quite something for me, as a high school English teacher to admit to; after all, there is bound to be one or two 'stupid's in every class, sometimes even three or four which would give me hives. OK, so I don't like stupid people. It goes way back. There are worse things… Intellectual bully you say? Sure, if you're into labels? Intelligence or 'Intel'-Bully..,perhaps.

This little "foible-trait" of mine was forever reinforced upon my return to Canada after one year spent backpacking my way through England, most of Europe , the Mediterranean and Morocco- all this, after having graduated(1982/B.A @U.B.C) 'Magnum Cum Normal'. I went to the store to pick up my developed pictures from probably a dozen twenty-four exposure rolls of film(about 300 snaps!) taken all during my extraordinary, once –in -a -lifetime adventure-travels.Excitedly, I walked up to the counter and handed the girl my ticket.

"I'm sorry to have to tell you this sir, but our developing machine-equipment broke down during processing and some of your pictures were destroyed…" she said, unblinking.

"How many? I gasped in horror, my heart rate climbing. I started calculating in my head. Two, even three rolls gone? I could live with that,maybe?.It would still leave me plenty of pictures.

"All of them," she replied. Sheepishly, she looked at me and added," I hope they weren't important..?" STOP RIGHT THERE!(What did you just say?) What I wanted to say, in all truth, was:" Important? No, of course not, just breath-taking photos from a ONCE-IN-A LIFETIME TRIP THROUGH Europe. Or.., "No, of course not, just my WEDDING photographs! They'll be plenty more of those, right?" Nah, just my first-born child!" How important could they possibly be? What pictures are ever not important? Why do you think people all over the world even take pictures to begin with? Some people out there, now, from The 'Save- the- Stupid- People-Conservancy' shush-in with, "There are no stupid people, just stupid comments. And that to me by itself is another example! Believe that if you want to. It was a stupid person to have said such a dumb thing-albeit in an effort to calm a disgruntled customer. That girl? I can't even give her an "A" for effort after saying something with so little thought behind it. Just stupid is all.(As Forest might have said)

 ## " A Bad Case of Crabs"

While on a terrific family holiday once to Jamaica, I guess I sort of sealed my twisted fate with the bottle, just as the Carpenters were singing their number one hit," I'm on the top of the world" (you can figure the rest out if you really want to; circa 1974 or so)

First off, they had one of those fairly typical (as I now understand things..) cabana-bars in the centre of the pool. How ingenious! Drinking and swimming put together like that- to keep 'Jack and Jill Tourist' happy, when they weren't dining out at the local town's McDonald's To me, that was just "crazy" …and more than a little enticing for a sixteen year old. I'd never seen anything like it; hell, I'd rarely seen the inside of a real, 'land' bar at that point(maybe a couple of exceptions in dingy hotel bars). They also had a mini liquor store in the lobby and a cigarette- vending machine. So, I was on my way…that is if you're into that sort of thing.

After a few rum'n'cokes at the pool one day, I started to make my way back to the room which I was sharing with my sister. On my way through the lobby, however, I bumped into a jovial, little Jamaican man wearing a Cincinnati Reds ball cap. In hindsight, it's become perfectly clear that he rather intentionally "bumped" into me, as a nice, juicy tourist mark and why he was so jovial. Ah well. He invited me to meet him there again, after dinner for a sample and possible transaction of ganja.

Of course, I met him that evening and we strolled down to the beach, sat in the sugary, light brown sand and smoked two joints together. He left me on my own by about nine or nine-thirty, and what happened next could only be described as a surreal experience. Not surprisingly , at that moment I was quite relaxed and at peace with the world….This was very potent Jamaican weed(as most of the ganja there is) and I was thoroughly looped, just sitting alone on the beach, listening to the lapping waves and all, and mesmerized by a gorgeous full moon that was so crystal clear, it was like a huge China plate in the night sky. It felt as though I could almost reach out and touch it(or so I thought anyways, after a couple of joints).What happened next was simply unforgettable. There I was, a happy soul but, admittedly, a wee bit paranoid as per the usual T.H.C.-induced euphoria, glancing around me often in all directions when I "suddenly" found myself sitting in the middle of a moving beach- a writhing carpet of hundreds or probably thousands of tiny , baby crabs which were wending their way this way and that. Most were, naturally, the same colour as the sand- for camouflage, I presume. This unnerving phenomenon seemed to give the beach around me a singular crawling-effect(thanks K. B.), at first a bit frightening and then just mesmerizing as I settled in to observe it. To a biologist, perhaps, it would be no big deal; I'm not a biologist.

 ## "The Goat and the Tree"

A friend of mine was recounting a story/parable he heard in a sermon by a minister who spent some time in Africa. In one of the thousands of tiny villages scattered throughout the land, one family carved out a fairly typical, tough existence, living in their thatched-roof mud hut, with their livestock- a single goat nearby. One end of a rope was tied around the goat's neck while the other end was tied around a tree to keep it tethered within view, and to prevent it from wandering off. Then, one day came after a month or so when they untied the beast from the tree, thinking that maybe, just maybe, it would walk the short distance across the field to a patch of land that clearly offered much better grass for grazing than the tired worn area under the tree that it was so used to. Alas, they were all surprised to see that, once released from its area by the tree, it made no effort whatsoever to seek out the new grazing possibility; instead, it stayed right there, in the area by the tree that it had grown accustomed to. There was no more grass to be had,but,at least, it felt safe there. And that was the message! What was the message? I asked my friend because for me, a man who loves his metaphors and analogies, I was having a rather stupid moment,myself.We all have our 'trees' (comfort zones, for the you- know- what..) Sometimes, it seems, we even tether ourselves to our own tree, rather than walk through unexplored grasses where – who knows?- a hungry lioness(or perhaps a mate..?) maybe lies waiting. But, if we don't cross the bridge (to mix metaphors!), then we will never know what treasures, or fertile grass, are on the other side, just waiting for us to discover and enjoy. Sure, there's risk. Who knows? Maybe that's what all those lemmings are thinking as they near the edge of the cliff?The sheer numbers of their mass migrations cause those in front to be shoved by those in the rear behind them-nature's way, I guess, of thinning the 'herd'?

Dee Bus Bee Comin' Soon,Mon

On yet another day, my sister and I(me, as her 'escort') decided to go into a nightclub in the nearby town of Ocho

Rios. We waited at a bus stop for twenty minutes or so before I asked a young Jamaican fellow with us, if he knew when the next bus was. His reply would become almost standard fare for brother and sister fun for years to come, whenever we were facing uncertain wait- times. He said, "Dee Bus Bee Comin' Soon,Mun." Sure enough, 45-50 minutes later, there it was! That trip taught us both about Jamaican time, a slow-zone not so common in North America; apparently, it's a very individual thing and the ganja is never too far away.

 ## "On the Sidewalk"

Whenever I had visitors come to Beijing and look in on me, I always tried to warn them about being a pedestrian; Normally, you would think that you're safe as a pedestrian up on the sidewalk and off the street in North America at least, but motorcyclists in China will frequently come up on the sidewalk just to avoid traffic. It is so common to see , in fact, that you need to have your wits about you at all times. Leaving the safety of your tree does have its dangers…

 ## "Cardboard Underwear"

For the most part, they don't have clothes-dryers in the homes and apartments in Beijing. Now, this is a good thing, right? Think of the electricity they are saving! Clothes there are all usually drip-dried and whenever possible hung out-side in the fresh air(?) and ample sunshine–the latter of which is abundant, even if the first is rare. This often neces-sitates ironing, if you care enough about the wrinkles. Me? I'm a man, remember? I couldn't care less. Give 'em a good pull-shake and they should be good. I had a nice, big sunny and often very cold enclosed balcony where I could hang my stuff.OK sure, sometimes the briefs were a little like cardboard, but they'd settle in to the right places after just a few uncomfortable strides!

"WESTWARD, HO!"

Those Winning Teams and Funerals came, just prior to the family packing up the household and moving to the WEST Coast in Vancouver. There, I would finish off high school, attend college and embark on my illustrious (big tongue firmly planted in cheek) high school English teaching career. You know, after more than fifteen years of marking tests and grading essays, I can honestly and still say, I've really loved it! OK- maybe not the marking part(although there are those out there who will also try to tell you they enjoy doing the laundry or washing the dishes, scrubbing the bathtub ring...same ones, I think, who say they "like the rain, really Zen-like!") uh huh !) and that was only because it cut so deeply into my Sunday NFL-watching time. For me, besides the complete autonomy of running my 'own show' once in the classroom, it was the truly magical process of bonding with individuals and whole classes alike that would develop a special synergy for each. Each student and every class has its own unique profile and dynamic when dominant personalities, or characteristics, come to the fore to blend with my own. Oh, always the mixed emotions as another year drew to a close! By then, it's already late spring, even early summer in some books, and then you can add in the electric energy of exam-fever and pending graduation, followed by dozens of yearbook signings H.A.G.S. should be banned! and maybe, privately, (shh..)the odd tear on the drive home as I would think back to those awful, drizzly, uninspired fall mornings when those special connections were first being forged; It was just like those winning teams I spoke of earlier; I.. was fortunate enough to be a part of something very special. I recognized that it was all about the process of having been together in a class or at an early morning practice on those dreary autumn days- spending time together. It would be that which made the effort worthwhile and unforgettable for many of us. It was time...precious time!

"Never Pitch Your Tent in a Wadi!"

One of my favourite stories that my Mom shared with me way- back- when related to "Show'n'Tell" (remember? At the time, still a popular, daily activity in grade school). Well, our family did spend maybe two years in Australia when my sister was still quite young. She's five years older. Me? I wasn't yet even a glint in my father's eye. However, here's the thing- I had grown up firmly believing that I was there in Australia. After all, I had heard so many stories at home which were only strengthened by my completing a few fascinating projects at school about Aussie flora and fauna, The Great Barrier Reef, and the Outback so that by grade five or six, I had convinced myself of my Australian experience. It seemed perfectly natural for me one day then to take the teddy-bear koala we had at home into the school with me and regale my classmates for twenty minutes with my extensive, personal knowledge of 'The Land Down Under'. It could only have been made better if I had a live aborigine standing next to me! A few weeks later, after my presentation, as my mother related to me long afterwards, she was attending a parent-teacher conference with my language-arts instructor. The teacher told her how much she and the class had enjoyed my wonderful talk on Australia and its native plants and animals. That's when my mother interrupted her to explain that I had not been born yet and certainly had never been to Australia. I guess they shared a laugh or two, and thus closed the book on my 'Australian adventures'. I've been making up stories- both oral and written- ever since, I guess. I could never say it better than best-selling author Tom Clancy who is attributed with, "Writing is so much damned fun. I play God. I feel like a kid at Christmas. I make people do what I want and I change things as I go along! Yep-wholehearted agreement there, T. C., and not just with writing It's fun, what can I say? These glowing coals of the imagination have been fanned red-hot to this day. Some people might be tempted to call it lying and even go as far as to suggest that a trip to the psychiatrist is in order. Perhaps. In response, first I pitsaw them then I say they probably have little or no imagination themselves and resent those among us who do(Na-Na-Na-Na-Na!). I do so enjoy good quotations by other writers and I will borrow from another here-Paul Fusell who was quoted once as saying, "If I didn't have writing, I'd be running down the street hurling grenades in people's faces." A bit extreme, perhaps, but I share the sentiment. There's something there about angry attention-getting, I think..? Sure beats a trip to the Principal's office!

  ## "Sneaking a Peek"

Remember Natasha, she of the butterfly panties? That was the really funny, ironic thing for many of us boys. Irony? We didn't have a clue at that point-it probably had something or other to do with what mothers did in the laundry room? We were so testosterone-pumped full of curiosity and misinformation (read stupidity) about what girls had between their legs that any and all glimpses and peeks into those nether regions could only ever meet with disappointment. Somehow many of us, I think, were expecting some sort of special appendage, probably, something like our own only different, but there was none to behold. In fact there was nothing, absolutely nothing! It would prove to be the subject of many recess and lunch discussions where speculation was rampant and fact, meagre to non-existent.

  ## "English Teacher, Huh?"

I've learned the hard way over a lot of years some of the curses and blessings of my chosen career-path. Once in a grocery store while checking out, I related to my cashier that I was a high school English teacher. All she could say to me then, and without hesitation I would add was," I hated English; it was my worst subject." "Hmm," Was all I could muster at that instant as I gathered my bags, turned and left dejectedly. I have several good friends who have always been made a little uncomfortable by my career choice, too, because, like many out there, English was not a favourite subject and so a few can be quite self-conscious about it in their dealings with me. Personally, I've always found it rather inviting and invigorating, myself, but I understand that is coming from someone who still enjoys getting lost in the dictionary from time to time. One friend actually prefers to this day to only send me funny -cartoons rather than any sort of text message in which she would risk the embarrassment from her atrocious spelling and bad grammar. Any number of times I've tried to explain how I don't "mark" or grade her writing(it's off the clock), and that's a good thing because she would most likely fail. Another good friend plants his uniquely irritating seeds quickly on his visits by using some of his own personal favourites from what has now become his own classic store of mala-propisms, including "more better" and"worser". He knows it rankles me, so he relishes any opportunity to do it.

"Mommy's Boy(2) & Stalwart"

When the family first up-rooted from our Sarnia, Ontario home, I hated my parents with a feverish passion (…who cares if it's somewhat redundant? I'm reminded of Cocteau's line that writing is "to kill something to death.") That feeling brings to mind also a line from William Gass who supposedly once replied to the question, 'Why Did He Write?' with, "I write because I hate a lot. Hard.". In hindsight, my parents must have known both some of the rumours and truth of my then-Sarnia circle of friends- and- acquaintances and a few of the escapades we were getting up to, and here,too,is my guilt-mongering Pulpit-Master out for a stroll. One childhood friend had been placed in drug-rehab twice by the time we were fifteen. He was back dealing within months of his first 'release'. Two others who were present for so many of my much younger money-cake birthday parties(!) had been caught one night after breaking and entering

An ex-Navy man and a Golden- Gael mechanical engineer (the only half-year grad class-due to WWII- of 481/2).

a private residence one night and then unleashing a real mean-streak, just a torrent of vandalism once inside; Clearly, they did not believe in journal-writing!? Fortunately, I remained only on the hearsay- periphery of such nasty events and criminal activities, so I could still almost look the minister in the eye, sort of, come Sunday when his gaze ever met mine. I can attribute some of that to my Pulpit- Master, some to blind luck and I believe the rest to my father.

He was a fairly serious-dispositioned man although certainly not without his sense of humour. He could often be impatient and loud while tutoring his kids(me and my sister) in our high school math homework, but there could be no denying his love of church, singing and choir, sailing and, of course, his wife - who would regularly intervene in those loud, often teary tutoring sessions to protect her kids. Whenever my peer circle-as it was- elevated our talks to include parents, marriages and affairs (real or imagined), several of my friends could only snicker and scoff at the mere idea of my father, Ken, ever being unfaithful toward my Mom; he rather exuded integrity and fidelity. To the best of my knowledge, he was true-blue and faithful until the day he died. If you know differently, keep it to yourself will ya?! I would wear his fidelity like a badge of honour in a group where some fathers collected and catalogued boxes of Playboy and Penthouse magazines (does that help to explain anything?)in their basements and still others were already breaking their marriage vows with messy affairs. My Dad was a stalwart in that way, or so I like to believe. His one and only but oh-so passionate 'mistress' was our sailboat which he first purchased when I was just six years old. She was a classic beauty, an all-wood (pine, oak, mahogany) 26 and one half-foot Atkin sloop built by G.W. Noble; she was family.

(The graceful "mistress", Panique, dockside in Vancouver, 1979)

My Mom even liked this 'other woman'! My older sister and I in some ways grew up on that boat, and on the water. He did so want to pass on his love of wind, sail and water to us all after his navy days during the war when his own less-than dignified nickname among shipmates had been "Two-Bucket Parrish(2BP)" (the North Atlantic will do that to a fellow, I hear). He served as radio- man aboard a corvette in North Atlantic convoy- duty. However, by the same token, he was never teased much by his shipmates about his tendency- perhaps because he was an excellent boxer and missed out on the championship in his weight class-middleweight/ light- heavyweight, then- by mere seconds-lack of killer instinct which he definitely passed on to me.... One bucket for cleaning up the deck, got it? And that came straight from the sailor's mouth, so to speak. The feeling of freedom one experiences when out on the deep, blue sea/ lake is really hard to fathom (excuse the all-too-easy pun..) and second to none(Well,ok, maybe a handful of things).

The rhythm of our lives ebbed and flowed like the tides and was dictated to by Fall "Haul-Out" and Spring "Launch" schedules for as long as I could remember. Even after launch, we still had to 'step' the mast which was a complicated, risky process all on its own. One year early on, he inexplicably failed to attend to all his own failsafe measures during the procedure and the over four hundred pound oak-pine mast came crashing down on my mother who-for some reason(we've never been clear on it)- was standing in the cockpit. It hit her almost full- on but luckily was a glancing blow to the side of her head and shoulder. She would be hospitalized for a day to help recover from a severe concussion and badly bruised shoulder. No one would ever again be allowed on the boat during the mast-stepping (except those doing the work), as Dad continued to fine-tune his safety measures over subsequent years. Even when he spoke of the incident years later to me over a breakfast-special, you would still sometimes see tears welling in his eyes: there had been this nightmarish moment in his life when he thought for an instant that he had killed his own lover-wife and best friend! I can't imagine, but I've tried lots. There could never be a doubt that he was a straight-shooting, honest, upright kind of Joe, except he was a Ken. He passed on most of that, and a weak heart to his boy, or at least I've tried to be (and, no, not weak-hearted!)Literally, so I've been told, what I have is a malfunctioning ventricular valve" ("re-gurgitating", they call it.; doesn't always close properly, so there's leakage, or "backwash"..) but neither was it enough to keep me from two championship sports teams as a teen nor from being physically active for all my life! I was still playing rec-hockey weekly (to my mid- fifties) in China until moving down to Beijing where I worked out three-four times each week at a nearby gym! So to me, it's always been sort of a non-issue…though I've always been very aware that heart disease has taken many of the family men, and would catch up to my branch.

Dad and I did have some rather special bonding-time, too. When we did first relocate to the West Coast, we did not take possession of our new home until the third week of that October. Dad and I came out in late August, so I could register and get prepared for that first week at my new high school. For the first six weeks, the two of us stayed in a mo-tel on Clarke Road in Coquitlam. I would do my homework sitting at the little arborite counter just outside the bathroom. We ate dinner out most of the time. Breakfast on the week-ends was the best, at a cheap diner-restaurant where smok-ing was still permitted, as by then we both were smoking. He had stopped for quite some time but picked it up again when he realized that his son was hooked. It was something for which I don't think my mother could ever forgive me. Let's go back to breaky for a bit, shall we?

There were those wonderful $2.99 bacon 'n' eggs specials with endless refills of weak coffee (thus the endless!) in those old, half-inch thick, always chipped porcelain mugs. I still remember the day he came back late one night to the motel because he had to go over to the North Shore to super-vise the unloading of our four-ton Atkin sloop (his mistress) from the railway car it was shipped out on from Ontario. On another note, before the move for us, personally, that year, I had accidently broken two of my father's ribs. He was tickling me from behind one day in the kitchen as I stood at the stove helping Mom prepare the dinner. I did warn him to stop, but he persisted,so,finally after my patience was out, I threw my arms around his chest, lifted him in a great bear-hug, lugged him across the floor and slammed him into our refrigerator on the other side of the kitchen- a bit too hard, I guess? He had trouble sleeping for a month or more, but he still proudly told most of his friends and colleagues that his fifteen year-old football-playing son had done the damage-quite by accident of course..., but still, it was. something to be proud of; it's a male thing, I guess? Up there with spitting and swearing,

 ## "And, Alcohol was Not even a Factor..."

I did have an even earlier near-death experience in my life (the stroke being first and foremost), as a 'twenty-something' when a friend and I were in a devastating car accident. We were driving the four-oh-one (#401) from Toronto to London/Sarnia for Christmas holidays. There was a little snow on the ground and roads. He, of course, as per usual, was speeding (as he had done from his first day behind the wheel) regardless of conditions. Well, we lost control and started sliding and fish-tailing right toward the back of a semi-trailer. He reefed on the wheel which took our front end away from the almost certain- death with a collision. However, we were now heading for the wide, grassy meridian in the centre of the highway. There was only a moment's relief and quick, mutual sighs before the driver's side tire caught the edge of the wet grass. In an instant we were completely sideways and began the first of three rollovers.

All said and done, we eventually came to a stop, upside-down on the interior shoulder-edge of the oncoming lanes. We slowly crawled out of the wreck through the front-side windows on our own and immediately realized with looking at each other that our faces were completely smeared with blood-quite frightening at first glance!. It did not look good at all. As it turned out, however, we were both OK and the blood was simply from the myriad of superficial cuts and nicks caused by the shattered windshield. We walked the two hundred metres or so to a gas-station where we cleaned up, grabbed a coffee and called a friend of mine in London to come and pick us up. Whew! No, alcohol was not a factor, just stupidity for the road conditions…. sorry, A. My friend and I still chuckle as we remember shaking hands with and thanking all of the dozen or so people who stopped and came back to check on us at the wreck on that wintry day. It was a weird moment in time, alright.

 ## "Bottom's Up!"

I remember reading somewhere as an adult- that a young person who has an alcoholic drink before the age of seventeen has a seventy-five (75 %!) percent greater likelihood of having alcohol-related problems later in life. Where they get those numbers I don't know, but it must be true; I know I can attest to that; I did the doctor Jekyll/Mr. Hyde thing for ten years or so. Then I mostly just hid a lot of my struggles by moving to another continent! Still, I'm often left wondering, too, about the other guys in my circle back then…Did they have struggles with the bottle, as well; did a few go on(God forbid!) to become alcoholic fathers perhaps?There's a few of them out there, I know. My Dad might have given me the occasional snort of beer while we were out on a family sail, but even then it was done hesitantly and accompanied by some stern looks from my mother. I point to early shyness that sprouted into a sheepish demeanor making me very susceptible to the flock's movements. In truth, I would often crumble in the face of peer-pressure then-being slow to recognize my own strengths and leadership skills… In grades eight and nine, we would mostly have to rely on a few, indulgent elder siblings- not mine), or sometimes complete strangers out in front of the beer store and, very occasionally, someone's alcoholic parents-the last of whom didn't really care too much as long as their own needs were looked after first. If we did ever land a case of 12 or 24, and a house was not available, usually our 'party' would happen in the woods next to our elementary school or else at one of its many covered entrances. It amazes me to think how much of that must go on with pre-teens/ tweenies across the country and a lot of it unbeknownst to their parents. Some otherwise intelligent parents do live in a state of ignorant- bliss('the ostrich state'), like the former U. S. army policy for gays...' Don't ask, don't tell'. Silence is golden. Out of sight, out of mind; if we can't see it, then it doesn't exist. "Wouldn't be our girl or boy. He's respectful, obedient, doing O.K. at school. There has been a very good advertising campaign echoing these exact sentiments on television: (Not our child) 'Our son or daughter is responsible, kind and intelligent;heck, he/she keeps the bedroom clean, cooks and even helps out around the house. No!!?' Really?

By grade 9, a couple of us had climbed outside the box long enough to contemplate fake I.D. After three or four hours at our downtown public library,A.G., my best childhood- buddy and I had crafted fake birth certificates which, while not especially brilliant, were close enough to pass inspection often enough at the beer store and even in a couple of hotel bars in town by people who didn't care enough to do their jobs thoroughly. I think for them or their boss , the golden rule was simply if you could pay, then you were helping business and to be welcomed, period. Sure.

 "Sheepish yet Happy"

For me, personally, there was an unforgettable year of Bantam hockey (13 and 14 year-olds) when my team had two older teenage boys(a mistake!) coaching us. Once, at an early morning Saturday practice they passed around a cold jug of Ripple-apricot wine and two or three joints as we were dressing and tying up our skates! (And, today, we're worried about 'head-hits!) True, we would not be a powerhouse- team that year, coincidentally enough; you might even say we were a bit sheepish…and we were, but we were a happy lot alright.

 ## "So Close Yet so Far"

One summer day, after attending the recreation-day camp in morning where we played checkers with bottle caps, made lace bracelets, and started to learn about flirting, we were returning home after a successful foray to the beer store in the afternoon. I was balancing the case of 24 on the handlebars of my ten-speed with a jacket thrown over it to hide it from inquisitive eyes, but just as we neared the entrance to the school parking lot and our woods-refuge, the R.C.M.P. pulled us over to the curb. They didn't believe any of our concocted story, promptly confiscated our hard-won case of beer, put it in the trunk of their cruiser and drove away,… probably to the family picnic! So close yet so far…

 ## "Cheers!"

We had some adventures, to be sure. One boy in our group almost died of hypothermia one New Year's Eve ,after four or five too many libations with the crew, but he was luckily discovered by one of his own parents passed out(or should that be 'pissed out' in his own vomit in a snow bank in their very own snow-covered backyard Whew! There's a story for the grand-kids, huh? (Yes, I might have a few of those, too) Some of us (no names, please) had even, at times, forged letters of permission from parents to buy and bring home cigarettes 'for them'-when some stores required that (no doubt to protect themselves.?).Yes, it was' party - central alright' and we were mostly all of four- teen and fifteen. Then there might be the occasional house party with someone's parents away for a week in Mexico or Hawaii. Underage drinking, young boys and girls and an empty house was a recipe that was bound to lead to other things and quite often did.

 ## " Gazebo Time"

By grade nine, there came a whole stage when I and some others had settled comfortably into a routine of skipping a few of our afternoon classes and drinking Southern Comfort and O.J. in the screened-in gazebo found in one of our back- yards. We could be there from early afternoon until maybe three-thirty or four when-sobering up some-it was time to make our way home for dinner, after watching The Three Stooges and the original Star Trek! Television show. When I was finally caught for cutting classes, I had skipped a grand total of 72(by their count anyways);of course, back then our classes were only forty-two minutes long! It wasn't like they were an hour long each, or anything!(Remember Idi Amin, and the catfish..?).

 ## " Death as a Gift"

After a few years in the home (remember? No reindeer games?)Mom had a debilitating stroke that stole much of her speech and left her pretty much bed-ridden. She would be transferred to first an acute care ward followed by a pal- liative care ward where she would later die with me at her side, holding her hand. How nice?

I had been out of town, as I've already mentioned, but she seemed to have waited for my return. In fact, I am con- vinced of it. This, in her indomitable way, was yet another of her profound gifts bestowed upon me, her son. I had been initiated long before to nursing- home life (elder care, now), as a young boy when we paid numerous visits to a home where she had placed both her own mother and an aunt. I remember my discomfort at those times, me-at thirteen or fourteen years old, and younger- so often perched on the side of a bed, gently holding a very small, withered hand and straining to listen to and understand the mumbled stories emanating from between doubtless ill-fitting dentures. Both women died alone in their beds in that nursing home; I know those days influenced my Mom greatly; she didn't want to go out in quite the same way though she sort of did, anyhow, when it was her turn. "We all must die alone," she told me once years before –even if the room is crowded….That is a solo journey, that one.

I shall always remember when my maternal grandmother died and my mother honoured me by asking me to be one of the pall-bearers, with a written card yet. Hell, I didn't even know what a "pall-bearer" was at that time. Within months, mind you, I felt like I was an old 'pro',and living in the shadow of death. You see, I would also be a pall-bearer at a friend's and hockey teammate's funeral –after he and two others died in a fiery car crash after a night of underage drinking. As I recall, the whole team wore our champion-ship jackets to the ceremony- or perhaps I just wanted that to happen.

 "Cry-Baby"

I guess when I was little, I was somewhat of a cry-baby(still am..) and my mother indulged me with the customary hushes, whispers and hugs. Of course, before long my mushrooming dinosaur-size began dictating all the expectations surround-ing me and consequently my behaviour, including no more crying, thereby creating the aura that I would carry with me into adulthood. It must be in the genes, however, because the 'waterworks' would never shut off or leave me completely; I was quite an emotional and philosophical young man-even then advocating hugging among hockey- teammates and

friends—unusual—I daresay, for many teenage boys That re-
flective nature led me to start writing poetry in earnest when
I was ten or twelve though my Mom kept even earlier efforts
from back when I was six or seven and first experimenting
with rhyme, and, no lie, she would collect them all(too much
for the fridge-door!),… in that famous shoebox, no less.Yes,I
was always an emotional person before my stroke; after it, I
felt like I was leaning much more to the "maudlin" side of
things. That "crying-thing", again. Sure, when I heard a favourite song or saw an old movie, I was gone. Like when the
alien- queen in the sequel Aliens is hunting the little waif,
'Newt' who is scurrying for her life under the gratings and
Ripley comes out to her rescue! "Get away from her, you
BITCH!" The Sound of Music is guaranteed to always turn
on my taps, especially when Captain Von Trappe starts losing
his voice on stage while singing "Edelweiss" (I mean Come
On!)", and Maria chimes in to support him and help him finish. My wife knows this side of me only too well now and does
a quick- check when she sees my eyes tearing up. To reassure
her some, I might just utter "song" or point to the image on
the television screen that has triggered me. What burns me
now is that a well- done tampon commercial can set me off
these days –and just leave me weeping and shaking my head
in disgust at myself. And those save-a-latte-adopt- an- Afri-
can child commercials? Forget it! I'm gone as soon as I see
the first picture of the mud-thatch hut beside the dusty field
that has not produced a food-crop in three years.….. You know
the ones: where they grind up the four kernels of corn they
found on the ground under the market stalls, add an ounce
of contaminated water to it and make a miniature corn- cake
to feed three children and one adult. What about snakes…?
For protein, I mean. 'Shut up!' says my Pulpit Master. Judge
Not! Of course, as usual, he's right. Let's return to crying for
a moment, shall we? Now, I could be seated in the semi-circular audience at one of my stroke-recovery clubs just listening to a volunteer singer-musician clumsily galloping through
an old Gordon Lightfoot tune while I and several others are

struggling to keep awake. Suddenly a phrase or chorus jolts me and I snap upright in my chair and only then do I realize my cheeks are wet with tears. Who's to say why exactly? Perhaps when I last remember hearing the song-which is true of most things now-I could still feel and use both my legs. I could still chase my girl around the room. Now, I have to tie her down first!(..before I chase her around the room, whispers S. L.of the non-sequitor)

 ## "The More Things Change, Yadda, Yadda,
Yadda, Not True"

Nothing is the same for me in the world any more. Now, think about that for a moment, if you will? All of the world's details seem different to me. The bigger things have remained mostly constant. Women have children. Men chase mostly women, predators hunt and eat prey, the sun continues to set and, as 'Papa' Hemingway so rightly observed, it continues to also rise. Some people are idiots. Some people are charitable, thoughtful and kind-hearted folk; Some are not. Some people wear "hoodies" because they are under the misguided belief that they are fashionable, or are simply too lazy to really dress; Still others wear the things purely to conceal their identities from the next surveillance cameras in the stores or homes they plan to rob.Nice,very nice,indeed.Oh,yes,they do also tend to draw attention to the wearer…as suspicious-why, like hats and sunglasses, people are asked to remove them when entering most banks . Some people still cannot parallel park. And fish still has far too many bones…But, like Gary Larson did years ago with his 'boneless chicken ranch cartoon', I'm sure people are out there somewhere working on boneless fish-farms. The bones tend to slow things down an awful lot and can even be dangerous. We, in the West prefer our food popcorn-easy and convenient-that way we can eat a lot and fast! Shovel it in! A –Lot-of-Fast-Food! "Fast-Express- Lane-Fast".

Some people steal the shopping carts from grocery- store parking lots, a few even believing the twenty-five cents entitles them to full- ownership.

Ozzy Osborn is still alive, a living fossil after a lifetime of multiple abuses; rumour is some scientists even want to research/investigate him and his genes for his astounding staying- power. Most of the other dinosaurs from the Jurassic forests of Rock 'n'Roll have long since passed on to halls of fame or museums or crematoria, the late sixties, early-seventies being an especially tough period. Poor Ozzie and rock-mate, Gene Simmons, Kiss' long time front-man after years of heavy make-up under hot lights, both their faces now have taken on the appearance of sad, melting ice-cream birthday cakes. like oozing stucco in the rain .That's all well and good-I happen to like 'oozing stucco faces, and both of them for their leadership and creativity in the 'rock world.'

Jean Cocteau is attributed with saying, "To write is to kill something to death." Of course, I like the humour, but I like the sentiment even more;If I presume for a moment in knowing exactly what to which he is alluding then it is the fact that most writers-me especially- first observe and then, -after finding something worthwhile- they stick with it and contemplate it as philosopher or pummel it as boxer or both - point is, they won't leave it alone, or as Liverpudlian Paul sang, "Let it be." They may be on a single thought for an entire morning or afternoon, perhaps longer and that is difficult for most people to comprehend, especially these days when "Look!I can change the image on my screen by touching my finger, right here! Remember Oscar's comma?Let me show you this one-it's great, a cat staring into an aquarium! And now with' Photoshop', what fun! You can paste O'Bama's head onto a ballerina! Funny, huh? (actually, no..)…

 "Three Coins…."

On both of my trips to Italy, I remember throwing coins into the famous Trevi fountain in Roma-squeezing my eyes tight and hoping,wishing,praying to meet a wonderful, beautiful girl who would become my life-partner (as the Mills bros. sang, "Be My Life's Companion!"); I did, so dreams/wishes do really come true in my books! I remember lighting a candle in Quasimodo's Parisien home, Notre Dame Cathedral, in memoriam to an uncle who had died when I was abroad.

 ## "Adrenalin- Junkie?"

Some folks need bungee-jumping or hang-gliding, rock-climbing or perhaps Para-gliding or white-water kayaking … to get their jollies, their kicks, that adrenalin-rush high. I guess, in hindsight, I had a rather low level of rush-seeking because backpacking through Europe on my own for a year and waking up most of those days not knowing where your next meal would be or where you would be sleeping that night was more than good enough for me: it was at once both exhilarating and frightening-riding the knife edge, as it were. In that mode, you are, essentially homeless, a "street person" which makes you alert and very aware- of your surroundings at all times. I can fully understand if many of them have suspicious natures,

Margo, Kim and Ronnie on Algarve beach in Portugal

even leading to paranoia in some. When all of your worldly belongings, from clothes to toiletries, from recreational needs to food and keepsakes are in one knapsack(or shopping cart, I guess), you learn quickly to never take your eyes off it and never to leave it unattended for more than a second or two at a time. I sometimes would play a coy but purposeful game of doing just that-leaving my bag unattended, but tether myself visually to it and test my own comfort-limits Quite simply, you trust absolutely no one except yourself; Soon you've become a masterful "control freak." It goes into every bathroom stall you visit and in some Mediterranean countries, you'll know, that is a feat by itself. Sure, as backpackers, most of us would steal at least one full roll ofT.P. in any restaurant that presented the opportunity. So, blame us, ok?

"Shrinking Circles & Burning Bridges"

Being a hugger from way-back-when, I always threw myself headlong, heart and soul into my friendships. For that, sadly enough, I have some regrets because my choices have not always responded in like-fashion with either time or similar enthusiasm for our connections. As singer-songwriter A.Marshall says in some of her lyrics, "Why don't you love me, the way I love you?" Guess that just makes us needier than most !All or Nothing, I believed, forever-but I've since learned that "forever" doesn't mean forever for some. It's just an empty word-meaningless (You know the kind of empty I mean here)" For sure, "says a friend, "We should get together for coffee!" Yeah right. Then pick a date and day , set a time and show up(!)…, but No…! . Now, I know better and, unfortunately, I'm a bit of a bridge- burner. If I sense that the fires have been lit on one side, then I'm going to light them on my side so they can join in the middle. How mature, I know! It just makes me sad to see and feel that process underway. Truth is, friendships don't last forever, much like many marriages, I guess, where the tectonic plates shift and give rise to all-new formations and the partners replace the meaningless "I Do's" they exchanged years before

with something akin to "I Give Up's and 'irreconcilable differences''. People drift apart and even stop making the time
and effort for each other. That's life, or just part of life. Of
course, so is getting caught in a terrible downpour or being
in a bad car accident, but that doesn't mean we have to like
it or embrace it! Hard enough just to "accept".. With me,
I'm often left wondering now if it's simply one of the inevi-
tables of aging, or if it's due at least in part to my infirmity
and the inconveniences and awkwardness which accompany
it, me being confined to a wheelchair and all.Hmmm...?

Either way, some of that residual inner nasty – boy(the
Bench-Voice, remember?) wants to shout," And F.U. too-
and have a great life! See ya. However, that puts me in the
same ranks as my toothless, cigarette-bumming acquaintance, a place I surely don't want to be. So, I will bite my
tongue some days 'til it bleeds and just shuffle along.

"Old Bridges"

These old bridges of brick and stone,
These old bridges of flesh and bone,
These old bridges that we once called home,
These old bridges...
These old bridges helped us both to pray and to cry,
These old bridges helped us laugh and sigh,
These old bridges between you and I,
These old bridges...
These old bridges so soaked with our tears,
These old bridges stood strong through the years,
These old bridges stood fast 'gainst our fears,
These old bridges...
These old bridges felt the rain, wind and sun,
These old bridges helped us first walk and then to run,
But these old bridges, they at last came undone.
These old bridges.... (New Mex.,1998-to help honour
  the end of a long-term relationship...)

"Write to Life"

Writing, for as long as I can remember, has always held a precious place in my heart. There are the two aspects for me as I've mentioned: one,the fun of working with ideas and words in my mind, in my imagination-that whole creative process and, two, the actual, physical process of feeling the pen glide across the page which is soon filling up with sentence after sentence-a very tactile experience that our friend, the computer, cannot match, I'm afraid. The computer simply does not have the right tools! Wow. Better than booze or drugs and there's no hangover or cotton-batten mouth in the morning. Whereas My Dad's 'mistress' as I've said, was our sailboat; mine-no question- is writing.

I've taken many and various writing courses in my day and,frankly,when I was looking for more inspiration, more knowledge about the publishing industry or television-I've usually come away somewhat disappointed. Hell, even the advertising industry seems full of many copywriters who are not really sure how they landed their creative, good-salaried positions. Second City? Improv? Closed circuits for the most part, where small tightly-knit groups of friends from high school or college have banded together, written and performed. Most of them perform only their own material-almost exclusively. So, the lesson there was to get into or create one of those circles early on. And film scripts? Forget it! Oftentimes you will see directors only doing scripts that they have written themselves. They're not open to 'external' or outside scripts – too many legal issues to contend with and complicate things ,and then there's the possible infringement of the financial pie which, in the film industry can be substantial.Nope, There's no demand or market, but that fact is little known or discussed in a world awash in the shiny-golden media coverage of the "underdog" and all- dreams-can- come- true- hype(the one-in- a- gazillion Rocky stories out there. Play the lottery, instead! No one is ever buying or producing scripts written-on-spec(written spontaneously by inspired-outsiders.) Am I bitter? You bet. Poison pen. Bitter grapes make fine vinegar. You might as well write in thin air, or pee in the snow because it will vanish before anyone of consequence ever reads it. It will sit at the back of the closet under some unused kitchen appliance from the shopping network for months which then become years. Rocky, you say! OK, have Stallone produce your movie-idea….

"Cheers!"

Sure, there was quite a bit of underage drinking in retrospect, mostly in the woods bordering our elementary school and sometimes in houses with parents away. Once even in peewee hockey(13&14) when the two older teenage boys who coached us(bad idea)thought it would be fun at one Saturday morning practice to provide a big bottle of chilled apricot Ripple wine and a couple of joints to their wide-eyed young charges-this, at 7:30 in the morning!). Not coincidentally, we were not a highly competitive team that year, as I've mentioned…,but we sure were a happy bunch of losers.

 ### "Busy is Good"

Surprisingly perhaps, but there was not too much more illicit drinking for the rest of high school for me, after the family resettled in Vancouver. I was on the football team, the editor of the student newspaper and had this wonderful steady girlfriend who I was mad about. In short, I was too busy, and too happy. Occasionally the two of us with a couple of friends might pick up a six pack or a 'twelver' and enjoy them on a White Rock beach, sometimes even with a fire. Ah, those were the days! A few times, the police would come by, have us pour out the beer and douse the fire; but it didn't matter ,really, as we had usually had our fun already by then.

 ### "Kiss & Cherry Brandy"

When college came, I stayed in residence with a few hundred other hormonally-challenged young men Great! There was touch-football on frosty weekend mornings, and a social event-dance called a "beer-bash" every Wednesday night to break up the week! As I recall, some of us nearly planned our schedules around the beer-bash on 'hump nights'- Get your mind out of the gutter; it was a Dance!

Many of the guys in the dorm would spend several thousand dollars of their summer earnings on new stereo systems by the end of August to listen to Leo Sayer, Linda Ronstadt and Meatloaf! Me ? When I would return to my inner sanctum at the residence, it was perhaps for a snort of cherry brandy and a wine-tipped cigar while listening to loud and scratchy Kiss on(no foolin') my 8-track tape/radio and trying to add more to the last essay.(There's just no explaining taste is there? Or lack of it…?) One weekend after stumbling upon the new word of "diatribe" and being utterly fascinated by it, I then went ahead and composed many and directed them toward each of my ten or twelve floor-mates and taped it to their doors , signing each only as "The Pen." It caused quite the stir for a while-and was a lot safer than hand grenades, I'll tell you.Why? Because I could; it seemed right.

 ## "Farts in a Windstorm"

I guess I've always been one never to turn down a bought beer offered to me(classy, huh?) and for being one-in some circles at least- who was known for being able to drink copious amounts of the stuff at most parties ever attended-thanks to that dinosaur-size I alluded to earlier. Add to that the fact that I have consumed more than my fair share of meat and potatoes over the years-and I quietly snuck up on the three hundred pound mark and shocked even myself when I learned of this truth. Yes, I cried! I told you: I cry at a lot of things… Buying clothes, then and now, has always been an issue for me. Then one day in China (where I was still a "svelte" 225/230lbs., I awoke to realize that I was surrounded by a sea of little men(people in general, I suppose). Don't get me wrong here, Chinese men are physically strong, tough-as-nails, sinewy,-just not in that stereotypical, beef-cake North American footballer- size. Not enough protein, I figure. They can eat a whole plate of stir-fried, chopped celery for lunch-and it might have 1-2 tablespoons of ham-burger meat sprinkled on top. No lie. This, while some of our guys here in the West are chowing down with two half-pound patties in just one "burger"- with enough meat to sat-isfy maybe five or six Chinese for one meal, possibly two.

 ## "Big Dads"

Is there any other kind? My father was not a huge man; he stood close to six feet at his peak and hovered around the 200 pound mark most of his adult life. So, his son "raised the bar" somewhat by taxing the scales with close to another one hundred pounds! Ouch. Not something I'm especially proud of. But it is what it is.

Small men, or as my father so delicately might have de-scribed them, "like farts in the proverbial windstorm"; they were of little consequence so not paid much heed. Thanks to our heavy-on-the-meat-diets here in the Western Hemi-sphere, many of our men, as the women will attest, must fart like Tyrannosaurus Rex, making the very earth tremble and scaring the cat out of the room. In those frivolous moments, I might sometimes call them "Richter-Farts" because I'm sure they must register on that earthquake scale. You know the kind….

 ## l.) (Funny Bits?) "Not a Day"

This condition of mine, being paralyzed on the left side of my body (not contagious, by the way; it is not-contrary to some thinking- a disease.) is not without its funny moments to be sure. In fact, I can honestly say that not a day goes by when I'm not facing some sort of funny, absurd moment or predicament.

Like for instance, I'm in a handicapped washroom stall where I cannot turn my wheelchair around once I've closed the door. Who designs these places anyways?.Do they want me to use the sink? It gets better: I've perched the roll of toilet paper in what I thought was a safe place for more timely use later, only to watch it inexplicably fall to the floor and sadly roll away from me under a partition and far out of reach, like in some weird cartoon while I sit helpless to stop it. Oh, yes, then there are the multitude of less-than-four-star eateries whose washrooms are inevitably hidden in the rear of the place usually down a narrow, poorly lit hallway which is crammed so full of boxes and supplies for lack of storage space that I can hardly squeeze by. Once I do get there, maybe I can't get through the door in my chair and have to stand and walk in the best I can by using the door and towel rack as support-guides. Once in position, then I can't close the door behind me. Fun stuff, alright .Does peeing and laughing simultaneously count as "multi-tasking"?

Even better – and this one happens most often with friends or family members when we're checking out a bathroom at a hotel/motel where I will be staying. Usually, one or two of them, after scanning the bathroom, will say excitedly," Look, they've got safety-grab bars beside the toilet!" I've learned by now, so am more hesitant until I do my own check. Just what I thought.., "Yes, they do… "I reply," but they're on the wrong side for me,huh?! A fifty-fifty chance at that point, I guess.

Sometimes, I'll get to just as far as the open door, looking at a john less than ten feet away-but, alas I can't get to it. Maybe it's like being on the shores of the River Jordan, seeing the promised land but not being able to complete the journey. That's when sometimes my smile turns into a deep, low absurd derisive laughter(being so close…yet so far to my objective-I've been told the laugh's a bit like F.D.' s the' nanny'.. I have to be especially careful at that moment because we all know at times how crying,laughing,coughing or sneezing can trigger incontinence; It's not something any of us want-especially when you've already been consciously crimping the hose hard for over an hour already.

Before going out anywhere these days, particularly some-where new, my mind immediately races with thinking of the washroom possibilities. There seems to be no standard in design or construction, so every washroom is a new adventure and often a challenging affair-not something,again,any of us welcome in moments of near –crisis. Once, I'll admit, while dining with a relative at a hotpot restaurant in Beijing and discovering there was only winding stairs with no railings up to the second floor washroom, he provided me some cover and distraction and I stood and peed in a plastic bowl the waitress had brought us in the back in a dark corner booth! Whew! Who knows? If you're having a Clint Eastwood moment and the punk in you is feeling lucky, you can occasionally find the episode reasonable, convenient and stress-free. Are you willing to take that chance, punk..? No.

Me, personally? I'm not much of a gambler,myself,as I've said; I would much prefer to go somewhere I know already works for me. That can be, understandably, tedious for some in my inner circle.

 ## " Pancakes, anyone?

Funny, stupid stuff, remember? I am no longer able to do some of the simplest tasks out there that most of us daily take for granted. I can no longer cut a lot of my own hard food into bite-sized bits because only my right arm is functional for the moment. Consequently, pancakes, French toast and waffles have become my standard breakfast favourites and, yes, porridge!. Oh,yes, can't very easily open any cans and jars also-if I'm cooking which I enjoy. Not that it's ever happened mind you but imagine, if you will, a grown man, slumped over in his wheelchair, nearly weeping in the kitchen because he's found the new bag of chocolateChipits,but can't get it open with his mouth and can't find the scissors... Grrrr!Do you really want to tug at my frustration strings? Give me one of those push-down first, then-turn childproof prescription drug containers Come on!Try it with one hand some time…

Let us backtrack some for a bit to that grade nine year of mine once more, back in early high school in my hometown. I took two very memorable courses; the one I wanted to take was Classical Studies 100 in which we studied Virgil's The Aeneid, and Homer's twins The Iliad and The Odyssey and the second course was my Mom's choice called 'Bachelor Survival' (groan..!which, of course was fabulous in the end!)

In' Bachelor Survival', we designed/ sewed our own shirts in one term and made a terrific roast beef feast in a second term which we all washed down with vodka and orange juice in class in front of the unsuspecting teacher(…such clever idiot- boys!). The course was terrific-and I don't just mean the 'screwdriver' part….Then in February came the opportunity of a lifetime-a school trip to Italy for eight days during Spring Break! With my parents' complete support, I was able to jump at it and off I went to Italy for the first time to see things and walk in places I had only read and dreamt about :The Vatican and Sistine Chapel, the Trevi Fountain, Piazza/ St. Peter's Square and in Venice, piazza san Marco, the Doge's Palace, Bridge of Sighs,Ponte-Veccio Florence, Pompeii, and finally, Sorrento, a picturesque mountain hamlet renowned for its cameo rings. Almost every female I knew back home at the time was destined to get one.

 "The Oldest in the Ancient."

The side trip to Pompeii was simply marvellous. It was a gorgeous clear day with the magnificent profile of Vesuvius as a backdrop and constant reminder of the catastrophe it birthed in 79 A.D for this bustling little seaport town. We would walk along those same cobble- stone roads with their deep chariot-wheel ruts. For me, it was mesmerizing to stand on a street corner, gaze up at the volcano-one of the 'three sisters' in Italy and imagine the horror and chaos of that terrible day so many years before. Wow! We saw the chilling plaster casts of the man –on –his –back and of the – dog -still –chained –to- wall, cowering, trying to cover its face with a paw to protect itself as the hot ash and smoke asphyxiated and buried him alive! Of course, no tour of ancient Pompeii, once a bustling seaport awash in sailors, could ever be complete without a visit to one of the ancient brothels. When our tour guide was asked about some of the messages carved into the stone walls, she snickered some and explained how they were just recommen-dations from earlier customers to subsequent clients about which girls to see and why! 'See Francis in Four for fellatio!' For me, it was easy to imagine myself there-not in the brothel, mind you, but just in ancient Pompeii, maybe working for one the local wine-merchants or in one of the dozens of bakeries that existed back then. Sure, Kim.

 ## "It's Our Heritage, Apparently…"

Now, let's jump back to modern times. These days, early on weekend mornings, I'll sometimes watch hunting and fishing shows in horror, disgust and some fascination.It's on those early mornings when nature's call precludes further sleep usually. Disgust, you ask? Yes, when I see a beautiful moose or caribou,or,even worse, a majestic black bear shot dead, yes- it disgusts me and then there's the hunter tug-ging the huge head up by the ears for the camera and his" trophy-shot". Seems to me it's all men pulling the triggers, of course. I'm left wondering what some of the compelling reasons are that make many of us men want to do that to begin with? I know so little about that life that it fascinates me; perhaps I will never understand the psyche involved. To watch so many small-bummed, big-bellied men, the kind who persist in wearing belts(decades after they've gone out of fashion), and even then trying to tuck- in their very small tee-shirts, and all this while balancing precariously in a small boat in the middle of the lake.

"A Many-Splendored Thing"

I will jump around a little now and then as you no doubt have noticed and land, for now, squarely in the hypocritical heart of our own multi-culturalist culture. To rant on, I think it's mostly a political and tourism-marketing sham:makes for good brochures and draws 'em in! It's all a façade, really-like that Cuban 'embargo' in the States. I mean, sure, there are many different cultures and races here in Canada, that's true-no argument. But they don't always blend so well as in a mural....thus the switch in metaphor, I guess from a 'quilt' a generation ago to the more accurate "mosaic" now, where all the little tiles are put side-by-side, maybe even touching some, including our own heritage of dual-founders, French and English. Golly, I know people who, because they can say "Ni Hao", and because they eat deep-fried chicken or some kind of mystery meat- balls once a month in sickening sweet orange sauce, consider themselves quite 'cosmopolitan'!

'Multicultural?' Sure, we love to eat Chinese!' (Women and babies? Do you stir-fry them?). These are the same people who can eat an omelette for breakfast without recognizing or caring about its French origins Of course, the Chinese had already been eating omelettes for a thousand years by the time 'our Wolfe and Montcalm' squared off on the Plains of Abraham, So there!.

If these pretenders do attend one of the many parades or festivals offered up every year by the city, then again, they're showing their 'deep' multicultural stripes! The fact that few are able to discern among the many Asian cultures, or even care to, is of no concern to them; I think when they're not so busy attending these multicultural festivals or eating some Chinese, then they're probably at home praying for a lottery win!. Many of us don't seem to care and have little motivation to actually learn about the other cultures in our midst once we've finished our class presentations on them in grade six. And that's really just too bad, and a little sad.

 ## "Golf Balls and Eye Infections"

Getting back on track now, I'd like to return to what I consider that fairly colourful childhood and tween/teenhood of mine; you know about some of the underage drinking-but how was it all financed, you ask? There was a base 'salary' of income which most of us at the time collected which was called an "allowance", but that was just a measly few dollars each week. So, it did take some ingenuity to handsomely supplement that with two main entrepreneurial ventures for my inner circle at least:golfballs and fishing lures. There was a nice, little Par-3 golf course close to the bridge connecting us to our southern cousins in Michigan. A few of us would sneak onto the course after hours in the dark and then retrieve lost balls by swimming in the water hazards. Before long ,we had perfected it to an art where we would carry our masks, snorkels and fins with us in a knapsack, like camouflaged navy seals on a black ops- mission. Some nights we could find almost two hundred balls. Three boys-two hundred balls We didn't need and rarely used the masks-we would just walk and feel the balls under our feet, dip down and get them.

Then, we would polish them up and be back out at the entrance to the course early the next morning to display our treasures on towels and sell them back to golfers on their way in at, say, three for five, five for ten etc.

Then there was our fishing- lure' industry'. We knew where most of the salmon fishermen gathered each morning on the shoreline where Lake Huron narrowed for its final rush under the bridge into the St. Clair River. We would go out swimming there later in the morning with masks, fins and PLIERS(here, the masks were invaluable!) to help easily dislodge the snagged lures from the debris at the bottom of the lake where they had been lost that same morning. Again, similar to the golf balls; we would clean them up and sell them back to the fishers in the next morning or two. This was also a lucrative, but much trickier business-exercise because each different lure required a careful, individual assessment and evaluation to set a price. Some research at our local Canadian Tire store helped us some in that way. Still, a good morning of sales could yield each of us between ten and forty dollars, more than enough for some cigarettes and beer- and perhaps even a late night pizza here and there, not to mention the occasional and much-prized" "Thai-stick." There we were, learning all about business management and finance with trying to juggle these two enterprises at once, and learning, too, about good partners, bad partners! Needless to say, it was a good summer if you were into those sorts of things. However, it did come to an abrupt end and came crashing down for me, after I con-tracted an eye infection from swimming in those cesspools called 'water hazards'; I came clean, so to speak, after some torturous parental interrogation and, after a week of antibiot-ics, had to give up my share of the golf ball retrieval trade under direct orders from home!

 " A Team Player"

Those who have never really played on a successful sports team(regardless of gender..) before cannot fully appreciate the camaraderie and bonding that goes on in those circles. Me? As mentioned, I was fortunate enough to have been a part of two such championship teams as an early teenager. In football, it was dreary, cold, drizzly fall mornings out in the muck charging the sled or doing pylon drills. Those best and cruellest coaches among them would burn memories of themselves(like brands) into so many of us by always reserving the wind-sprints for the final few moments of each practice(maybe common, I wouldn't know..) with all of us exhausted, panting and only thinking of hot-showers just moments away. Our team-building evening consisted of pizza and a Woody Allen movie. Maybe that one's uni-versal? It is precisely those moments, as real coaches and players know, that build the otherwise elusive "chemistry" that helps bond those winning teams. They provide those painful, joyous memories that are shared among the select few who were there and experienced it for themselves.

 ## "In the Trenches"

Each of those teams was like an additional,quasi-family because of the time spent together and those unforgettable moments in the trenches. To a one, I'm sure, each of us has harkened back to the one or two terrific plays that we maybe made some twenty or twenty-five years earlier. Some might characterize that sort of thing as "sad", even pathetic. Those people are generally women, and usually wives, many of whom did not play team-sports, I bet. We men are pathetic, in so many ways- no argument, here. Those 'family-teams' not everyone is aware also shared much with Snow White's crew of dwarves because each had to have: a sleepy-head, a doc-wannabe, a sneezy and always 1-2 grumpees

Inspiration*

As I've shared already and will some more I'm sure, my beautiful, adoring wife is-without question- my biggest inspiration. Her smile is the ultimate reward I continue to chase day after day. It lightens my entire being when I see her. Still… give it time.' the one old cynical friend murmurs….

 ## "A Depressing Inspiration"

Truth to tell, many of these rehabilitation centres where I've spent a lot of time these past few years, whether they be in China or Canada-anywhere, I suppose- are at once both depressing and inspirational places to be in. You see people, some of whom will never even stand again much less walk and who need much assistance just in transferring from chair to bed or john. Think about that for a moment: there will always be an attendant with them every time they go to the toilet. Or the ones who can't even manage that much and do all their business in diapers on the bed! While in China in the one facility, while attending to my own stand-up business, a man would be regularly wheeled in from his room down the hall and left in the middle of the washroom to do his thing. You see, his wheelchair had obviously been adapted with a custom- hole in the seat that allowed him to 'evacuate'. Seeing that would make me sad. When done, he would turn and wheel himself away, leaving the proof of his visit on the floor behind him. It was hard to be a witness to any aspect of that sort of thing, if you know what I mean; You can't really chit-chat while it's going on. I wonder, though, how did he feel about it all? Talk about your dignity, or lack thereof?

Then… you can watch as a two-legged dog hops out onto the stage of the Oprah Winfrey show, or a dolphin has been given a prosthetic tail….I've seen many double-amputees re-learning to walk on artificial limbs, burn victims, and people who have suffered simply unimaginable pain and anguish-but there they are getting up, opening their eyes and trying to walk a little further every day. Wow! The spirit we have all been gifted with is truly precious and remarkable.

 "The Hillside"

Of course, my Dad, as part of his relocation deal to the West Coast, had negotiated all new accommodation for his twenty-six foot mistress-sloop, the family sailboat. It had been shipped out to the coast on a flatbed train car and thus saw what most large sailboats never see: the Prairies. She seemed to take smoothly to her new salty home after most of her life spent in the freshwater Great Lakes(Lake Ontario, Huron). She would now be berthed in a small, quaint yacht club attached to his new work place, one of the few oil refineries in the Lower Mainland on Burrard Inlet. The club was a self-sufficient joint that had railway tracks and a heavy-duty dolly which could then be hauled up onto the tiny beach where a concrete platform awaited. An old electric motor and winch was located up on the crest of the hill and did the work in bringing members' boats up to dry land for repairs and annual upkeep. Now, ours, you may remember, was a four and one-half ton boat, so the process was not without a fair amount of anxiety because, like a small whale, if she were to ever topple over on the way out or on the beach-platform, it would have been disastrous. We would put her 'up on the ways' every spring for a few weeks, sand and paint, sand some more and varnish, getting her ship-shape for the upcoming season. It was always exhausting yet somehow exhilarating work, having become a labour of love for all of us by then!

 ## "Chocolate Chip Cookies"

The final time father and son performed this ritual together ended, I think, on rather a low note. My Mom and sister would stand on the hillside working the controls for the winch-motor as my father and I guided the four- ton boat gently into the waiting upright, metal arms of the dolly-which had been positioned at the end of the track at low tide. The electric motor, winch and drum, had seen its hay- day by now, so the stop- and- go controls were a bit finicky and overly sensitive, sometimes working for only ten or fifteen feet at a go!

Dad would give what we both thought was a very clear 'stop' signal with an unmistakeable slashing motion across his throat in exaggerated movements. Still, however, to both of our surprise, the boat, its keel now resting firmly on the dolly, continued to lurch forward toward the shore and the concrete platform, What the hell was going on? His frustration grew and before long we were engrossed in sarcastic ridicule of our 'winch-mates' at the top of the hill. Dad growled," What the hell are they doing, anyway? To us, it seemed like they were disobeying the golden rule-never take your eyes off the skipper and his hand signals. A moment later, I countered with," Oh, probably discussing recipes and how many chocolate chips to put into the chocolate chip cookies. Whatever it was, it was 'like farts in a windstorm': inconsequential, irrelevant. Nothing was ever to interfere with the communication between us during those critical moments. Clearly, they were busy chirping away merrily about something, and not paying attention to us on the boat! There would definitely be a follow-up conversation to this matter! .My Mom and sister left the club first that night to head home(maybe to hide…?). The process did continue and eventually, the sloop was safely positioned on the ways, and soon ,high ,dry and safe on the beach platform. There would definitely be a follow-up conversation to the matter….My Mom and sister left the club first to head home, as I've said. My Dad and I would stay for a few more hours, putting up support struts, her overnight tarpaulin and the like, to ensure she was secure for her first night on dry land. It would be eleven or eleven-thirty before I started thinking of my own fifty minute drive home to Kitsilano. I left finally, but not before my father and I had a heated, unforgettable exchange on that dark hillside beside the boat and the old winch. How heated, you ask? As we did some last-minute adjustments with the safety cables holding the dolly and boat in place, his patience snapped with me for not working fast enough and I felt like he was treating me like a child all over again; This simply wouldn't do, so, playing the oh- so-mature male game of you- pushed- me- first, I pushed back with my tolerance at zero-no more of that stuff, thank you very much! I went off the deep end and for the first and only time in my life, I told my father, to go fuck himself!! Then, I got in my car and drove away, leaving him standing by himself in the yacht club's dark parking lot. I was feeling some sense of relief but also a nearly overwhelming sense of that heavy, Presbyterian guilt I've talked of which clings to you like skunk spray. Two days later, I would embark on a long-awaited three week European adventure-holiday with my then common-law partner. I would never see my father alive again.

For months, even a few years after, I stewed in that same guilt about how our final exchange had ended on that dark hillside by the water. It's been pretty hard to shake that one-for what I said to my own father, the man who helped teach me to walk, skate (even if only to turn in one direction well!) and ride a bicycle, (the engineer who finally saw his one and only,big,ole mouth-breathing son graduate not only from high school, but also university!)

 ## "Mr. Bigness" (No, not Carrie's fellow)

As I've mentioned before, I've always been "a big boy". Everything about me(pretty much) was big, and my mother was good at reminding me of that with each clothes-shopping foray. My hands are big, my feet have always been enormous, my arms long. Even my lips are quite big,and,oh yeah, my tongue. The latter two were just two of many contributing factors in my penchant for mouth-breathing and for the early lisping and stuttering difficulties. I don't really know, but I wouldn't be surprised to learn they probably have tongue-reduction surgery these days for those who need it.Even then I knew a fellow who had a pronounced "lateral s" lisp causing him to froth at the mouth which made mine sound like nothing. My Mom, bless her heart, used to also tell me that when I was little because I would sit on a chair and often breathe through my gaping mouth, even her husband, that's right-my own father- thought early on that maybe, just maybe, I was retarded. Nice, huh?

So, you can just imagine the thrill it must have been for him to see me, his behemoth, spluttering boy graduate from two academic institutions! Now, Back to Vancouver these days. My wife and I just saw that excellent film "The King's Speech" the other day and I so strongly identified with George the sixth and his speech travails that at some moments it made me shudder to my very core. It brought back a flood of all not-pleasant memories; I never had to do the marbles-in-the-mouth exercise, but I did have to stumble my way through a terrible maze of trying tongue- twisters just full of "Susie's and Sally's. And that would lead to me making up a few nastier ones of my own which I won't share, sorry.

 ## 'The Slow Joy-Ride!

A lot of we stupid, young men(somewhat redundant, yes..?)-teenagers, mostly- seemed to do it, so finally the opportunity presented itself to me, and I grabbed at it-bleating all the time-: my parents were away, I had found the keys to our Volkswagen Beetle, and, most importantly, there was to be a house-party in the area that night!. I was all of fourteen, maybe fifteen by then, pre-most smarts(&license)… and , like any, stupid, self-loathing sheep or lemming is wont to do, I loaded up the car with a few friends and illegally drove(you didn't know that lemmings drove cars?) the six or seven blocks it was to the party- house; well, we eventually did arrive after an excruciatingly long trip which was made ,really, in ten or fifteen foot increments: I had next to no idea what driving a standard transmission entailed and nor did any of my accomplices. Sort of like that women-thing, too, where we knew what they should look like, but had no operating knowledge. Yep, that was one more of very few truly idiotic, adolescent moments and I (we) survived it! Some don't…survive the 'stupids' My parents never mentioned it although I know the snoopy next-door neighbour doubtlessly informed them when she saw me jerkily reversing out of our driveway with three other heads silhouetted in the vehicle besides mine- knowing my parents were out of town.

 ## "Dad-in-a-Bag"

As it turns out, I did go to Europe with my partner at that time for several weeks; we had a wonderful time, but I did arrive back in Canada only to learn that my father had died in

my absence and my Mom had already cremated him . There
he was now, his ash-remains in a plastic bag inside a small
cardbox box which lay on the floor of his bedroom beside the
desk where, for so many hours, he would sit, handicapping
the thoroughbreds in preparation for his big weekend at the
races; boy, he sure did love 'watching the nags.' There were
loads of memories, of course, but the freshest was still the
one that happened just prior to my departure for Europe and
of how I told him, 'to go fuck himself' on that dark hillside,
before I did go to Europe–not exactly what you hope your
last exchange will be with your father. I would do a lot of
internal dialoguing with my Pulpit Master... who eventually
was able to console me some with the fact that, all things considered, I was a pretty good, decent man and a good-hearted
son. The truth was that that one moment on the hillside was a
mere instant in a 'century of life' we shared together and one
not to be dwelt upon. That summer,we would eventually take
Dad out for his' final sail' aboard Panique and return his ashes
to the brine on a gloriously sunny day! My Mom, sister and
I held a special little ceremony on board in the cockpit and
said our farewells. Just the following day, it's true, the new
neighbours across the street welcomed their first-born into the
world; after all, there was a vacancy

"Heartspring"

So differently those shades appear:
A weakened pulse is gone yet near;
A friendly sparkle in a stranger's eye
But so, too, a sudden strangeness in an old friend's sigh
The evening dusk blends with the dawn;
Our father's here, our father's gone.
We do see your face there in the stars above,
In the wide delta's giant tidal sweep;
And in the blinding sunlit ripples of the sea,
And the cool rainbow shade of the deep.
Some rhyme is lost to reason
Much reason lacks all rhyme-
How I'll always wish to hold him,

Just once more, a final time.
I wish they knew, the other five billion,
How much I loved my father.
I can only hope he knew.
Many sons are not so lucky; this one was.
The life-cycle is moved on,
Faster than anticipated but nevertheless
Precisely on time;
Dust to dust, dust to water, ashes to water,
And when my soul is parched with having lost your
    fragile body to the ages,
I shall drink plentifully from your strong spirit
At the Heartspring of memory.
A chorus of angels will sing a hallelujah welcome-
As is their custom for gentle souls and pure hearts.
Each new day will be a baptism of sorts,
To wash away the anger and fears-yours and mine, both-
And to leave only the sounds of a new life
Whose crown glistens with the tears of God.
   (August 18, 1991)

 ## "Best Game!"

I could, also, quite easily, remember one of my much earlier hockey games from the time when I was maybe fourteen(making it 'Bantam' level for those keeping score, I guess). I had run (boarded) an opponent quite hard in behind our net, and he slumped to the ice unconscious. In my feeble defense, it was not a brutal or cheap hit, and long before players had "STOP! Signs stitched into the BACK of our jerseys. He was out for a moment or two and, finally, would be helped by teammates back to their bench and then to the dressing room. Well, the boy's father was so furious with me that he climbed down several seat-rows and was soon trying to grab at me over the plexiglass at our bench and swearing a 'blue streak!' My father intervened to protect me. It didn't escalate beyond a shoving and light wrestling match between the two dads and that was probably a good thing. My dad had come within seconds of being a golden glove champion during his navy days as a middleweight or light heavyweight; he could throw a meaningful punch if ever he wanted to. He wouldn't tolerate me ever street-fighting at school, but he did tutor me some and set me up with gloves and a speed-bag down in our basement by the workbench.

Eventually, they escorted the other still angry dad toward an exit, and my folklore grew immensely with my peers that day. Not only had I knocked an opponent out of the game, but I also scored a goal on a rare slap shot after an end-to-end rush!(I might have had three of those rushes in my whole hockey 'career').Generally, I was a reserved, -stay-at- home defenseman . 'A spider-D- man'- let them come to me, then annihilate them-put them down, with good, clean hits, mind you. Without question, it was the best game for me as a youngster. I was simply not mean-spirited and, in fact, held back often in earlier days because of my tremendous size advantage!

  "Fish-Killer!"

I had almost every kind of pet imaginable when I was growing up. Go ahead, name one! (OK,, maybe no primates..) I had them all : dogs,cats,rabbits,birds, goldfish and exotic fish(Siamese fighter and an 'angelfish'), turtles(painted, snapping), garter snakes, mice, seahorses and, of course, my beloved crocodile! And here's my father holding little "Cronky".He was named after favorite broadcaster Walter "-And that's the way it was.!" Cronkite! Most of our pet names seemed to end with," y" in those days.

There were two orange goldfish (aren't they all?)No, I know; I've seen yellow ones, too, but I think "yellowfish" just doesn't have the same, strong ring to it. However, it became apparent after a while that they both had developed

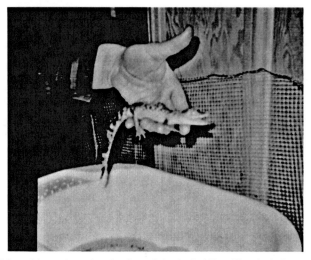

One of those big engineer hands of my father's, holding 'Cronky', the pet croco-
dile- a S. American black caiman who would never come to know the mangrove
swamp he was born in.

some sort of virus or fungus which caused pronounced holes
in the top of their head(like pencil holders); it was clear that
something was wrong. This ugliness/unhealthiness could not
be tolerated by my young aesthetic. The fish were unhealthy-
that was clear, perhaps even dying..? Consequently, I took it
upon myself one day after school to euthanize them. As I
couldn't find syringes small enough for their petite frames,
I took them out from their watery home, marched out in our
backyard with them cupped in one hand, lay them down in
what once had been my childhood sandpit and then promptly
cut them in half with one of my Mom's sharp garden spades.
The deed was done. I felt quite good about what I had done.
My parents, on the other hand, did not...party –poopers! I
was royally admonished for killing our little fish, for making that dreadful sort of decision on my own - without ever
consulting my folks. Would I now go straight to hell? Doubt
it. For what? Fish-killer (First catfish, now goldfish-but still
cold-blooded. It could have been much worse. I guess).

"Animal Shelter"

We had almost every kind of animal imaginable as a pet when I was growing up, as I've said. Go ahead, name one (OK, no primates!): dogs,cats,goldfish,turtles, small snakes, mice, seahorses and ,of course, my beloved crocodile. It wasn't until much later when I brought a black-widow spider on board! And that one I found in the wild-no kidding- at a toilet in a provincial campground in the Okanagan.

 ## "Jabba-jabba-do!"

There are some days now when I feel just like a big blob sitting in my wheelchair, especially on those rainy days when I'm wearing my giant, tent-sized poncho which makes me seem even bigger than I am - which is huge!. Those are my 'jabba-the-hut –days', where I'm feeling a little down perhaps and somewhat useless, not entirely there in my being, you know… a little dislocated, disconnected. I do ,however, have a big ball of sunshine inside on most days, regardless of weather. It is that energy I daw from every day to help keep me going. I think I've been quite fortunate that way from long before , and since the stroke that ,generally speaking, I have a good attitude and rather positive, happy demeanor. I believe it's true: there's a heck of a lot more good in the world than bad, like the water to land ratio(or right-handed to left-handed,70:30) I want to believe. I have so much to live for and to be thankful for and, at the top of the list, is my wife who still manages to be number one by a mile, with glorious, breath-taking sunrises that distant second. She's just a remarkable person whose inner warmth and grace match her outer beauty and charm. Personally, I think she oozes life and goodness and she has that gorgeous smile that first won me over!. What's even more, she loves me,hah! That is, quite simply, a blessing!

"Red-Handed on the Wrong Side of the Bridge!"

Once earlier on in that deep childhood of mine, I was foolish enough to get caught stealing while on foreign soil, a risky proposition to be sure although, I suppose much later as a young man it could have been a Spanish or Moroccan jail for a golf ball-sized chunk of hashish! On 'home and native land,' it was something that many of us did quite often in those early days: shoplifting for chocolate bars or gum (with hockey cards) was quite common in those days; we didn't consider it a "real" crime, after all(Idi Amin?). Much later, we would even joke amongst ourselves that the 'lifting' of gum, chocolate bars and other sundry items from the lower shelves was a contributing factor to our local Mac's Milk store's demise and eventual shutting down. While across the border one day in the United States, an acquaintance and I got caught red-handed while shoplifting. Rolex watches, you ask? Perhaps diamond rings? No, no,no.We were trying to steal the very best, the most popular item around at the time. That's right: Hot wheel cars! We were threatened with a trip to the police station during our initial in-store interrogation. I may have peed my pants, but can't recall for sure! Oh, Yeah! Well, the guy did give me a Dr. Pepper, after all!

"Hard to find a good Spittoon these Days"

I was just never a good spitter and, for a guy, that is problematic because, apparently, we are supposed to be good at it? Is it in our genes or what? Even with me being on two championship sports' teams, I still could never spit very well at all; It was never covered during our practice time or else I missed it! I could talk the talk in most every other way, but when stalking the sidelines or sitting on the bench, I simply could not make it happen. More than a few times in football, I would try spitting through the big, metal cage protecting my face, only to have it hit one of the horizontal steel struts and then have to watch for the next ten minutes as my gooey green-egg gob(sorry..) slowly made its way downward,yikes . Hell, to this day, both before and after my stroke I sometimes have trouble even clearing my own body. The worst ones are when I can't even clear my own face and chin! Nice. Hm mm.

 ## "Funny,ha ha"

For as long as I can remember, wherever I was, whatever the situation was…, I wanted to see, find or manufacture humour in the moment. I was very likely an intellectual and humour-bully. Weren't smart enough to keep up with me? Then you were a perfect target for my ridicule… a sitting duck! Didn't understand my humour? Perfect target! When I was a young boy in elementary school, I was a rear-seat heckler(rarely do we sit in the front rows); I was always there with a snide, or sarcastic remark or some form of wise-crack when the teacher paused long enough while talking up at the front of class. I have forever felt the need to inject levity into most any situation that presented itself. Of course, my elementary school days happened during the hay-days of the corporal- punishment era, the sixties, so my 'naughty' behaviour was consistently rewarded with a solemn and painful visit to the Principal's Office, Twice and sometimes three times a week, I would be pulled from class unceremoniously, escorted down the hall and left waiting for 'the big guy'. He wasn't really that big, just tall. Truth to tell, I was already bigger than he would probably ever be, and with his nearing retirement it's safe to assume his growth spurts were behind him by then. That's right, it was "strap time." I don't, honestly, remember the bum-whacking's(except at home..), but you had to hold one hand out very still in mid-air as he whipped the wide, hard leather belt down several times for some serious contact with the palm of your hand. What was scary beyond the "dead- man walking" thing down the hall or the wait-time outside of his office(which would always get the anxiety- motor revving) was the fact that our principal was missing two fingers on the hand that held the instrument of torture/ . You just needed to glimpse that damaged hand to start hyperventilating. Legend had it he had lost the fingers because he struck so hard with the strap!

There was- to go back a bit- one teacher of mine who, after putting her laser-sights on me for a trip down the hall-way, would pull me up out of my desk to a standing posi-tion by using only an earlobe. Being a big boy, as I've said, that was a lot of weight to pull up by a poor little flap of fat. That, by itself, was hardly an enjoyable experience. My earlobes responded sometimes with some sad swelling, and always by turning neon red, like Rudolph's nose! At the end of the day, my mother could often see at a glance or examine my ears more closely to know if I had been in trouble that day. The school, of course, would always call home to tell parents about such indiscretions and the punishments they meted out were, according to my parents, always justified and well-deserved. I could always try to conceal my ears, but those damn phone calls did me in every time! Whenever I did get the strap at school, I knew that after some interro-gation I would be getting it again, doubly hard, from an ex-Navy man with all of his fingers and toes! That's right: Dear Ole Dad! It was tough-love alright. Hell, even my piano teacher was in on it; she was a little, shrivelled up old nun (no kidding..);however, she wielded a small, metal rod just above my fingers as I nervously attempted to play. Whap! Whap! My parents couldn't understand all my anxiety over my weekly piano lessons -something that was intended to be fun and joyful! I guess ,I was probably in grades four and five at the time and had started biting my fingernails. Today, I could probably successfully sue for abuse? Ah, the times they are a-changin'.Or to discover every second kid out there had his piano-playing knuckles rapped hard, too! And, there, I thought I was the only one to have a crocodile?

 ## "Higgledy-Piggledy"

Higgledy-piggledy, here, there and everywhere... scat-terbrained. I feel strongly that that is how our brains work (at least mine), stroke or no stroke- you know, all over the place, all the time (a little disclaimer, I suppose.) To jump back a bit to 2003 when I was still teaching at the international school in China's North-East and all the Canadian teachers lived in furnished apartments in what I'll call the 'Teacher Compound', every day I would pass by a gaggle of women, all maids and a few baby-sitters and all preparing to go to work themselves ..for us. The only thing I could ever really say that first year was "Ni Hao" –that was pretty much it for me and several others. As I walked by, smiled, nodded and exhausted my Chinese, they would all snicker and laugh at the big, ignorant, foreign man. There was a collection of us who did not understand much Mandarin at all and could speak even less. It sure made for some funny, interesting moments every day –if you could look past the awkwardness.

 ## "Outdoor strip-mall housing"

Woops! We're now back in Beijing where I was English Trainer for an international high-tech company. Daily, on my way to work in a taxi from the subway station, we would drive through these shanty-town, slum neighbourhoods where I would see tarpaulins or sections of corrugated plastic and metal balanced precariously across an alleyway between ramshackle, old, red-brick buildings. People lived in or near these places which were mostly exposed to the elements and they just did what needed to be done to carry on with the daily business of life. For one stretch of time, after waving goodbye to my girlfriend(and future-wife!) at the subway station, my cab would pass by one of these strip-malls of the poor and I regularly saw a man out by the street, squatting at curb side, still brushing his teeth and spitting the leftover paste into the gutter. Then, we would drive the remaining 5-6 blocks to my job, on the twelfth floor of a luxury office tower that had two restaurants and a bar in the lobby. Old world-new world/HaveNot's-Have 's. The impoverished next to or embedded in, if you will, the new, wealthy class. That's the China, I know, the one that has been booming economically for a decade or more.

This juxtaposition was found everywhere, and to me this blending (or clash) was fascinating!

 "Two Men and a Urinal"

Earlier on, I said you would be hard-pressed to find more gracious hosts in the world than the Chinese. I do honestly and heartily believe that, still. However, after living in my Beijing suburb for a few months and having established fairly comfortable daily and weekly routines, I finally gathered the wherewithal and jam(peas in a pod) to venture out and try to taste what nightlife there was there in my vicinity It was time to move a little farther away from my own 'tree'. So, I took one of the dozens of pedicabs/motorcycle taxis to a local luxury hotel with a karaoke-nightclub joint attached Many of those establishments, as it turns out, are simply brothels. What did I know..? I drank a few beers then had to do what most others do at that moment-I went to the washroom. I made my way to a urinal and was standing there, attending to business. A moment into it all, I felt another, third hand gently chopping at my backside, massaging me. No lie. As male patrons of the place stood and peed at the urinals, the club would have young male attendants start giving them back rubs and massages. Now, this is very much a cultural thing and simply another example of their strange or bizarre ways of "providing for you, especially rich foreigners, as often as they can. Guess you can do that sort of thing when you have an over-flowing pool of labour to draw from and each is getting pennies for an six or eight hour shift(a little more than the 'napkin-fluffers'! When this first happened to me, my initial impulse was to turn, grab the hand's owner and slam him up against the wall while spitting out, "What the F- are you doing?!!?" A Chinese man with some English who was also present in the nightclub was kind enough to explain the whole matter to me. In hindsight that would have been too much like some homophobic Hollywood actors who freak out when a Frenchman tries to kiss them on both cheeks! Should get out more, I say…) I have very few hard and fast rules in this life; however, one remains that whenever I'm doing any toileting business, my hands are the only ones ever allowed to get that close! Yow!! Case closed.

However, having said that, at least just in my personal experience, too, sometimes individually they can be some of the rudest and most thoughtless folk around. This, now, is coming from me remember, a man in a wheelchair, got it? It is, I feel, very much a cultural issue: oftentimes, whereas the elderly are traditionally revered, the infirmed, deformed or handicapped are not simply neglected but actually shunned and almost left alone on the boulevard to the elements to dispose of like other unwanted things. Many times I've been sitting at a doorway waiting to enter somewhere and I've had a younger, and ,able-bodied man or woman rush or squeeze by me to get through first without a thought to hold the door for me. I am not their responsibility, so why would they care? That's education, but even more…sensibility.

They have yet to embrace the handicapped, the misshapen and deformed (except during their brief Olympic phase some, when they put on their 'happy face'/facade for the world) who are then treated with an almost disdain normally reserved for the diseased. There still exists a terrible old-world ignorance and prejudice toward the abnormal and 'imperfect' among us, and this will only change slowly like a creeping glacier. It is beginning to happen; I'm seeing more and more ramps.

 ## "Don't All Men?"

Yep, it's true: I've had some therapy, alright.How did you know? Add that to my naturally introspective self and I'm always exploring or searching for that greater context in my mind(Qualifying, second-guessing, predicting..). I think this

way as a man, so don't all men? It's taken me a while to realize that the answer to that is, the cliché- resounding, "No."
Sure, there's the easy stuff. For example, women; it's safe I
think to assume that most all of us men wonder about them,
THINK about them, and many of us lust after them because
we so enjoy the intensely pleasurable act itself: so much of
our current culture is premised on that. That reasoning is
simple enough because after some time and experience on
the planet, we learn just what kind of incredible physical/
sexual pleasure they can bring us. And, who doesn't like
pleasure, after all? You don't have to be an hedonist to appreciate it. No man who is still breathing and walking upright, that's who. Another one of those wonderful paradoxes
at the heart of our human nature, don't you think: first and
foremost due to survival instincts, we are very selfish, self-
serving animals, but we are at the same time very social- beings who need and crave companionship and contact with
the group. Doesn't everybody? Some more than others. In
the end, we are little more than human-bees who have managed to ruin much of their own hive.

 ## "On the Sidewalk"

Whenever I had visitors come to Beijing and look in on me,
I always tried to warn them about being a pedestrian; Normally, you would think that you're safe as a pedestrian up
on the sidewalk and off the street in North America at least,
but motorcyclists in China will frequently come up on the
sidewalk just to avoid traffic. It is so common to see , in fact,
that you need to have your wits about you at all times.Leav-
ing the safety of your tree does have its dangers…

 ## "Cardboard Underwear" Redux

For the most part, they don't have clothes-dryers in the
homes and apartments in Beijing. Now, this is a good thing,
right? Think of the electricity they are saving! Clothes there

are all usually drip-dried and whenever possible hung out-side in the fresh air and ample sunshine. This often neces-sitates ironing, if you care enough about the wrinkles; who irons their underwear?-Please don't raise your hands! Me? I'm a man, remember? I couldn't care less. Give 'em a good pull-shake and they should be good. I had a nice, big sunny and often very cold enclosed balcony where I could hang my stuff.OK sure, sometimes the briefs were a little like cardboard, but they'd settle in to the right places after just a few uncomfortabe strides!

 ## "Hypertension"

Hypertension has been a part of my make-up, I guess since birth, though I was probably a tweenie before I became fully cognizant of it. You want to know what it's like? On Monday morning, I would start getting anxious about playing Santa Claus at the staff party on Friday afternoon. I could worry about every aspect of my 'performance' from how round my belly-pillows would be, the angle of my hat and my "ho, ho, ho's"… After finishing a Saturday morning hockey game when I was younger, the anxiety for the next game would start mounting as I was taking off my skates from the game just played! I can and will always remember being asked to read aloud from a novel in those early grades when I was spluttering and blundering my way through two pronounced speech impediments: lisping and stuttering(which the Brits would be want to call stammering. As our teacher called on all of the students, desk after desk, I would be sitting there, trying to shrink my enormous bulk and calculating…' eleven before me, ten, nine more…, etc.

 ## "The Nearby Town"

Again we boomerang backwards to that first year of living in China, again, when I was teaching at the international school, remember? The apartment complex for the Canadian teach-ers was directly across the street from the school, maybe a three minute walk if you took your time. We were also about a twenty minute walk from the local town(40 minutes when really cold out!), a little fishing village called Jinshitan/ Manjitan. It had a few small stores, lots of bakeries and hair salons(most of which were fronts for brothels I would later discover-nope, never got my haircut there!) and several different restaurants that would all become favourites –of ours. On the weekends, it had quite a sizable open- air produce market which always made for fun adventures, considering most of us did not speak or understand Mandarin at all.

 ## "Early Shopping Forays"

Wash Your Meat! In that first year of living in the teacher compound across from the school, and a twenty minute walk to the nearby little fishing- village with its attendant small stores and restaurants, a weekend tour for groceries at the open-air market was enlightening in so many ways. The fresh fruit and veggies and meats were laid out on the ground, sometimes on towels, tarps, sometimes not, sometimes just on the dusty concrete. We just pointed at what we wanted and fingered how many. Then, when it was time to pay, we'd reach into a pocket, retrieve a twenty or fifty Yuan bill, hand it to the vendor and hope/wait for change . At the time, fifty was approximately ten bucks- Canadian; at the high point, it was about 8 yuan to the dollar!. After getting the change back, only then could we figure out roughly how much a tomato or bunch of celery cost. None of us could speak any Chinese, really, beyond the cursory, "Ni Hao"-so there was always a lot of gesturing and pointing. We had our favourite, little store for buying cigarettes, pop and stuff and the very occasional but very cheap and oh-so foul-tasting bijou(a native-favorite and clear liquor relative to ouzo and bad vodka!). For some of us, just seeing an "Oh Henry" chocolate bar could be cause for minor celebration as it was a recognizable little treat with understandable English packaging!

For most of that first year, I also had developed another very enjoyable, personal routine whereby, after my first quick coffee at home, I would don my swim shorts, grab a bag with a couple of towels and then walk briskly the twenty minutes down to the shoreline and beach and go for a swim in the always murky-milky cold ocean I. did this through September and October. The murk-milk came from the many fish-farms just off-shore. I loved it! Not the semen-like appearance mind you, but being submersed in the cold water! Nice way to wake up into the day, any day. I could sit, towelling off, have a cigarette and watch the sun rise every day! Lone time-Beauty..

 ## "Ah, Shucks!"

One night, I remember walking down to the village by myself to get a few things and I came cross a group of women sitting on a dark sidewalk, laughing and shucking oysters from a pile that was maybe four feet high at its centre. They offered me one and I accepted. Soon their laughter rose and through broken-toothed smiles and giggles, they offered another and a third. I ate ; I laughed along, wondering, right then I remember, if I would spend most of the next day on the john..?Happily, no.

 ## "Field of Dreams"

Nobody could ever adequately explain or cared enough to try why , but on the walk to one of our favourite restaurants in the village, we would have to cross through a wide-open hard-packed dirt lot of undeveloped land. To one side of this grungy, rocky field, we would pass by an older, decrepit, abandoned brick building. Now, It was commonly understood that one corner of the ground floor was regularly being used by some local townsfolk as an 'in house'- outhouse. It was covered from the rains and offered protection from the wind and prying eyes… and it was ready-made! Such odd sights to behold!

 ## "How Much Is that Turtle in the Window..?"

Now., To jump forward again to after my move down to Beijing the following year. There was one day when I was in my taxi, going home after work and we were stopped at a large intersection for at least twenty minutes. During this time, I noticed a man with a white plastic grocery- bag making his way between all the cars, stopping often and leaning down to speak to the drivers; I was curious. Finally, he was at my driver's window. He leaned in some, grinning, and then revealed a small painted turtle in his hand that he was trying to sell for someone's lunch. Not knowing how to cook turtle, and just remembering how I loved those animals as a kid, I had to decline his nice turtle offer. It could be chalked up as yet another of many and daily surreal moments in the China adventure.Another one, much late,r would be going to a local "corner store" and finding a huge sow-pig leashed to the railing out front! Pork chops, anyone?

 ## "Number 47,Please!"

To again jump in time and back to Beijing where my wife and I resided after my initial hospitalization and subsequent stints in rehabilitation clinics following my stroke. One early routine found us visiting a neighbourhood acupuncture clinic on a weekly basis. It was a small family-run affair, first-come- first serve basis with maybe twenty to twenty-five beds. And they were small beds at that-no sir, not built for your big-boned foreigners. Upon arrival, they would scratch out your number on a little scrap piece of paper and then you would wait for them to call you up. I dreaded the place..,not for its needles so much, but for its washroom facilities. It was a small, almost closet-sized room which was directly across from a set of stairs going down to the basement. The stairs were, I swear, built at a seventy degree angle That was a bit frightening for me because you had to stand and turn around in this itty,bitty landing at the top of the stairs just to get into the washroom. In those bad, fleeting moments, I knew a fall down those stairs would certainly end any and all frustrations I had in this life. Going to pee there was something I dreaded, but when you're thirsty, you know?

" Excuse me, "You Forgot Something."

So, anyways, we would go once a week to this little acupuncture clinic. Once I remember, I was already stretched out on my bed-cot when I just couldn't help notice(sure!) a young woman standing at the adjacent cot in red brassiere and panties, getting ready for her treatment. I tried my best not to ogle, but failed miserably After all, the colour was a bright, fire-engine red!The lingerie called out for attention, so I obliged is all.. She had a near-perfect figure and I'm a man, after all. It was just one of the very occasional perks to the weekly trip, I suppose. On another day, mind you, I saw something quite different. There was clearly going to be quite a wait, so I took myself outside to the boulevard to have a puff by the entrance stairs and ramp. As I sat there, doing my thing, I could not help but observe as a mother and her, I guess, seven or eight year old daughter stopped nearby and squatted down together. The little girl, hardly a "toddler" any more, pooped on the sidewalk and then they both 'upped' and walked away, leaving her special little deposit behind on the sidewalk. That's right, just like that. I don't know if a special edict had been passed during the Olympics or not to prevent such behaviour from being captured on some American cell-phones but I would not doubt it. For me, and many others here in the West, this was rather a disturbing and somewhat offensive sight to chance upon . No effort was made to remove it or even cover it. Think about this for a moment. Well, many if not most of China's landfills are not overbrimming with poopy non-biodegradable diapers. Most of the toddlers' pants have big airy splits in them that run up the crotch and bum, allowing for more convenient evacuation, if you know what I mean? At first when I saw these I tried to tell the parents their child had a big rip in its shorts! Many are also much enviro-friendlier than the mother I saw because they'll take the child to a park and find a tree to squat beside. Still, for my Western sensibility, it's bizarre to witness. This episode is just one of those ge-zillion naughty bits from China that my wife, bless her heart, would prefer I don't dwell on or even discuss. Fair enough....

 ## "Night Soil."

Speaking of strange sights and oddities, many of we teachers in our first year marvelled at the sheer size of some of the produce available at the weekend markets. Finally, one of the "vets" explained to us about the 'magical fertilizer' euphemistically nicknamed "night soil" which would often be spread on many fields under cover of darkness; that's right-human waste.

 ## "T.O.' s Lil Italy"

We have to back pedal some now to my pre-stroke days, when I had moved myself back to Toronto, after my European backpacking adventures. I eventually settled into an apartment on St. Clair Ave W. near Oakwood and Ossington. I could call the area 'Little Med', as in Mediterranean- for its solid representations of people from Portugal, Italy and Greece. It was, in truth, the Northern part of the city's "Little Italy" which turned all the colours of the Italian flag and erupted in celebration when they won the World Cup that one year. This was a stage when I, appropriately enough, worked as a temporary-fulltime employee for every major brewery in the land, and finally found good fulltime work as an order-selector in a produce warehouse (no cuisinarts!). It was mostly shift work, afternoons and nights, so during

most days when at home, I was busy writing my weird and I
hoped funny, angst-ridden first novel as a younger man.

"Kim, Ha ha!"

Anyways, I lived across the street from an Italian grocer's,
Darrigo's, and a little convenience store whose proprietors
were a lovely young Korean couple. Early one hot summer's
day , the husband had a small step ladder set up in the entrance and was struggling to lift an air-conditioning unit up
above the door. I was there for a quick 'pop-in' when I decided to do it for him. Amazed, he stood and steadied the
ladder as I hoisted the behemoth up on one of those wide
shoulders I've told you about, stepped up the rest of the way
and placed it on its new roost-shelf above the door. He was
just stupefied and thanked me profusely. He was an engineer and his lovely wife a clothes-designer, but here they
were with their two young daughters, selling cigarettes, pop,
ding-dongs and lottery tickets to the neighbourhood because
that's what life had dictated to them for the moment.

 ## "The Fridge in the Hall"

Also, during that same time for me in T. O.,I had sort of
befriended a neighbour from across the hall from my fourth
floor walk-up apartment,by the name of Bill. We never really conversed much at all because we didn't like each other
for some reason, so we just chirped at each other in passing
in the mornings on my return from work or breakfast, him
commenting on my girth and me on his bad teeth and per-
petually glum demeanour(tit for tat, you know..). Well, that
same summer, an old refrigerator was put out in the hallway
against the wall between our units. I thought it had an awful,
unworldly smell to it and it was left there for several weeks
almost two months in fact! As it turned out, it was not the old
fridge at all emitting the foul, oh-so offensive odour. Instead,
it was my bad-toothed neighbour, Bill who, apparently-as I
understand things- was much glummer than I could ever have
imagined and shot himself one day and then fell backwards

on his heated waterbed,-the warmth of which accelerated the decomposition of his corpse during what was a warm spell for Toronto. For all those weeks that summer, as I wrote my first novel, while listening to Webber's Evita(she was my 'white noise') repeatedly, I would walk by that old, 'smelly' fridge and wonder when, in Heaven's name, they were going to remove it! Now, I can say confidently that I know exactly what a rotting human corpse smells like – something that not too many of us can put on our resumes… and a novel topic for the kitchen cluster at any cocktail party!(Start with a generous cup of the worst underarm odour, add three tablespoons of toe jam whose fumes you can SEE and you're on the right track!.

 ## "That's Love!"

Tina famously roared out," What's love got to do with it?" Well, Just last spring-summer, my wife and I were brunching at a friend's and former colleague's of mine. We were sitting outside on his backyard patio, when he asked us to remind him of the timeline of our relationship. From our first meeting at a MacDonald's restaurant in Beijing, through the early dates and wooing, cohabitating, my hospitalization and surgery in 2006 to our marriage in 2007 less than a year later. My friend profoundly commented on the fact that my then- girlfriend had stayed by my side through it all, the insanely difficult time of my stroke, surgery, hospitalization and early rehab, and had hung around … to become my wife. My friend then commented that many young women in that situation might have abandoned me after such an incapacitating stroke; he was right, too. He looked quizzically at my wife with a ," but you stayed with him..?" I'm so happy to report that she replied without hesitation and just her smile, "That's love." It was just another of many marvellous moments that continue to mount in our growing relationship encyclopedia.

"And Still He Sighs".

I can remember vividly partaking in the teacher de-brief regularly on Friday afternoons(with my 'Boyo' for a dozen or so years at some local area pub. There we could congregate, raise a few glasses of beer and vent all we wanted about the education system from funding issues, class-size, zealous parents to photocopier foibles and , of course, the endless meetings. One friend-colleague has always had a rather distinct way of joining any social- gathering around a table whether it be in the staffroom or at the pub. He lets out this hugely exaggerated 'I'm here' sigh when he joins the rest of us, coupled with a little cough (It reminds me of Melvin Udall's phone mannerisms in As Good As It Gets(remember Jack Nicholson trying to talk to Helen Hunt?). Now, after being away from that circle nearly ten years when I was abroad in Asia, it was almost heartening to hear that he had not lost his signature sigh. Almost. Those afternoons were one of a myriad of reasons for me to pack up, change my routines and escape my life here in Vancouver to begin with. Some of me had become numb and did things only from familiarity and cellular memory.

 " Hard to find a good Spittoon these Days!"

You know, I've never been a good spitter and, for a guy, that's problematic. We are expected to be good at spitting, apparently. Even with being on two championship sports' teams, I guess it's in our genes? However, some of us missed that boat. I could talk the talk in most every other way, but when stalking the sidelines or sitting on the bench, I simply could not execute this simple function. More than a couple of times in football, I would try spitting through the heavy metal cage protecting my face, only to have my effort hit one of those horizontal struts and watch for the next five minutes as gravity slowly forced it downward. Hell, to this day and, again, after my stroke, I sometimes have trouble even clearing my own body. Spitting on yourself is rather a humiliating thing to do, especially if it's one of those raw egg kind of deals. Jumping Jehosaphat (as Mom used to say!)There are those times still when I barely clear my own mouth and chin. Nice, mm mm.

 ## "Ni Hao!"

Higgledy-Piggledy, here, there and everywhere-…scatterbrained. That's what we all are and we spend a good portion of our lives just trying to organize the unorganized from calenders to spice racks; I strongly feel that is how our brains work, stroke or no stroke-all over the place, all the time! Let us jump back again to my first year in China(forgive me, or swear at me under your breath!) and living in the teacher-compound across from the international school where I worked. Every day, I would pass by that gaggle of Chinese women, all maids , themselves, going to work for the Canadian teachers. The only thing I knew and could ever say was, "Ni Hao". That was it, so they would all snicker and laugh at the big, ignorant foreign man, as I went by. or were they? However, I wasn't alone in that regard, mind you, as there was a collection of us who did not understand a lot of Mandarin and could speak even less; it sure made for a lot of interesting, fun and awkward moments every day though.

 ## "Juxtaposition"

Jumping forward once more in time, we are now back in Beijing for my second year there on my own. I was then employed as English Trainer for an international high-tech company For me, it was quite an eye-opening adventure suddenly being in the business- world, after a dozen or so years in the classroom! Often on my way to work, my taxicab would drive through these shanty-town neighbourhoods where I would see tarpaulins and sections of corrugated plastic or metal balanced precariously between the old, ramshackle brick buildings. Some people were actually living around and under these things which were little more than canopies, really. For several weeks one spring, we would pass by these weird strip-mall sections of the poor and every day I would see a man out squatting next to the curb at the same place, coffee mug in one hand while the other was busy brushing his teeth, leaving him to spit excess paste into the gutter; it made me think of Elizabethan England or almost anywhere in the Nineteenth Century; I saw him there regularly doing his daily morning routine on the boulevard, something he had done for months, perhaps years – all this as I was in my taxi being driven to work on the twelfth floor of a luxury office tower two hundred metres away.

Yin- Yang, side by side, the old and the new, the shiny and the decrepit. This is one element, I think, that makes China such a fascinating place That was the China I saw every day, and the one not found in the picture-perfect postcard view that most tourists want to see!. Now, further down the street from the tooth-brusher, I could also see someone-not always a youngster- squatting down and taking care of entirely different personal business. It's ok, everyone does it. From super models to the Pope and Queen, all of us animals with digestive systems and alimentary canals do it. So what? It's just that most of us don't do it in plain sight on the sidewalk, or even in the nearby park and then leave it behind for the rains. They usually don't pick up after their toddlers; they're sure as hell not about to to pick up after dogs!

I would also see, almost daily, what I will call 'platoons' of restaurant workers(servers,cooks,cleaners) out on the boulevard standing at attention(no, really!) in military style-all wearing their matching uniforms and being sternly addressed by their drill-sergeant/supervisor. Wow! In fact, that sight was very common. Again, not found in the dragon-dance parade!

"Two Men, Three Hands, and a Urinal."

Earlier on, I said anyone would be hard-pressed to find any more gracious hosts in the world than the Chinese. I do honestly and heartily believe that,… still. However, having said that, just in my personal experience, too, sometimes-individually-they can be some of the rudest, most thoughtless folk around. There is still a lot of ignorance, I feel, in this regard, in many underdeveloped countries- of which China is most assuredly. This now remember, is coming from me, a man, somewhat incapacitated and in a wheelchair. Of course, I felt that way earlier, too, as an able-bodied man. It becomes very much a cultural issue: oftentimes, the infirmed, misshapen and handicapped among us are not simply neglected, but actually shunned- and that goes back, too, thousands of years. In that sense, it's awful. Many times I've been at a doorway entrance waiting to enter and there's been a young Chinese man or woman rush in and squeeze by me first because they are unwilling and too thoughtless to wait. Worse then, most do not even help me with the door. I am not their responsibility; why would they? For centuries, traditionally, many Chinese have revered the elderly in their midst and afforded them great respect and status, especially within their own families. Having said that, they have yet to embrace the handicapped and furthermore, the deformed/disabled people there are often treated with a disdain normally reserved for the diseased. There still exists a lot of terrible old-world ignorance and prejudice toward the physically-challenged who need any sort of mobility aids, whether it's canes, walkers or wheelchairs such as myself(Yes, even after they hosted the Olympics; for that they put on quite a show, I think). That, in itself, is very unfortunate and it will only ever change slowly like a creeping glacier.

 ### "Human Bees!

If I think a certain way as a man, don't all men? Well, it's sure taken a while for me to realize the answer to that is a resounding "No!" Sure, there's the easy stuff. For example,… women; I know most of us think about them, wonder about and lust after them because after some time and experience on this planet, we understand exactly what kind of intensely pleasurable moments they can bring to us. And, who doesn't like those, after all? It's just another one of those paradoxical aspects to our nature: Instinct dictates that we are, first and foremost, selfish and self-serving animals – but we are also very social creatures who need group support/validation and crave intimate connections with others regularly. In this context then, we are little more than human-bees who have managed to harm much of their own hive.

 ## "The Coffee Shop Spider-Man"

Spiders must have their lonely moments, sitting and waiting, sitting and waiting- perhaps I am one? Personally, I would think that they must be contemplative creatures with all that time on their legs-but that would suggest a sentience which we know, or presume they don't have. Of course, I don't know HOW we know that because no one has ever interviewed one, or even conversed with one except Wilbur in Charlotte's Web!. In my local coffee shop, there sits a man most mornings and some afternoons who lies in wait for unsuspecting, or stupid- enough prey to touch or get entangled in his conversation-web. If ever you're lured in to his web, then you might be told what the best time is to go to the grocery store and buy your roast chicken, or that his son will be coming soon to visit him from Asia. Lotteries are my favourite 'If only I had those first five numbers different, I'd be sitting on 4.2 million dollars right now! It's the same every week. He's not only one of those to count his chickens before they hatch, but to count chicks without ever having had a hen! Then, there's the pictures of Christ he's taken over the years, one in the clouds while flying at 37,000 feet, one in his bowl of mushroom soup. If ever you are lured into his dreadfully sad web(Yes,ok, I have my stupid moments..), then be prepared for lotteries, roast chickens and rare images of Jesus Christ. After all, very few photographs from Biblical times still exist And yet he has exclusive access to some!! Of course, they are in black and white. Wait. Wait! Wait! You know, the more I think about it, the more I start to think that maybe this fellow is more of a fisherman than a spider. (it's just that I've always so enjoyed spiders, I guess.)

"No Dryers!" (aka High and No Dry!China)

It's a good thing, I guess-the fact that there are no clothes-dryers to be found in any of the apartments in Beijing-just think of the saving in electricity! Clothes are all drip-dried, outside if possible in the sun and 'fresh' air or else in the many huge, enclosed balconies like I had. True it could be very cold(subzero), but it was sunny quite often, too. OK, sure, sometimes the gaunch would be a bit stiff but being a man-as I've explained- I couldn't have cared less about wrinkles A couple of good, hard shakes and they would then settle into place the rest of the way by themselves after just a few strides. (Vancouver)

"View from the Rear".

In the area where I live now with my wife, there is a cozy, little neighbourhood café which I've been known to frequent. It presents a fine venue for the mandatory, daily people-watching. But, let's get back to me , shall we? It's fascinating in a few ways to be sitting in a chair all day- although, granted, it is hard on the petunia!. It offers a completely different perspective on the world which I would give up in an instant; I'll call it, "bum –level" and it is. My head is usually at about the same level as most derrieres. That's fine when you're in line somewhere and you've got a gorgeous young woman ahead of you with a knockout figure and a cute, round bum whose incredibly tight jeans separate the ass-cheeks with mathematical precision, the seam running just so between the twin orbs, like a (meridian?! Stretch pants are nice also, and even mini-skirts and warmer weather's short-shorts-you know the kind-with each glute squeezing out a bit from under the fabric to peek out at the world. My oh, My! Relax. Yes, she knows and ,yes, she has one of the cutest tushes I've ever ogled. Curiously enough, the day we first met she was sitting on it.

"The Flip Side"

Of course, on the flip side of that perspective there does exist a few drawbacks. Once, while in a line-up like that, I was almost overcome by the exhaust fumes emitted by the man ahead of me; he did turn around and glance at me briefly, but there was still no acknowledgment at all. Nothing. He was not about to take ownership of the bad air hovering nearby, but there could be no doubt that he was, indeed, the perpetrator. In moments like those, again, I just can't leave well enough alone, or bad enough alone, so I forced his hand some (I'll often do that sort of thing which, as you can imagine, leads to some bizarre interactions..). I tapped him lightly on the shoulder to get his attention. There was a pretty, young woman standing behind me and there was just no way I was going to let her think that the offence was mine! When the man turned around again and looked down at me, I simply asked him point-blank, "Did you just fart?" He confirmed my already solid suspicions with a sheepish grin and small nod." Sorry about that.." he murmured. I moved sideways a bit so the woman behind could better see and hear his confession.

"Welcome to the Neighbourhood."

I get to know many of the people in the neighbourhood from the clerk-cashiers at the grocery store to the many neighbours and locals in the area, including even a few homeless folks. I figure, by now, I probably know the names of close to one hundred people! Just keeping everybody's name straight is an issue, but I play with it and try to make it a fun, challenging game for myself.

There's one woman whose name I do not know, but who I see regularly as she walks by me on the sidewalk Her face is a pasty white and, honestly, seems too big for her head- there's just too much dough for the pizza and its toppings; she has a mouth that reminds me of Heath Ledger's 'Joker' although the weird slash is made even scarier because it's usually painted in some gaudy neon red or orange lipstick. It is frightening to look at, but it does inspire ideas for my next Halloween costume. A second woman, thin as a rail, has this immaculately coiffed short hair-do where never a single hair is out of place, or even moves for that matter! When I see her, she is always on her way to the local hair salon, go figure.

"The Girl in the Orange Bikini-no tats." (Vancouver)

O.K., question. Is it cheating on your wife when you're down in the laundry room and you see a beautiful young woman who is wearing only a shiny, orange bikini and, worse, she's bending over and trying to fish out the last couple of items from the dryer? This is happening, you were a witness to it all and you neglect to mention it to your wife?? I think not. I had no lewd, lascivious thoughts(well, maybe just the one and it was fleeting, almost premature you might say).

When we first noticed each other, she was only slightly self-conscious as I said, "Nice bathing suit." As if an explanation were even warranted, she said.,.. "this is all I had left."

(Later that same day…)

'Funny thing happened this morning, honey, when I was downstairs doing the laundry.' And, no, I don't really call my wife, "honey" Nope. Some things are better left un-shared, you know, and I think that's understood in most re-lationships. Why create a problem where there need not be one? Maybe it comes out a month later when you're both talking about how strange it is that you will not vary your laundry- routines on Tuesday mornings one iota, in the faint hopes orange-lightning does strike twice..

"Funny Bits?"

This condition of mine-being essentially a paraplegic….be-ing paralyzed on the left side of my body (arm and leg..) is not without its funny/absurd moments. For sure. In fact, in hindsight, there is no doubt at all that my sense of humour has been one of my saving graces, seeing ridiculous, absurd, and at times perhaps even painful moments…as humorous. I was told once by an acquaintance who had apparently, tired of my humour(..?) that, "not everything is funny, Kim." I beg to differ with him. If you look close enough, you will always find humour; I still feel that way! And it's those 'comic relief' moments that help make life more bearable at times.

"Too Much English…"

After even my second year in the Honours English program at U.B.C. which, admittedly, I only squeaked into and that even with special consideration- only to quickly fade away, I'll never- ever forget my meeting with a course-counsellor who looked over my tentative chosen schedule of desired courses and flatly said, "Oh, you're taking much too much English, here, Kim; You'll be overwhelmed with reading and inundated with essay writing-just too much. She was right, too, but I loved the essay-writing part! Funny, too, now that I think about it how I also "squeaked" into the Creative Writing department with a 'special portfolio submission! I've been doing a lot of squeaking in, I guess..?And I'll be the first to admit so much squeaking can cause some resentment Squeak, squeak!

 ## "Bums Away!" (aka Sexist Pig It chafes!)

As I've mentioned earlier and unapologetically, I'm a serious 'bum-man'. It's all about the bum for me. I found a like-minded floor mate in my first year in residence at U.B. C. and he introduced the notion of ' V.PL'. to me which is short for "Visible Panty Line". Generally, the guys love them because they reveal a certain degree of confidence depending on what type is worn, but they are a bane for a lot of women, some of whom refuse to leave the house in the morning if they suspect they are sporting one!. You can judge a lot by how much you see, and where it's located exactly. We even developed a silent signalling 'alert' when a young gal walked by with a V.P.L. worthy of note! Now, remember that I lived and worked in China for six years? Well, it's hard to find any more perfect balloon-bums than on young, Asian women, especially the Chinese girls. Alright, I have a brief confession for you: Prior to my moving to Asia, it was never beyond me to adjust my position or, even at times, change my location, to provide a better, unobstructed view of a marvellous "caboose." Another quick confession since we're on this topic; Once, during my backpacking adventure of Europe and the Mediterranean, I was hovering close to a bus depot one morning in the seaport of Piraeus, Greece when I caught a glimpse of a bod with a jaw-dropping, nearly –perfect tush in tight, cheek-splitting jeans. I moved some to observe more of her and her parts and then, truth to tell, I followed her as she boarded one of the several buses in the near vicinity. Yes, I guess you could say I was stalking those glutes..?I had no idea whatsoever where the bus was heading-and, it didn't matter one iota. I was having a Carpe - Diem/Gluteus moment(a 'seize the bum-moment'). I was going to behold more of that behind and that was that. As it turned out, the bus drove north up into the mountains for a couple of hours and eventually came to a stop in a small town whose name I don't recall. I was treated like royalty and stayed there for two days, even had a beer and ouzo with the owner of the perfect rear orbs. Leaving any possible conversation to my imagination would have been a much better thing to have done in that instance, but, still, it was worth it in the rear-end…

There is sea-level, and then there is "bum-level". Because I'm sitting in a chair most of the day, my head is usually about the same height as most derrieres for better or worse.

Now, that's all fine and well when you're in a line-up somewhere and you've got a gorgeous, young woman with a knockout figure ahead of you whose ever-so-tight jeans separate the ass-cheeks with a mathematical precision, you know, with the seam running exactly down the centre between the twin orbs. Sure, that is definitely preferred to the pot-of- chilli-for-a thirty-boy-scout-troop- bum, otherwise known as the multiple-convergent, or elephant-bum(E.B.). Stretch pants are good, as are the mini-skirts and with warmer weather those lip-smacking short-shorts!(sexist-pig!) You know the kind I mean: the ones where each lower gluteal fold is squeezing/peaking out from beneath the hem-line to glance around out at the world. I can tell you one thing for sure- a pair of glutes like that is attached to one-heck-of confident young woman. Geez, 'confidence' is a sexy thing, isn't it? My oh, my! Oh, hush, relax. She knows. And, yes, she has one of the cutest tushes I've ever stalked-and, oddly enough, she was sitting on it when we first met; She could have had three cheeks for all I knew!

"The Flip Side" (reprise)

The good with the bad. Of course, a little rain must fall…. On the flip side of the positives I've mentioned is the other kind. Once, while in one of those aforementioned line-ups, I was nearly overcome by the exhaust fumes emitted by the man ahead of me. He did turn around and glance at me briefly at one point, but there was still no clear acknowledgment at all. Nothing. This fellow was not taking ownership of something that obviously belonged to him. There could be no doubt that he was the perpetrator of this noxious gas cloud now lingering in the area. It's in moments like those, when I just can't leave well enough alone, so I forced his hand a bit (I'll often do that sort of thing which leads to some bizarre interactions, hilarity, absurdity, confrontations… you name it. I tapped him lightly on the shoulder to get his attention. There was a pretty young woman standing immediately behind us and I was not about to let her think the offence was mine! When the man turned around this last time and looked down at me, I asked him point-blank, "Did you just fart?" He confirmed my already solid suspicions with a sheepish grin and barely perceptible nod. "Sorry about that," he whispered. I moved a little side-ways in the line so the young woman behind me could better hear his feeble confession, catch wind of it you might say.

"Neighbourhood Lost and Found"

If the infamous Downtown Eastside is the 'crotch of Van-couver, then Marpole,orSouth Vancouver as it is also called must be a poor cousin, maybe an 'armpit.' It, too, is home to a lot of "down-and-outers," a lot of dises:disenfranchised, disabled, disordered, dysfunctional and even self-talking street folk. We in Marpole must have the greatest proportion of disabled people with scooters, wheelchairs and walkers in all the Metro Van area. Many are on disability pensions, some others on social assistance, throw a smattering of crack- heads into the mix and you've got this shanty-town some of us like to call Marpole, with its wacky collection of the hobbled and disenfranchised

There's this one woman whose name I do not know, but who I see regularly as she walks by me on the sidewalk on her way to the local hair salon. Her face is a ghastly, pasty-white and, honestly, seems much too big for the head that carries it; she has a mouth that reminds me of Heath Ledger's the 'Joker' except that the weird, slanted slash is usually painted in some very gaudy neon orange or red. It's scary and gives me inspiration for my next Halloween costume. A second woman in the area that I see, thinner than a rail, has this absolutely perfectly-coiffed short comb-back hairdo where never a single hair is ever, ever out of place- or even moves for that matter. When I see her, too, she is doing her rigidly upright walk... down the street for her weekly appointment at the hair salon .. whether she needs it or not. It takes we men a while to understand that it's never really about the hair at all! No, a good salon with regular, loyal patrons is a place they go to be complimented by the stylists and to screen the latest neighbourhood gossip. For some of the older or disabled women, it's one of few trips they can still make on their own, and it is therefore a treasured and much looked-forward to outing!

 ## "Bad Wings in Wawa"

Not to damage the tiny town's booming "tourism industry" at all, but on my wonderful touring trek-adventure way back in 2001,when I drove from Vancouver back to Toronto and then on to my hometown of Sarnia- I did have an overnight in

Wawa in northern Ontario. I found a diner-restaurant, maybe attached to a hotel..? I forget, honestly. I ordered and ate just the worst platter of chicken wings imaginable. They were sort of droopy after swimming in the special sauce which tasted much too much like tomato soup and ketchup to be pure coincidence. Makes me shudder still to revisit that memory.

"Teacher-Mills."

Oops, here we go again… Let's go back to my early Chinese days in the Northeast at the international school where I taught for my first year while in China. I have reached some final thoughts about my international school experience; you know "puppy-mills", infamous in most places for their neglect and often sad treatment..? It really wasn't all that bad for us -but I do think much of that industry promotes and is fuelled by "teacher-mills"… get 'em while their young(er and hungry),(or retired and desperate) squeeze all you can out of 'em for 1-2 years and discard them…. They served their purpose:helped bring in revenue, and to cement the school's growing reputation Those places are a bit like cable companies these days, at least to me, whose profit-margins and bottom-lines depend on the newbie's, the new kids, the new customers,and who are not so great with looking after them after they've been signed up! Their naïveté then becomes' need to know basis', so information is doled out achingly slowly and only in small bytes!

 ### "Shard Stew!"

O.K., As I've mentioned, all the Canadian teachers were accommodated in private apartments in the teacher-compound, located directly across the street from the school. There was a rec-facility there, with a gymnasium, a restaurant and a staff cafeteria on the ground floor which most of us frequented for breakfast, lunch and occasionally dinner because often little groups of us would band together and do the twenty minute walk into town where we had choices of several little restaurants and a couple of little stores to go to. So, one day, there we were eating lunch in the "caf"-,some delicious, but labour-intensive stew? Lamb? Beef? Who knows? The dear friend sitting next to me quickly and so aptly nicknamed the dish, "shard stew" because, in fear of our lives, we spent half of our lunch time carefully removing fine shards of bone from between our teeth, until we each had a small pile of potential life-spoilers on the plates in front of us. No question that the Chinese have some very flavourful stews and soups because their ancient history and wisdom told them-as Graham Kerr told us years ago – there's a lot more flavour to most things if you cook by using more of the animal and its parts. I remember another moment, for a quick aside, when I bit down into the very hard, crackly head of a chicken rather unexpectantly while dining with Chinese friends and eating soup. You will often see a lot of teeth- picking and cleaning by Chinese diners after a meal; you soon learn to appreciate the 'why?'

"The Exploding Chair!"

Kaboom! Ouch!

In the one smaller hospital in Beijing(SiuJiQing..?)where we stayed for seven or eight months...Rm205. That was early on when I was still mostly bed-ridden, that's right, doing all of my business from a prostrate position. Of course it was there where I retrained and sat on the toilet for the first time again-it was quite painful! They did get most of us up and down the hall to the very communal shower room once or twice a week. Are you kidding? That was absolutely .wonderful, a godsend. It was always quite an experience-both exhilarating and frightening. Well , one day, my 24 hr/day helper/care-caregiver(most of us needed one) who slept on the couch in my room beside my bed, helped take me down there and get ready to be clean again! Once there, they had one tiny, wooden chair, the kind built for children- I've seen them., I know; it would allow us to sit and rest after standing at the grab-safety bar and sudsing up nicely. After I rinsed myself off the best I could, we sat me down on the chair for a break and shampoo. Then, after just a moment or two and with no warning signs at all(like in a Jacques Cousteau documentary..) the tiny little chair exploded apart underneath me into fragments and sent me crashing down to the slippery wet floor, bum first! After the initial shock and surprise- there I was naked, of course,(as most people tend to be when showering) and sprawled out on the floor. Feeling vulnerable? Do you think? Oh, yeah, you might say so. My helper, a tiny, little fart of a man was shell-shocked, pacing like a caged miniature tiger, doubtless fearing for my well-being some and most certainly his good job. He ran down the hall after a moment to the doctors' office, most of whom were female and he returned in a flash with maybe six or seven of the female staff who promptly stood out in the hallway by the entrance in a huddle gawking in at the huge, , foreign man spread out naked on their shower-room floor. Nice! There I was, still sitting in the midst of the shattered chair , looking at its remains and actually laughing a little at this absurdity , thinking how lucky I was that I did not land squarely on one of those small wooden legs to impale myself through the asshole. Ouch! Count your blessings. Admittedly, that's tough to do when you're sprawled wet, soapy, naked and helpless on the floor with six or seven strange women staring at you and alternating between giggling and shouting down the hall for more help! Unless you happen to be a 'big person', you just can't imagine the fear some of us have about chairs disintegrating from underneath us. The plastic patio chairs don't shatter; No, those tend to melt!

 "Mom's Shoebox."

My mother and father knew from quite early on that I loved writing and wanted to be a "writer." That must have been quite disconcerting for them-not something most parents would probably want to hear; after all, it didn't rhyme with either "octor" or " sawyer". Ah, yes, I wanted to be a "writer." Whatever that means? Screaming fans, adulation and then, of course, there's the infamous writing-groupies! The 'Penny Lanes' of the literature world, that's right. Yep, from early on, I looked forward to those feminine, literary-rhamoras(Go ahead, attach yourselves!). Whaddya mean there aren't any literary- groupies?!! Anyways, back to Mom for a minute. Before she moved into the "elder care facility" in New Westminster, I remember well those last few years leading up to that transition; she was still living on her own in our Coquitlam family-home. Hell, while still in her chair, she joined a travel- tour for three weeks to China where she recalled to me how several young Chinese men actually carried her-in her chair!- up the twenty-five, maybe even forty steps to land her atop The Great Wall! When she returned to Vancouver, I found she had contracted some aw-ful bug that needed antibiotics to defeat – maybe something that even Genghis Khan had experienced upon invading….

" A Real Sleeper…"

My Mom used to love telling a couple of stories in particular about me, her baby boy and Number One Son! The First was that when I was just a baby, just days old and back in my new home from the hospital, she and Dad would often have to come into the room and over to my cradle-pen and actu-ally wake me to start a new day. This came on the heels of me asking if I had kept them both up to all hours as a baby. No way she said definitively, "You were a dream-baby(but of course)… You'd sleep right through the night and usually we would have to even wake you in the mornings and tell you it was time to get up, start a new day and maybe eat something! Of course, maybe all mothers tell their children that, I realize; However, from what I've ever heard or read, I thought not. Then later, as a toddler, when the family was living in an international compound close to the oil refin-ery where my engineer-Dad worked when we were stationed in the Middle East. This was when we were living in Iran-Abadan and Isfahan to be more precise. We were there for two –two and a half years. I was all of five or six months old when we went. While wending our way back home to North America, we had a stopover in Roma.First, for a quick addendum to my docile early nature, let us skip back to Iran… We had a maid, and care-giver to help look after me - and my Mom, to use her own words, would regularly, "chew her out" after finding her next to me, the both of us sitting on the cool terrazzo floor under the table in the kitchen(the coolest place in the house) with the maid smoking hashish from her bubbly, hookah pipe. Mom, in recounting the story to me so many years later, would even giggle slightly as she said, "You were a very happy little boy." Now, we all know why. And when my urine is dope-tested, I will simply have to plead the'2nd-Hand- smoke-'skate-boarders' Defence.' Yes, I was always a good, little sleeper and, I guess, a hash-induced happy, smiling, young kid, yes sir!

 ## "More 'Teps, Daddy, More 'Teps!"

I'm not quite sure when children start talking (18-25 months?), but my speech impediments began quite normally, I gather, when I had difficulty with the INITIAL "s" sound of many words. When we were in Roma, one favourite story of my parents was how on the one day my father took me to the famous Spanish Steps and all I could say –as much as I was enthusiastic with seeing so many stairs to climb, was, "More 'Teps, Daddy, More 'Teps!"

"Quasimodo's Orange House.(Canada)"

I'm not sure why , but I figured if 'Quasi' ever did have his own single-family detached dwelling (apart from 'Our Mother' in Paris, I mean), then it would probably be orange-coloured. This was back in my hometown again when I was a tweenie/teeny; it was a bright pumpkin-orange colour, rather hard to miss. This was where some friends and former hockey team-mates lived- and it was our 'party house'. We consumed so much beer downstairs in their rec-room, laughed and cried, smoked and drank, listened to loud rock'n' roll, drank some more beer and talked about "forever" like it was a saleable commodity to be bought and sold by the pound like teenagers are prone to!

At least we were dry and safe and warm; it was sure a luxurious alternative to our mossy logs in the often cool, damp woods. All of us fully recognized that the parents were both drinkers, but if their needs were met early enough in the evening, then the rest of us were pretty much free and left to ourselves to carry on as we pleased down in the 'bowels' of the house – and we did!

'New World, New Life."

Let's go back now to revisit my first year in China where everything was so new and so different. Once we landed and deplaned in Dalian city, it was a freeforall,really, and one that left most of us shaking our heads and laughing. After they had us all loaded on a bus in the parking lot, we watched in horror as they hurriedly and randomly threw and piled our luggage onto an old blue open-air flatbed truck beside the bus. There are thousands of those ubiquitous blue trucks on the roads here, all dating to their hay- days during the Cultural Revolution! Some you'd swear are held together with rubber bands, tape and msg. We sat on the bus, amazed and more than a little stunned by what we saw. The truck did have short, rickety wooden rails on either side, but the growing mountain of bags between them would not even get one tie-down strap; Instead, two of the five little men who had shared in the loading operation would actually crawl atop the mound, spread themselves out some and act as "weigh-downs" for the one hour drive to our new homes in the complex across from the school.

When we did reach our 'new homes', the apartments in the teacher compound beside the school, all of our bags were, once more, unceremoniously off-loaded from the truck and dumped in yet another pile on the pavement where we were left to dig out our own belongings. We were told to take one of our bags with us and to simply choose one of the open apartments which we would then call home for a year. Three floors. Choose a door, walk in and stake your claim. This was the first of countless adventures in our great Chinese tour.

 ## "Thai-ing One On..."

Thailand was an exotic, tropical place chock- a –block full of gorgeous, willing male and female sexual partners known then only to me through legend, mostly media and movies. After experiencing it some first-hand, now, I have a much greater; full-bodied, you could say, understanding of its enticements, particularly of its appeal to adult males of almost any age. German men, I know, sure like it a lot- I couldn't believe how many German fellows I met when there. They were there, surrounded by beautiful young women, while the "frau"/ Mrs. was back home , holding down the fort and minding the kids, he was off to Phuket for ten days of "dental work" and golf, and- oh yes!- limit- less sex with his weeklong Thai 'girlfriend' who happened to be his junior by twenty-five years! When I was there, it was often almost impossible for me to spend any time alone in the bars, without being approached by, or joined by some gorgeous, young Thai woman. It doesn't take long (even for us slow- guys) to realize that that is their job- and that the place is awash with prostitutes, Yeah, yeah,yeah, kid in a candy store at first, I suppose, but the novelty of attracting such exquisite company does wear off some, or did for me at least. To begin with, as a Western man, you stand out like the 'proverbial sore thumb (was there a lot of 'carpentry' in "Proverbs..?) and are therefore targeted- not at all for your sex appeal , unfortunately, but because you probably have a mitfull of cash and are doubtlessly ready to part with some of it for the right feminine charms. It is their job to see that you do.

 ## "She-He's"

I did spend some time in the original "sin-city" (Bangkok), but for of all things and I kid you not, a dental check-up and a quick tour of backpackers' alley. Once, I was walking along on one of the hugely busy, noisy streets of the dozens there are and I had just finished a cigarette when I was approached by a Thai policeman. He escorted me back thirty or forty feet to where I had mindlessly discarded and stomped on my cigarette but on the pavement; He picked the stupid thing up, waved it in my face then motioned for me to follow him to a nearby police kiosk where he promptly cited me and wrote out a ticket for twenty dollars! (Most of that, I'm sure, went into his own private coffers..; It's like that in a lot of S. E. Asia, from what I could tell..) In Chiang Mai, several of us stayed at the same funky hostel, surrounded by the open-air bars everywhere all bedecked in the mini-Christmas lights so common there.

 ## " If a Bear Farts in the Woods, Does He Grunt, 'Excuse Me?'"

We all know that at least they must fart! Well, I was always taught(no,not to fart!) and had drilled into me from a young age to be very polite and respectful of others, especially elders, and hosts("lions and tigers and bears! Oh yeah!). It probably started with just having a lunch or dinner over at a friend's house ("Always, always say please and thank you to your hosts, Kim! Always.) and that would lead, of course, to the occasional sleepover. Sure, we all know that real bears can't talk, but then, by the same token, we should know that because of their omnivorous animal natures and anatomies, of course they fart. Me, too, I must admit, but I can be out hiking in the woods of B. C. or northern Thailand and if I do burp or God forbid, fart, then I'm the kind of fellow who will always say, "Excuse Me!" It doesn't matter, if the only sign of another living creature in the vicinity is the persistent buzzing of a mosquito; I will feel sheepish and always, always ask to be forgiven. I did use to in my "abler days," love to go camping each summer by myself, it's true. It was a pilgrimage of sorts, a quiet, peaceful refuge and time away from most everyone-where I could recharge my batteries with cold early morning, mist-covered lake-swims, some beach-reading, lots of campfires and,oh yes, some solitary writing(is there any other kind..?)!How can anyone not remember, and love "tent-sleep" when you had that same nuisance-mosquito buzzing in your ears most of the night.? I'm quite sure the buzzing we hear is really mosquito laughter! Though they tell us it's wings ...

"The House in the Field."

It was a condemned, abandoned house that was located in a huge, undeveloped field on the edge of our woods, in behind and quite close to our local convenience store which meant that we would bicycle by it several times a day through all those springs and summers on our way to the local Mac's Milk store. Fortunately for us, this was in the days before they used loud classical music to chase away the vagrants and gangs of adolescents! During elementary school, One of our classmates lived with his family(for a year) in that house! I was only ever inside the house once to observe the huge sheets of linoleum peeling away from the kitchen floor to reveal the wood sub-framing underneath enough to see and talk to someone who was downstairs in the basement. I was able also to see up- close the skeleton of some kind of car whose back seat had been yanked out and now acted as a lone-sofa on the storage-room porch and, of course, the urine-stained single mattress downstairs in the wrecked-room that doubled as a bed for the occasional, unfortunate overnight guest, and as a disgusting wrestling mat for the three or four sons and their

Idiot-friends.' This was a family clearly living life on the edge- and not just of the woods, but of life itself. If my parents had ever known about it, they would have, I'm sure, forbidden any subsequent visits.

There was another family, too, much closer to home in the neighbourhood which had at least four, maybe five boys, one of whom was approximate to me in both age and size. What that meant was he and I would always end-up paired together during P.E. class in early high school. Because that testosterone-laced brood did not bathe regularly, their hygiene was always questionable and because of that, their body odour was not; it was offensive, no two ways about it.

More "' Teps, Daddy, More 'Teps!"

I'm not quite sure when children start talking (20-24 months..?), but my speech impediments began quite normally, I gather, when I had difficulty articulating the INITIAL "s" sound of many words. When we were in Roma on the return leg back to Ontario, one favourite story of my folks' was about the afternoon my father took me to the famous Spanish Steps and all I could muster-as much as I was enthusiastic with seeing so many steps to conquer was, "More 'teps, Daddy, More 'teps!"

Quasimodo's House

It was a bright pumpkin-orange colour, rather hard to miss; it was where some friends and former teammates lived- and it was the 'party house.' We consumed so much beer downstairs in their rec-room, smoked and drank, listened to Uriah Heep albums, drank some more beer and talked about "forever" like it was a saleable commodity to be bought and sold by the pound. At least we were dry and safe and warm. Compared to our usual retreat in the often cool, damp woods, it was a luxurious alternative. Most of us recognized that the parents were both drinkers, but if their needs were met early enough in the evening then the rest of us were pretty much free to carry on as we pleased down in the bowels of the place- and we did just that!

"Pine Knob."

What a spectacular outdoor concert venue this was! It was a large outdoor amphitheatre in Michigan, like in ancient times, only more comfortable and with flush-toilets! I saw both Todd Rungren and Joe Walsh on separate occasions there, while not knowing either very much at all. It didn't really matter who the headliner was because we could easily find pot there and the bus ride always began with a stop at a cold beer and wine store over the border, so my friends and I would load up on the clay jugs full of sickly sweet apricot or cherry wine and some awful Old Something-or-other- beer. Funny, all these many years later, I can vividly remember getting lost at the Rungren concert after a washroom stop. It was only blind luck, really, and a lot of monitoring one suspected area before I could finally identify one of my friends and return to my seat!

(Addenbums)

 ## "Fannies-Come –Hither"

Join me back in China for my first year there, again. One of the two younger women who worked in our front office of the international school, I'll call V.V., scored an 8.5 on the 'perfect-bum-scale', so I would always be on the alert for times if ever she got off it long enough to leave the office and walk somewhere for an errand- Pathetic, huh? There I was, like I was back in grade 9, but now I was in my mid-forties following an exquisite bum down hallways, judging symmetry and firmness and checking out 'convergence points'.

Even later, after my stroke, my wife and I found a couple of tutoring jobs for me in Beijing's downtown core in office buildings. At one of them, there was a receptionist- and I'm a fair to hard marker- who had a "9.0" on the bum scale. If I timed things just right while getting off the crowded elevator, I would sometimes end up directly behind her behind for the last one hundred foot walk to her desk in the lobby. My, oh my! There we are, again, with life's simple pleasures. The 'architecture' was simply superb, astounding even. Her big, bold name tag sat squarely on the counter in front of her desk as she answered phones and greeted people. I couldn't resist, so broached the topic one morning with her, "Do you know the meaning behind your name? I asked, having a few silent, pointed thoughts all of my own! I explained half in English, half in Mandarin that "fanny" also meant "behind," derriere, bum, caboose,etc and even added a quiet compliment connecting the obvious dots for her with," You have a very attractive bum."

Ridiculous, you say!? How can a bum be "attractive? It doesn't smile; it has no eyes, no face, no mouth! Of course, that's not entirely true. You simply have to tilt your head about ninety degrees to one side or the other to see it! (The smile, that is..)

" Rockin' the Kasbah!"

On my gargantuan, year-long tour through Europe and the Mediterranean, I did also take a wee sojourn across into North Africa, getting across Gibraltar to Tangiers and after a week or so, made my way by bus to a small town down the West coast called, Asilah, where I and my two travel-mates at the time were "picked up" rather quickly as we got off the bus at the local depot. A young local man persuaded us to join him and his family for our indefinite stay there; we accepted the offer. This village was, at best, two hundred metres from the ocean's edge. I learned two things fairly quickly after settling in some: first, was there were no toilets or running water and the second thing.. well.. was not to indulge in too much of the "hookah" before negotiating any purchase. There was not even an outhouse though the principle remained the same: a hole in the ground; there was a walled in area just inside the front entrance way to the home- but there were neither doors of any kind nor were there even curtains to hide behind! It was the 'honour-system', sort of….

Hell, I could have been happy if they had a curtain, but nope. Toilet paper? Yeah, right! In your dreams, maybe. Forget it!. What they did have were two small bowls, one to either side of the small squatter's hole. One of the bowls held water, the other just loose sand- these to take care of your business finger! On one of the first nights of our stay in this private residence, our hosts invited over some friends and other family to join us all in huge communal feast! It was lamb couscous and, as I recall, it was delicious, just fabulous! There was no cutlery; so, as is the custom, everyone used his or her left hand to scoop a spoonful-sized amount from the communal dish in the middle onto your flatbread. There must have been a dozen of us and we all sat squat-legged on the rug surrounding the food. Because most of us in the world operate everything and navigate our way with our right hands, it made perfect sense to me then why you would want people using only their left hands when rooting around in the communal food-dish! Yes, sir!(If I have my facts straight, the right to left- handed ratio in the world is 70:30, like the water to land ratio. Coincidence? I think not! And we think double-dipping is "bad".

" Every Ocean"

On the second or perhaps third day with our Moroccan hosts, the young man explained to us how an uncle owned a clothing shop near the market(but of course!) and we should, naturally, come visit and browse. Well, we did just that and before long I had found a "jilabba", the ankle-length male robe that just called out to me. Soon, the uncle took me into a separate, curtained-off room at the rear of the store. Once there, he made the first of several pots of marvellous mint tea and packed the first of many bowls of hashish in his grand hookah. We sat(they do a lot of that there..), drank tea and smoked, it seems, continually, for four hours as we "negotiated" the final-deal price for my jilabba; suffice it to say, I left happy, on several different levels! Yes, for those who care…, I did go swimming off that Northwest coast of Africa! I have to swim in every ocean I get close enough to; it is a compulsion. There was an earlier episode when I was touring through the ruins of the World War Two German bunkers on the Normandy beaches with a former partner. I would eventually take a break and find myself through the dunes and down to the surf for a swim! It's a compulsion, really. So what!? I just love it. It's exhilarating! Every Ocean.

On a somewhat related matter, I've rarely written erotic-poems, but the following squeezed itself out one day and voila!

"Her Ocean"

I followed the arrow,
And hit her bullseye square;
Then I hit the button, once my point was there.
I felt the shudder, and I felt the rush-
To swim in her ocean, with just a gentle touch.
Yes, I found the grey among the black and white,
In this worldly game of chess;
I followed those contours well and carefully
Beneath that summer dress.
I studied her geometry, both her angles and her curves
And I punctuated sentences when I found there, unclear
   words.
I climbed her scented mountains, and reached a high
   plateau;
To swim in her loving and the melting snow.
I found her spirit soaring in that clean, crisp mountain
   air,
As I wrapped myself in pleasure, and in her tousled hair.
Oh, yes, I felt the shudder; I felt the kick, the rush-
And long swam I there in her ocean,
\with just a gentle touch. (Sept 3,1998)

*** CAT STORIES***

"There's More Than One Way to Skin a Cat"
   Of course there is. Be creative! Some people have been
over the years. It does, however, tend to gloss over the whole
brutal- sadistic aspect of that popular idiom. I used to hear
my Mom say that, too- and I never fully understood. I guess,
there is more than one way to do almost anything in this
world – and that maybe we should try our best to stay open
minded to alternative thoughts or positions…to occasionally
let our loops go over the lines?

However, I had one early high school English teacher who, quite obviously, took that expression much too literally and too much to heart when younger. He only lasted the one year before being released from his post, but not before he had regaled us with some of his boyhood tales when he and his like-minded, sadistic pals caught, tortured and killed many of the stray cats in their neighbourhood in London!More frightening still was the smile of perverse-pride he often permitted himself in the telling of such tales.

"Fire in the Hole!"

After a couple of years at U.B.C., a dear friend convinced me to join him with going up north, since we were both looking to take a year off from studies, so off we went to seek our fame and fortune to Fort St. John in B.C.' s Peace River area in the northeast corner of the province(to the oilfields!) where I worked as a "swamper" for a time, a helper, a go-pher, where you do the driver's bidding or what he is simply too lazy to do himself(often one in the same..) Before long, we were both working for a rat- holing company. That's right: rat-hole! It's ok, I didn't know what it meant either when I started! We had a fleet of three huge drill trucks that would go out and be first on the "lease site", that area of land that has been cleared to make room for an oil drilling rig and its accompanying camp.Those were the big jobs and the rest of our time was spent doing holes for foundation-pilings in the many new subdivisions sprouting up through the city For the lease-sites,You're out in the middle of nowhere with the snowy owls and occasional moose and black bear wandering around. Once we were on a site and had drilled down twenty-seven feet with a 48" auger wide bore-hole (one of the bigger sizes!) when we struck rock; suddenly, the drill was useless. What to do? It didn't take us long to come up with the answer: DYNAMITE! I was given a small bundle of dynamite(about five or six sticks) and lowered down into the hole as I stood on the top of the auger(drill bit). Being the girthy fellow I've always been, it was a tight fit. Soon, however, there I was twenty-seven feet down in the earth with a bundle of explosives in my hand to set in place. I did just that-and will never forget the one moment of looking up at the night stars and wondering if this was the last I would ever see of them? Just a six volt battery and an electric blasting cap separated me from the Almighty at that instant. My driver and I took refuge under the carriage-deck of the drill truck, did the deed and stayed there for a good four or five minutes as the rock and debris rained down all around us. Yessiree! Never to be forgotten.

"Oscar's Comma"

People who are not writers, themselves, simply don't get it for the most part; I have one friend who sees me with a lot of time on my hands and thinks I should be at home to write a book, if not a 'bestseller.' Others figure that through some magical, alchemical process, a book just brimming with words and dressed in an attractive, shiny cover suddenly appears on the bookstore shelves one day; another for me is how when there's even a hint that you might be published, these people around you all start coming forward with ideas of what you should be writing about next! Reminds me of an old Seinfeld episode when another comic keeps feeding Jerry these terrible lines that he thinks are funny! Aghhh!. They miss the hours and hours at all times of the day and night when the writer is languishing, wrestling with every idea initially- and, then, with every word with which to express it. It is a marriage, really, and anyone who has ever been down that path should know- it takes time and energy to make happen and sustain, to nurture it and make it thrive. It can be both exhausting and exhilarating work and, at least in my case, it must be done on a daily basis for it is, quite simply, an addiction I must feed. One of my favourite stories around the writing process comes from the wit and pen of Oscar Wilde who replied one day to a friend at the pub who asked him what he had done the day before,

To that, legend has it he replied, "I spent the morning putting a comma in, and the afternoon taking it out! "If you get that, then you have an inkling of what it's like; shepherds might have some insight, too.

"Unseamly"

To revisit some my preoccupation/fetish (no!) with bums (preferably of the round, firm female variety..),they don't make the grade for me if they're too skinny. In fact, to be fair, male or female, for a long time now I'm always immediately suspicious of those people with little or no bottoms; you know, where the bum-cheeks don't even meet at the 'seam.' Not only does it not look right and hold much less appeal, but it leaves me wondering how they manage to do the simplest things daily that most of us with bums take for granted. I worry for some that they might fall into the bowl, unless they always use one of those special barbershop kids'-boards that stretch across the arms of the chair. I imagine those things must be pretty inconvenient and awkward to tote around all the time.

"Don't Call Me Avuncular!"

Let's hop, skip and jump our way back to China, again, to my first year there at the international school. I was a bachelor in my early fifties and I was asked to head up the English Department, clearly for my charm and good looks! While there, I befriended a very personable younger couple of Canadian teachers, both of whom were nice, good people but gooey, sickly-sweet in love which you can take only so much of, especially if you're single. We would dine and occasionally party together. One day, she informed me that I so reminded her of an uncle in her family. Then, too, I had easily slipped into the role of 'surrogate uncle' with another couple and their teenaged son who was attending the same school that both his father and I taught at. There weren't too many school choices in the vicinity then. I was lucky enough to be 'adopted' by this family and we would subsequently hang out and be seen a lot together. Given this context, she-of the personable younger, gooey couple told me there was one very special adjective I made her think of. As it turned out, that word was "avuncular." I would have been upset earlier had I known what the word meant, but within a day or two I did: 'uncle-like, you know, the red-faced tubby, poorly-dressed man at the cocktail party who everyone likes- if he doesn't drink too much, or make passes at the hostess! Whew, I was quite insulted, unbeknownst to them. There I was, again, as a bachelor, satisfying some lusty urges every weekend in the big city about an hour away, and working out in the teachers' gym 3-4 times per week, playing hockey every week and confidently believing that I was very much still an attractive, funny, intelligent, virile youngish professional man with lots of libido and adventure yet to come! "Avuncular!??" It was like a death-knell. No thank you, please.

I was no over-the-hill-to be-tolerated-uncle…!

"Hazing the Newbies!"

The deal was, with the international school, that the "vets", those who had already served some time in this foreign land/ culture for a year or more, would quite intentionally hold back their knowledge and wisdom of the place and keep it close to their chests and, then, only reveal it to us new recruits bit by bit, card by card, like some sort of game they thought was funny; I guess it was part of a long-standing tradition, making up some of the initiation rites for this international school at least and, I imagine, many others around the globe. It could have been worse, I suppose: at least no one turned me upside down to dunk my head and flush a toilet. Like the first time two of these veterans took me into the big city "for drinks" and we started the evening off at a rather famous drinking establishment where half of the faux-clientele are absolutely gorgeous young working- women whose sole job it was was to make any men- especially new, rich foreign guys- feel right at home—and, boy oh boy, were they good at their jobs! One of them, in fact, became my first 'girl-friend' on foreign soil and we lasted over a year together though, admittedly, our relationship centered mostly on sex, money and laughter-like any new relationship.Huh- huh, so shallow. Yes, she had a cute derriere(Hi J).

"So Little Time…"

Occasionally, whenever I might indulge myself with few happy and fleeting dreams of becoming a successful writer, then I'm not just attending conventions and festivals and doing book-signings. No, I have a nice maybe three-storey, older red-brick house, with a huge, ten-people-can-sit-with-their-drinks front porch, a nice, screened-in back porch or, better yet, a roofed-in gazebo in the backyard where I can spend a lot of my time peacefully writing in the afternoons. I do, I must admit, often feel like the proverbial kid in a candy store which has some similarities to the 'lusty uncle' experienced in most Thai bars, constantly surrounded by beautiful young women, all of whom are wanting to accompany you home and pleasure you sexually all night long. That feeling will usually wash over me like a tsunami, when it comes to writing time: I can go anywhere, do any thing, choose whatever I want to disappear and have some fun with! I remember once seeing a documentary, or portion thereof on Timothy Findlay, one of Canada's premier, most renowned writers. He and his partner at that time lived, I think, in the Orillia area, had a nice older home and a great gazebo in their backyard where, coincidentally enough, he would spend a lot of afternoons writing! It would be my second gazebo. Maybe no Southern Comfort, this time, O.K. perhaps the 'odd' one…

" An Olympian Bum." (Addenbums)

I remember watching our winter Olympics in Vancouver. One of the woman bobsledders split her skin-tight spandex pants right down the seam in the rear when in the starting gate. Of course, a cameraman was positioned directly behind her to catch all of the push-starts and 'action'. What he caught in that moment was a near-perfect balloon-gluteus along with the mere hint of a rather sexy dark thong-panty. My, oh, my! It being very much a man's- world still, I watched as that sports channel re-played the clip four or five times in just a few minutes. Perchance to dream!

One of my early high school English teachers, a friend of my mother's, indulged me regularly with our grade nine book reviews. I did six or seven James Bond novels in a row.. until there came a point when I felt almost comfortable fabricating my own "double-o- seven" plot and presenting it as original Ian Fleming. I remember the teacher more than once, giving me a big smile and asking," O.K., Kim, what did Mr. Bond do this week?" (Hi, Mr. C!)

Yet another early high school English teacher was not nearly as much fun; in fact, he was horrible. The actual teaching itself whenever he did some was alright, I guess, but as a man and a human being he was obviously an evil, twisted thing, destined for greatness perhaps one day in the Kingston Penitentiary. I've always been a little surprised that I have yet to see his name appear in the media as a serial killer. He regaled those of us in his class with some of his sadistic, teenaged exploits as hinted at earlier..

CAT STORIES b) "Some favor"

Apparently, in his day, cats were a dime a dozen-there were many stray cats that roamed freely through the neighbour-hood. So, he and a few equally-twisted close buddies would catch them, torture and kill them in a variety of ways. It was, in his words (which I would hear many years later echoed by 'pig-farmer/serial killer Robert Pickton...), 'doing the larger community and society as a whole a favour- a good deed!). One method they liked was simply collecting four to six cats(like it was a recipe!) and putting them all together in one big, burlap bag, tying off the top so there could be no chance of escape and then watch excitedly as the bag changed shape after they threw it off the local bridge into the river-and the drowning,panic-stricken cats clawed each other to death in their final throes, desperate for freedom and life! Another method and judging from the enthusiasm in his voice, obviously one of his gang's favourites was to take one cat at a time and throw it into a large furnace they had access to- and then take turns watching through the porthole in the door as it was literally burned alive! Nice, huh? Of course, I was often mercifully distracted from his 'Poean' ramblings by the pretty owner of an oh-so-cute bum who sat in the desk ahead of mine. "And how was school, today?" my mother might ask later at the dinner table.

Marsdom: keep it simple-"Just fine, I would answer, glancing at our Persian cat stretched out on the living room floor across the room. Yes, Marsdom: plain and simple-very male. In fact, the simpler the better, less chance to incriminate yourself or get drawn into a conversation where you still might do just that. Mind you, that grunting style, so common among thirteen and fourteen old boys (and even girls) would not be long tolerated by my father, not under his roof!

"Nuthin'"

Back in grade nine, my Dad would quite regularly ask me at the end of the day, "What did you see today, on your walk to school (thirty minutes either way..)? My standard fourteen year-old response, to try shutting him down was, "Nuthin." He would not accept that any more, even, at times, getting irate! Things were about to change. And, so, the interrogation would begin on his boy, the 'reluctant conversationalist'… He would bring that same thinking ,or strategy to bear with my dining-out habits, too. One day, as the family sat ready to eat in a restaurant, I had just delivered my standard-cliché order of "hamburger, French Fries and Coke" to the waitress- when my Dad jumped into the fray, with both guns blaring, "No. Not today, you don't, Kim. There's more to the world then hamburger, French fries and a coke! You're going to try something different, something new, starting NOW. My mumbled protests were summarily dismissed. Suddenly, I found myself eating something called 'liver and onions' and you know what? It wasn't half bad. Of course the dish did come with a serving of fries, some small solace for glum- me who still had to choke down the ahhhh-arghh.. asparagus- the smelly-pee vegetable! Yuck.

CAT STORIES (Cont'd)

" The Cat Woman of Venice" (Advisory: no cats are harmed in the following anecdote)

Back-tracking to my back-packing exploits again in the early/ mid eighties (for which I have only memories, no pic-tures-remember?), I did get the most out of that wonderful "Eurail Pass" of mine and in Italy, it would eventually get me up to the legendary, romantic city of canals, Venice! I ended up finding a cheap hotel very close to the Piazza san Marco and the Doge's Palace (the older, cheaper hotels always sound better when you call them "pensionnes", don't they?) It was raining a lot for the three or four days I was there and in the lagoon- city, an interesting phenomenon occurs during those overly wet times. Not surprisingly, as it sinks a little lower every year, it is increasingly vulnerable to flooding. And Vancouverites think they got it bad..?! What they do there is set up these elevated 'catwalks' that extend in some places a couple of hundred metres to allow pedestrian traffic to con-tinue over what soon becomes ankle-deep water. These little raised walkways are probably eighteen to twenty inches high and a little over a foot wide! Well., I explored every museum and gallery I could find within city limits- as was my way in any new city on the tour- in the first day or two… One night, after enjoying a few libations in a local taverna (por favour), I strolled down to the huge "boulevard"/ shore-walk at the wa-ter's edge next to the Doge's Palace and the famous moored, bobbing gondolas. Before long, I had slunk into the shadows of an alleyway, or side street, to have a cigarette and enjoy the sound of lapping waves on the gondolas when, out of the darkness, appeared an older, hunched over 'bag-lady' (she was carrying a white plastic bag full of something..) She came closer and closer to my place of concealment nattering gibber-ish to herself the whole time, with me all the while trying to be quiet and even cupping the burning tip of my cigarette so as not to be seen. As it turned out, this woman wasn't speak-ing gibberish entirely; instead, she was calling out names in the night. First, one cat appeared, then another, and another. She kept calling out until she was surrounded-no lie- by at least thirty to forty cats! Every now and then she would reach into her bag, retrieve something which I would later learn was fish heads and sundry parts. What got me, was the fact that she seemed to know each of them by name, individually. It made me wonder if she had been doing this act of kindness for years-probably.

 ## "Muffin Tops and Groin Dimples."

I think, for the record, it's time that something should be clarified once and for all around the whole issue of "love handles" which in the past few years have been granted the much cuter and friendlier epithet of "muffin-tops." I get it. Who doesn't like muffin-tops? Most of us know, they are the best part! "love handles" was always a poor, if not inadequate and inaccurate moniker. Those of us who have ever "been there", you know-when pieced together the male and female puzzle-parts how the little gentle rolls of fat high on the sides of the waist are not the "handles" at all; in fact, they're actually superfluous with little to no importance. No, the real handles of love are those glorious gluteal cheeks, the buns, which is one reason so many of us guys are always checking out the female's backside. 'Quelle Surprise! Buns of steel or even balloons, as I've mentioned, hold immeasurably more appeal to try and grasp than does a ladle or two of chilli con carne. Let's face it!

"Porridge and Titties, anyone?"

It's happening to me, too, that aging thing. As my shabby sideburns add more grey every day, I realize, too, that like my father before me and a few fathers before him, my hearing is weakening, getting poorer. It does, however, bring with it some humour and absurd moments. For the past few months, I've been watching a Tim Horton's television commercial where four typically idiot-men friends are waist deep in the cold lake, just offshore from the cabin and grappling with the big, wooden, summer-time diving platform, trying to position it in preparation for swim-season. Their wives and/or girlfriends, all carrying coffee cups and little bowls, come down to the shoreline (with the cottage in the background) to greet their hard-working men and shout happily to the cold four," Thought we'd help warm you up a little - with some porridge and titties!" Of course, what they're really saying is "Timmy's.., as in coffee, but I don't hear it articulated that clearly, and it's true maybe we hear what we want to. Again, it's life's little weird, absurd moments that can bring such pleasure and giggles! Even of the prurient kind-

"Secrets of the Bum."

I can't speak for Japan, having never been there, but at least in Thailand and China where the female behinds, as I've said earlier, tend to be of the near-perfect balloon variety, I do know one secret of success for many of them. A lot, if not most of the younger women (18-40) wear girdles and all sorts of strap-it-in, lift-it-up harnesses and undergarments, (Shape Wear) giving their rear ends at least a fighting chance against that gravity-thing!. And, after all that under apparel is laced or hooked up in place, many will then go on to pull on another layer of skin in whatever style pants they choose to wear. God Bless lift- and- hold technologies.' Careful says a Pulpit Master, 'Don't blaspheme!

"Groin Dimples."

It's not a medical term to my knowledge and just the best I can come up with so far, but another one of those very appealing parts of the female anatomy is what I describe as the 'groin dimples,' and they're really more like "troughs" those soft, runway depressions that run along the girl's inner thighs until they converge and disappear into the crotch. Both of us, men and women, have them-but here I speak only of the latter. They are seen most prominently when she's in her bathing suit and sitting cross-legged in front of you. And maybe that's why most of them try to avoid that position.

" Tiger, Tiger.. Chicken, anyone?"

A few of us from the international school also made another side trip, during Christmas holidays, up north or, more accurately, further north of where we already were- to the province of Heilongjiang and its capital city of Harbin which is, I think, the second largest in China at a cozy twelve million or so. It was a huge, sprawling industrial city, just a few hours by train from the Russian border and world-renowned for its marvellous annual snow and ice-carving festival. Many of the sculptures are simply enormous and then beautifully flood-lit at night with these rainbow-neon colours. To walk around in minus twenty degree weather, taking in the sights and occasionally risking frostbite by taking your camera out from your coat pocket was an amazing experience! After a couple of hours, we were all ready to have a break and find one of the many Russian restaurants for some hot, delicious borscht and jaw-exercising homemade bread! It was one of those most memorable adventures I had while on the Asian continent.

It didn't end there, either because Harbin also has another rather extraordinary attraction not to miss in its "Tiger Park" on the outskirts of the city! To imagine this place, think of Spielberg's Jurassic Park. It was a huge compound consisting of numerous fenced-in but open expanses of land(Paddocks-I might guess 15-20 acres! each) with its own "pride" or group of tigers stalking around. We were all on a mini-bus and watched in amazement as some of these large cats obviously preferred to stay close to the perimeter fence-line(like the veloceraptors),... , or else were simply looking for a gap to escape! The company that ran this 'park' had a deal whereby, after perusing their 'tourists-can-feed-the-tigers-menu in the lobby, you could then watch something being fed to the great cats. Several of us menfolk wanted to buy a small cow (calf) and watch it being fed to the big cats, but the wives and girlfriends protested so vehemently that we were forced to relent and lower our expectations dramatically to 'chicken-level'. The bus stopped here and there for photo-ops, as a few tigers, recognizing the food-mobile was present, shadowed the vehicle everywhere we went.

They stopped just long enough at one point for one of the workers to grab our chicken and quickly throw it out of the opened doors onto the ground nearby. Everything was over in a flash. I can assure you, after a couple of muffled squawks, the chicken felt no pain. Mind you, even if it had, I would not have cared. This one at least was not going to end up in a bucket with some French fries! One tiger, perhaps the alpha in the group, was on it instantly and with one crushing swipe from a huge clawed paw-any and all movement and noise ceased. The next five minutes saw that victorious cat spitting the feathers out in an almost-cartoonish effort to clean its face and mouth.

"Do My Boobs Bounce Too Much?"

It happened one day back when I was still teaching full time in Vancouver. It was over the photocopiers one morning, just before classes were to begin. Apparently, she and her fiancé often went jogging together, but before that she would do jumping jacks and some running-on-the-spot in the early mornings before they headed off to separate work places. She, (since she, too, is no longer among the living) turned to face me, jumped up and down for a moment very quickly and then asked me point-blank, "Do you think my boobs bounce too much?" Although I may have been thinking 'show me again, please, for a repeat performance, Instead, the best I could do was, "What do you mean?" My fiancé says when I run, my boobs jiggle and bounce too much," she said naively, cupping her breasts some, as if to point out to me exactly where they were located.... Really? And, there, I always thought she had delightfully perky boobs-not too big, not too small, firm with those 'Bob Seger' straight-at-cha headlights." No," I opined honestly. Clearly, there was anxiety in her voice at the prospect of already displeasing her fiancé. "Look," I said, flatly(no pun), trying to console a little-the biologist in me coming out, "breasts are mounds of fatty tissue over specialized glands whose principal purpose in life is to produce milk for newborn babies. Of course, they're going to bounce when you run; if they didn't, then you wouldn't have any at all! She seemed to accept my weak explanation and we continued on our ways, me lasering her firm, little, round behind (which didn't bounce at all) as she walked away down the hall.

 ## "Scooter for Two?"

Suddenly we find ourselves back on my European-Mediterranean travels once more. I had such a blast during my stay on the island of Crete! As I've mentioned, there was this gorgeous, ancient stone harbour of Hania, some olive tree-beating, some time on the chicken farm and several days of just puttering in and around the harbour, itself, over coffee for many sunrises and sunsets. There did come a time when I paired up with yet another American fellow who had a Vespa scooter and was planning on touring across the northern coast of the island and asked if I wanted to join him on his travels to Iraklion, another small ancient port-town at the other end of Crete. Sure! It was November by then, mostly overcast skies and getting cooler by the day. I would spend (Christmas that year, 1983) in Iraklion. Before we got there, however, midway on the journey we did split up briefly for one day and night close to some nameless small town along the way. I ended up walking for several miles by myself with my knapsack (in which I had packed some bread, sausage, cheese and a modest-sized bottle of ouzo!)At some point along the road, I was approached by an older Greek couple who invited me back to their farm just as the clouds were darkening threateningly on the horizon. Good timing, indeed. I stayed the one night in their' sort of' guest house-garage for a few drachma; it had a sleeping cot and a rickety card-table with a light; it was perfect for me. I would sit and write most of the evening and drink some ouzo while carrying on a rather one-sided conversation with this huge, hairy black spider that had obviously called the place home long before I arrived. Yep, after convincing myself that he was not a tarantula, not remotely interested in me and having one last shot of liquid-liquorice courage, I was able to catch four or five hours of sleep before outside morning sounds and slivers of sunshine filtering through the tattered curtains woke me in the early morning. I eventually rendezvoused with my scooter-friend in the nearby town by lunch time and, soon, we were back on the road.

Upon reaching Iraklion, it was not long at all before we found a bustling, inviting little taverna stocked with plenty of cheap, ice-cold draft beer and-surprise, surprise- more ouzo! The tables and patrons of this place had earlier in the evening spilt out onto the angled cobblestone streets where seatbelts would have been helpful. The whole town was decked out with Christmas lights which were at once gaudy and reassuring; we joined a few other revellers to sing a couple of bad carols, before stumbling away to find some sleeping quarters.

"The Grocery Lady."

Back at the international school in my first year in China-that's what we called her, this enterprising, younger, foreign woman who would first stock up her own car with 1-2 trips to the closest city's Wal-Mart and then drive the one hour out to us once a week to sell –off her ' Western' inventory, with a mark-up, of course. It was cause for minor celebration among us when it was "grocery- lady day!". We could buy our Corn Flakes, Raisin Bran or Oatmeal all from the trunk of her car!

 ### "The French Fry Truck."

We skip back now again to my childhood and place of my birth. Under our very famous bridge in the ole hometown which connects us to our American cousins in Michigan, was this sort of landmark- tourist and local attraction known as "The French Fry Truck". You see, it was this truck that would be parked under our side of the bridge all spring and summer (I don't know if the other side had a version, too? Yes, apparently!) where you could buy a cheap, small plate or a "cup" of chips. What made this vendor so extraordinary for most of us, as kids, was the "vinegar hose and gun" they used to spray the fries with. All this took place maybe one hundred feet from the sheer drop-off to the boiling, churning whirlpools of the St. Clair River as it passed under the Blue-water bridge from the southern tip of Lake Huron. There were always a few smelt fishermen and a couple of native kids there diving and swimming in the swirling, angry rush of water!

" Under the Bleachers"

The girl I had the hugest crush on in grade nine did happen,(how'd you guess?) to have one of the cutest bums in the whole high school- but she was already dating full-time, a small-bummed Catholic boy who was, admittedly, a better all-round athlete, especially in hockey and football. Ping –pong didn't hold much weight back then, or else it would have been a closer race, for sure! So, at the big, annual football festival- game, plan 'B' was hatched and soon found me seeking solace with another- a nice, pretty, young girl who was also a 'minor-niner'-under the bleachers. When something exciting happened elsewhere like on the field, the full bleachers would explode with a thunderous roar of shouting and stomping feet directly above us, making it all the more exhilarating as I got closer and closer to first-base at a football game! The smell of hot-dogs and mustard was in your nostrils! It was early male multi-tasking: breathing, listening, groping and more breathing (not necessarily in that order..)-all the while watching a football game between people's calves!

"Good Lines!"

Once, as a kid, I was on my bike at the school yard with two friends when across the field from us, another, strange boy arrived to the field and looked around, appearing some-what lost; clearly, he was on foreign turf; he was not from our neighbourhood, from our 'neck of the woods'. Within moments, one of my friends shouted at him from across the field," Get the freak outta here before I tear off your arm and beat you with it! If you had known this friend, you would have known he had the strength of a grown man inside his otherwise fourteen year old body and would have been fully capable of ripping off a limb and making good on his word! Friendly circle, eh? The young stranger left at once.

 ## "Two Trainees and a Beer Trolley."

In Europe I found that you got so used to the common train travel that it actually became fun after a while, while still novel to me- as a North American! Of course, it sure helps that the word for "beer" in several languages sounds very similar to how it does in English; making it hard to go wrong, really- and that finger-pointing, thankfully, is universal! After my sojourn for a few weeks on the Iberian peninsula where I had hooked up with those four Canadian gals and an American fellow and packed through Spain and Portugal, my American buddy decided to take off for France and asked me to join him, as he knew no French. I had my grade 9 Quebecois-French but compared to his zero, I was "bilingual" in his eyes. On the train they had some cheap, awful American beer(sorry, that's just the way it is..) and "T" and I managed to create quite a pyramid in our cabin from the empty cans; they make it so easy with a well-stocked cold beer and pop cart rolling by every twenty minutes or so! We were off then to gay,ole Paree!

"Pub Crawls."

We went on a few of these when I was an "inmate"-resident of Totem Park residence at U.B.C.in my first year. At the first one, I had never heard of such a thing, of course. "A what?" That's also when I learned about after participating in a couple of "Eat and Runs," later renamed, I believe, "Dine and Dash." From "E&R's to D&D'S." |

" TheRaperbahn".(?)

The German leg of my European backpacking tour was ostensibly to visit a former college floor-mate who lived just outside of Hamburg. I would find him, eventually, after walking for miles through the nicely- wooded countryside and passing by a few smaller villages, nearing his family's estate. He treated me to a visit to his local, private yacht club where most of the fifteen or so good friends he introduced me to each had to buy the Canadian pal "ein bier fomfasse" (draft beer, if I have it right?). We also managed to find a house-party later that night where, as the 'special guest', I was treated like a celebrity! It was a fun party to be sure! And so memorable-even with drink(!). My buddy introduced me to another of his friends from the 'kitchen cluster', one of several large paratroopers – and one of few young men comparable to me in age and size!. Of course, after a few chest-bounces, some friendly, garbled verbal sparing, and head-butting with each of us feeling out the other like the stupid, rutting- muskoxen we were, we took our contest outside for a fun "wrestle" in the neighbouring park, to determine "alpha-dom. "It was, really, the only time I can ever recall as an adult man ever being lifted off my feet completely by another man. This one then slammed me down on the hood of a parked car, thereby creating the bone chips in my one elbow that I still carry with me today! We finally shook hands, even hugged a bit awkwardly and stood by stupidly, as a group of curious fellow- partiers who had gathered to watch the action actually applauded our efforts('Hey, Stupid, young

men-that was great!'). This adventure was more painful perhaps but less embarrassing than the following evening when
my friend and I and a few more of his paratrooper-buddies
went out for dinner and some beer. The dinner was delicious,
but there came a point when he told me to hurry up because
we were leaving! "Why?" I asked, surprised. He leaned over
and told me in hushed tones that one of his buddies had just
pissed under the table! I couldn't believe it(No!), so I did
a quick visual check under the tablecloth. Sure enough, a
large , foaming, steaming puddle of urine was growing and
moving quickly out toward the aisle-way! So, the four of us
young big, strong, stupid and ugly beer-drinking men beat a
hasty retreat from the restaurant and went laughing into the
night.Ah- yes, "y" chromosome- fun!

"Mundane and Magical Matters."

Let's revisit China again for a spell, shall we? We shall. In
those early months following the stroke, I was a patient in
this monstrous red-brick rehabilitation centre in the heart of
Beijing for at least seven or eight months. There were some
moments of despair and hopelessness, sure, as I lay in the
bed and did all of my business right there from a prostrate
position and drifted from one DVD movie to the next all day
and night for weeks on end. My 24-7 care-giver would lay
a diaper down behind me on the bed and cart away any deposit I was good enough to make for analysis. Dignity? So
long, farewell.., aufiedezein-goodbye..goodbye! 'Nuff said
on such mundane matters More importantly, there came one
afternoon, or evening when my wife-to-be-unlocked and
lowered one of the safety side- rails of my bed, climbed up
and lay next to me so we could snuggle and hug some. This
was one of the many precious moments she has shared with
me during our time together. Some of me thinks she could
not have known what an impact such a gesture would have
on me- but, then again, the more we have walked our marriage path together, the more I understand she very likely did

know exactly how she was boosting my sorely lagging confidence and nearly crushed male ego with such an amazing show of tenderness and affection. Maybe, just maybe I was, still, a handsome and virile man who held some allure and appeal? No "avuncular", here, thank you very much! This was the same rehab centre where I was wrestled with initially and re-introduced to being vertical, to standing on two feet again!

"The 'Franken-Bed"

It reminded me of most every Frankenstein movie I've ever seen: the "standing bed"… My wife and my helper would accompany me down into the bowels of the facility to where a very large physiotherapy room was located(aren't they always?). There, they had the firm, shallow mats and pads on low, wide beds , or simply, on the floor where one to three physios would work their magic. They also had the aforementioned "standing beds" With help, I would get up on , lay down and be strapped onto; then they would start the gyro-machine that would pivot me into an upright position-for thirty to forty minutes at a stretch! They have to help you to teach yourself, your legs, mind and heart(all muscles and organs, really) again about that pesky little thing called," gravity," after you've been lying prostrate for months on end with all those organs and muscles atrophying a great deal. The bed did also have a small table-tray which came out around your ribs and chest in the front and allowed you to at least rest your arms a little, or play with food if you had any, like those infant high-chairs of old. As they raised me closer to right-angles, I would always do my 'silly monster-imitation' by extending straight out my right and only functional arm, making some low grumbling noises as I did. I would also from that position call out loudly for the waitress to bring me another cold beer, as if I were in a restaurant! That line became everyone's favourite, and every afternoon I would not disappoint the regulars!

(Addenbum) "That's Some Bumper!"

Once, in Vancouver while sitting out in the glorious, infrequent sunshine at my regular place on the sidewalk in front of my building doing my 'nicotine thing,' I was sort of hidden behind one of many trees lining the boulevard when I noticed a young woman at curb side just a few feet away, rummaging through the trunk of her parked car. Obviously she was unaware of my presence, with me being mostly obscured by a big tree trunk. So, for a few moments ,I guess I was a voyeur. There was an ever so slight breeze that day and, I must admit, I did put in a small wish to the wind-gods for a bigger gust or two, as she happened to be wearing one of those very flouncy, silky sort of mid-thigh dresses; well, my wishes were answered and within a moment, as she leaned once more into the trunk, a little wind-gust lifted her dress up fully on one side to reveal one entire wonderful ass-cheek and the dark thong she was wearing at the time. Ahhh! Just delightful. A Nice little gift that this "bum- man" thoroughly appreciated; again, it's sometimes those smallest moments or breezes that can bring us such joy!

 ### "L.D. B. Syndrome (L.D. B. S.)"

I feel like I should explain a bit about a personal 'syndrome' and the label I've coined for it-something I've lived with most of my life: 'Little Drummer-Boy Syndrome!' Much better-sounding to my ears than the tedious' F.O.I'. (Feelings of Inadequacy); I've been writing, it seems, forever and a lot of that has come out in the form of poetry and a sub-group of which, when pressed, I could call simply, "ditties" (a blend of lyric and ,-simple song-poem wannabe's). For as long as I can remember, I have always had a fascination for and gift with rhyme and was enthralled from a young age wherever I found it from Dr. Seuss' Cat in the Hat and Grinch to Ludwig Bemmelman's Madeleine series. Then, of course, with age, came Robert Service(with his McGee's and McGrew's)

the Carpenters, the Beatles,then Elton John and Bernie Taupin and- Tim Rice, Rice and Webber(name anyone, really.) I
am still quite naturally drawn to rhyme, and choose rhyming
verse often to express myself whether it be in the form of a
serious poem, a parody, or a "ditty" for a birthday party or
a retiring colleague! It seems only natural to me; I often see
the world around me through a rhyming-filter-it's true. Anyways, there have been numerous moments in my life when I
have crafted a poem or ditty to help celebrate a" liaison", a
love, a milestone of some kind for someone I know, attended
a party in his/her honour, and then found that I was the only
one in attendance not bearing a wrapped, traditional gift
of some kind. Oops. No, I just brought my "words" to the
celebration and would stand, rather sheepishly (a recurrent
theme, as most are..) in one corner of the "manger" and bang
gently on my drum, as I read aloud my words composed in
their honour . Right then in those moments, I might feel how
I imagined the Little Drummer Boy must have felt, humming to himself, standing beside a donkey, those many centuries ago in the manger; coincidentally enough and a little-
known fact was he was standing directly behind the farmer's
daughter and looking at her bum. I hear a gentle rebuke from
the Pulpit Master… who whispers, 'Inadequacy', Kim; they
call it, 'Inadequacy'. Yeah, thanks.

(FUNNY BITS)

"Toilet Humour, sorry!"

Being this close to the ground in my manual wheelchair, I
tend to 'rub shoulders' (or ankles, if you like?) with what
you might term a lot of low(er) life, other disabled folk in
chairs or scooters, street people who are sitting or laying all
day in the parking lot or alleyway as I pass by. As I've come
to discover all-too-well about this' barely-above-ground-
'sub-culture' is that most of them are usually able to tell you
exactly where all the best handicapped public washrooms
are located in the vicinity This is since many of them, of

course, take care of all their hygiene needs(if they do at all..) once there. They can scrub-up some with a "birdbath"... where the soap is free and they have(or used to have) a limitless supply of paper towels to dry-off with; some places have stopped providing paper-towels all-together, ever notice or wonder why? Environmental concerns, sure! Like the miniature shampoos once supplied by hotels Yep, unfortunately, there's always some who are less hygienic, who even have trouble transferring from scooter/chair to john- and still others who are able to spread/spray their fecal deposits from seat to floor to wall and sink like it was some sort of obscene performance- art, leaving at least me for one wondering when it's my turn, 'How the hell did they do this?? Of course, the golden arches are a favourite for many: spacious, well-lit and regularly cleaned and re-stocked! This is my competition, these days, whoah, me!

Once, however, I found one of these washrooms to be in such revolting shape that, upon entering, I had those involuntary oesophageal writhing- bursts which usually precede vomiting! I had to ask and then wait another half an hour for an attendant to clean up the mess. I nearly peed my pants in the interim and thought for sure my eyes might be permanently crossed!. When out and about, I drink beverages like everyone else and then soon have to pee-so, now, I've become somewhat of a slave to the washroom facilities because it has to be wheelchair- accessible, and many are not. In some coffee shops I've been in, I can't even get my chair through the door. Now, there's another of those weird, funny moments: I'm within ten feet of the necessary, usable bowl but I can't access it.I'm so close that if I was a good spitter, I could get one in the bowl; sometimes, I am able to stand, use the door some to take the few steps required to get closer to something like a counter or sink for temporary support. Several times in those smaller, less-than-four-star-restaurants, I can't even wheel my chair down the always dark, always crowded hallway-corridor in the very back of the place because it's being used to store boxes full of inventory-supplies…! So, it is the fast-food joints when I'm out and about that are preferred- and those are the people I'm mostly competing with- Youch!

(FUNNY BITS)

"Do you smell that?"

I'll always remember one of my initial interviews for the China teaching position. The interviewer asked me what I thought was one of the oddest questions I'd ever been asked in an interview, "How's your sense of smell" he queried. "You're not overly sensitive to smells, are you?" Turns out- in his bigoted preparation- he was alluding to the fact that some Chinese public toilets have not been properly sanitized or deodorized since they were first constructed in the Sung Dynasty, so their generally and extremely offensive odours waft outside to uneasily blend with the more pleasing smells of nearby food-carts on the sidewalk- leaving the nostrils heaving and the brain in utter chaos. Always, the 'old with the new', or is that, 'the old and the poo?'

"Baring My Fangs!"

For what I thought, at least at the time, was another good line, we will have to step back in time to my high school days and one night when I attended a house-party with my adorable, long-time girlfriend, K. I was angered somewhat by another strange man whom none of us knew- and how this fellow kept approaching and chatting-up my girlfriend, but he would do so only when I left the laundry room where we were, and popped outside for a cigarette, it seemed to me. I thought this slinking behaviour rather suspicious and that he seemed to like 'my girl' a little too much; he had a beard, this fellow, did I mention? Finally, I approached to confront him and just sternly said," Stop doing that, before I tear off your beard and shove it down your throat. His questionable behaviour (and mine, too)did cease immediately, but my aggressive outburst which was out of character for me-honestly- did not sit well with my girlfriend at all! I thought I was only doing the right thing, the 'alpha-male-baboon-baring-his fangs to an intruder and giving him a chance to exit peacefully. Many of us men think that behaviour entirely appropriate, even impressive and expected, but, it seems, it can leave a lot of our females just shaking their heads at our testosterone-fuelled stupidity. She would soon enlighten me and smooth my ruffled feathers (and you didn't even know baboons had feathers, did you..?) Apparently, that kind of potentially-violent anger and aggression is usually not found cooking a nice dinner in the home, or fluffing the freshly-cleaned sheets on the bed! I guess it's better reserved genuinely as a males-only-thing. We convince ourselves maybe that it's for the others, to protect what 'belongs' to us and it is our "lion's pride"- when, really, it's all about our own indivdual pride and egos! We are-by far- the most egocentric in the species without doubt! Even with food-bits stuck to our face or clothes.

"Day Camp"

It was held at our local elementary school/yard every spring and summer, and was always fun. It was where and when we learned those all-important "life-skills", like how to make lace bracelets, play checkers using pop bottle caps, play "Capture the Flag!" in the neighbouring woods, and, of course, continue trying to peek down girls' or counsellors' blouses, to see both underdeveloped and developed "nations". For the girls, most of whom were our long- time regular friends and classmates, according to the magazines, there should have been some appealing mounds or, at the very least, the promise of mounds on the way. Again, try as we might, there was usually nothing there; in fact most of them looked pretty much the same as the boys did. Whoop-deedo! Before long, however, some of those same girls would find themselves mercilessly teased and humiliated by a small circle of a few boys (myself included, sadly enough..) who would make a game and contest out of revealing to the world which of them actually had genuine 'starter-breasts' and which ones were "stuffing" Kleenex down there to give the appearance that nature was doing its job. In class, mind you, we would take turns walking by the desk of a suspected stuffing- girl, pause, actually reach quickly down her blouse and pull up Kleenex-if any were there, then wave it around victoriously to everyone, I'm sure bolstering their egos to lower than deflated and stepped on! Lovely, huh?Today, that same group of us would be arrested for at least assault, I'm sure! The girls, it seemed, wanted breasts almost as much- perhaps even more – as most of us boys wanted them to get them! On our side, for the boys, it was almost always about needing to shave, an indicator that you had crossed over into the "man's realm" from boyhood Again, showing the inequality among we "men", a few could have started shaving probably by sixth grade!. Little could we have known then the sheer tedium that accompanies facial hair and our society's expectation that it(like dust) be removed daily to look respectable. It is a lot like dusting, perhaps: you've got to do it regularly because it just keeps coming! Even when we die, apparently(different schools of thought on this...?!); do they have barber shops in Heaven, presuming I go in that direction?

"Sheer Little Shorts."

Maybe what Marshall McLuhan meant those many years ago was the 'massage is the medium. 'I know my first one in Beijing was, yes, quite an eye-opener, alright. I was given something vaguely resembling a hospital gown – only shorter and more gauze-like if possible and a pair of what might pass for shorts, it's true –not much imagination needed, I'm afraid. It began with me face-down on the bed and my pretty young Chinese masseuse kneading my back, and legs (thighs and calves), but her magic fingers and sexy tight silk gown soon had me levitating from the table –if you know what I mean(wink, wink)?Of course, by the time she had me roll over onto my back, there could be no hiding the fact in my sheer little shorts that I was very much enjoying the experience. She took note of my enjoyment also, briefly left the room and returned a moment later with her boss/'Mamasan' who then explained to me that for a mere one hundred dollars(U.S.) my masseuse would take care of all my pressing needs! The innocence was gone, now- and at what cost?($0.00, so far..)

"Dib,Dib,Dib/ Dob,Dob,Dob."

I was both a cub, and later a Boy Scout and have wonderful memories from both periods. Those organizations (along with 'Toastmasters' much later..) were about as close to 'military' as I ever came or wanted to, but I guess I did learn some discipline and all about the concept of teamwork from the former- hmm mm , I guess those are reasonably important life skills, or, at least people keep saying they are. Plus, of course, they are just so golly-darn age-appropriate for young boys who definitely have a pack- mentality and, otherwise, can get up to some no-good. And leadership skills…? When we learned it's much easier to allow someone else to assume that mantle whenever possible…, and then watch as they "delegate!" Yes, sir, one of the keys to successful leadership!

 ## "Sword- Fights!"

Now, there's something all the girls miss out on! As young boys, a situation would often present itself when there were two or more of us taking a pee at the same time. Using our urine-streams, we could angle ourselves just enough to cross our golden- liquid swords! Hah, girls just don't have the necessary weaponry for duels like that; this is probably how the whole notion of penis-envy really originated. One day, some little girls saw the boys off peeing and laughing together, occasionally turning toward one another. If anything at all, it's the convenience only they might envy… (of having only to shake another finger-like appendage and not the entire 'fuselage'.

(Addenbum) "Strangers in the Alley"

Now that I've at least mentioned a few male bums along the way, including my own, I must share another quick tale regarding mine. Usually, viewing a person's naked bottom is the sole preserve of and a partner's only privilege- but me, on occasion, I have been known to share that perk with complete strangers, it's true. Am I a flasher? No, not really. When I go for my dry- day constitutional cane- walk in a nearby alley way, I park my chair at one end of a chain link fence on those mornings and walk beside the fence for a hundred feet or more. Like most other people I know, I have several different sweatpants that I wear. Trouble is is that each is somewhat different from the next in its style and certainly the cut or fit- and the tightness of the waistband, etc. Some are a little too tight, but that makes them good for walking while other much looser ones are better for everything else. Occasionally, I will find myself over at that fence some mornings with pants that need constant pulling up, if you know what I mean? Twice now, I've had to ask perfect strangers walking by to help me pull up my pants to cover my behind after they slid down to almost my ankles during a walk! Novel way to meet new people, don't you think?

"Idiots and Urine Puddles."

Being a man most of my life, I have to vehemently complain about my peers (or should I say 'pee-ers?), those other adult humans with penises (penii?) between their legs. My God! Now, many women out there might not know or care – having never been inside a man's washroom before unless you've got tinkling todlers, but we have these special, vertical "urinal-things", like bassinettes that are vertically attached to the walls-allowing us to just walk right up to them and tinkle to our hearts' content; they should have fire hydrants and trees painted on the walls behind them for us. Well, frankly, I'm sick and tired of all of those idiot-peers of mine out there who still don't fully grasp the concept behind the "urinal". So, as a result, they stand a little too far away and then up diddling some on the floor in front of it for others, including me, to stand in when it's our turn next. Lovely! Of course to me, it goes a long way in explaining the insecurity and anger that many of my male cohorts exhibit out there – if their 'thingamabobs' are far too short to even dangle over the bottom portion of the gaping white porcelain mouth which is waiting for their stream! Fish in a barrel, I say. Obviously not. Why not check the rear and side-view mirror more, look down occasionally and do a 'stream-check'. Is it going where it should? Instead, we are left with urine puddles in front of four out of five urinals! Thank you very much, you thoughtless dolts! You know who you are- and you probably can't read, so will never see this. Too bad, really. Maybe they're the same ones who paint the walls of the handicapped rooms at the golden arches..?

"Leakage, Seepage and Spillage."

Sure, so the gals can't have "sword-fights" while peeing, or write their names in the snow(more like Rorschadt Blots) but they have so much else to deal with that most of us men can never fathom. There's that monthly-egg-purge-thing they have to contend with from a young age when nature reminds them not 'periodically' but monthly, 'If you're not going to use them, you're going to lose them…' And it won't be pretty. And, Lord- knows, there's plenty of men out there who actually get squeamish at the mere thought or mention of blood between her legs "down there." I guess they won't be there to see their children being birthed or to help lick away the afterbirth! After all, there was never a hint of that kind of stuff or other basic biological functions in the centerfold pictures, after hours of plucking, waxing, Only later in life would we learn that life does not always imitate art. Then there's the boobs for women, those delightful, utilitarian mammary glands; the more "mature" the bustier ones become, the more chance there will be of "spillage"- where little tucks of fat from the breast under the arms "spill" out and over the brassiere lines- very unsightly and to be avoided, apparently. So, after removing their hair from pretty much everywhere else it grows on the body- except maybe trying to add more of it to their eyelashes, the more bosomy among them would have to tuck some of their ' hangout' into- what some pre-teen boys would call with a giggle, their "over- the –shoulder- boulder- holders." Of course, during the monthly egg-purge, many have to be wary of leakage and seepage problems up in the crotch and not wearing white on certain days. Yeast in-fections? Warm, dark, moist places are favoured by not just men,but yeast colonies, too! Some of me, when queried on the matter, wouldn't be completely surprised to learn that some men out there might guess it has something to do with bread-making!? Wrong. I see them occasionally on that afternoon bell-ringing show- try as I might to avoid it. Many simply don't care enough to listen or learn about it- and just know they want the woman to be clean and 'ready to go' when they are. Great! That's empathy, for you….

"The Naming of Stuff!"

When I was much younger than I am now, I would some-times sit writing my stories and ideas down- and I just loved creating names for characters! A lot of the time even ,as part of a challenge-game, the names would come first, then char-acters would have to be designed to "fit" them. What kind of job/career, life, family would a person with that name most likely have? Jack?(construction) Or Fraser(accountant)? The stupid, monosyllabic ones came easily, like "Stew the chef" You see, it didn't really matter how stupid or ridiculous-sounding (and even.. the spellings i.e. Memee,Lindah and Shellee/Trudee?) they were because 'Goober' and 'Festus' ,' Opie' and 'Potsie' were already being used and well-estab-lished. We'll leave Lenny & Squiggy out of it for now! So, the sky was the limit! Anything goes,Newt.

Where, on earth, did they come from anyhow? "Ah, he's such a cute little 'Goober', isn't he? It sounded an awful lot like 'booger' to me! Zelda and Esmeralda and even my wife's, Miranda, were names that always held some pizzazz-fascination for me and conjured up images of magicians' assistants (pun intended)in sparkly leotards. The Chinese have a long-standing tradition of child-naming often that reflects either nature or the immediate environment or weather of the moment at birth. Then, because we all start out quite small in this life, many Chinese will also have the moniker "Xiao" meaning 'small' attached to their names; it remains roughly their equivalent to the former Communist- tradition of naming everyone 'Comrade-friend' to help create an air of equality, superficial though it is- like the tile work.... This gives us an endless stream of little drinks, little houses, little apples, little lambs, little horses, little moons, little winds – you get the idea To this, my father would doubtlessly have added, "little farts",but I have yet to meet anyone with that name.". It's nice, I suppose, A wee bit whimsical in fact,if not somewhat unoriginal and tedious after a while, especially for a fellow whose one principal epithet through life has been 'big guy'! "Brave Achilles" and his friend, "Big Guy."

" Toilet Paper Blackmail!"

Whoops, here we are back again, back-packing with me through Europe, O.K? Once, somewhere during my visit to Greece, after a night of Calamari and a bit too much ouzo, my bowels were writing a script entirely unto themselves the following morning. I would, eventually, find a much-needed public washroom (no mermaid in sight..) and, there, sitting out on a single chair in a weird sort of reception area between the men's' and ladies' washrooms was an older, potato-faced Greek woman who would sell you a few squares of toilet paper in return for a few Drachma. We smiled at each other. I gave her a few Drachmas and she gave me uh… three squares of the precious paper. My sphincter was already burping for help by that point. So, I dug down deep, found some more coins and gave those to her also-and she would give me two more sheets! (You gotta be kiddin' me!) "No! my mind was shouting, "You don't understand!" Some more Drachmas still netted me a few more urgently-needed squares. Only then did I feel armed enough to proceed with my pressing operation! As I headed in, I can admit that my last look at her was not a pleasant one. She had complete control of the game. It was toilet-paper blackmail!

"Finger-in-the-Bum-Club" (Different Day, not related)

It's not as bad as it sounds; First-off, it's not a real club, so please do not write to ask me how you join,O.K.? It reminded me some of that old favourite show, The Littlest Hobo". It was the 'littlest oil refinery', one of few in the lower mainland of Vancouver, and purportedly, at the time, considered on paper to be one of the most cost-effective in the country!. Perhaps it was inevitable that for those first two years of mine as a student out at U.B. C., I would find myself as a summer-student at the same refinery where my father worked For several of us 'sons and daughters, it was all part of the package offered by the company to children of employees (those were the days!), those of us fortunate enough to win their scholarship-awards (which paid full-tuition costs to post-secondary. for four years!! Most of us worked in the "pipe- gang" alongside the pipefitters and welders in the plant. We got to know the tradesmen quite well, of course and were each regularly assigned to one man- but we students, mostly young, stupid men would form close bonds, regularly strengthened by beer-drinking outings to local bars on the weekends! I learned a lot of rudimentary pipefitting/plumbing skills and, that, when coupled with my time assembling toilet- tanks would help make me reasonably comfortable around threaded pipes, t-joints, elbows and ball-valves. It was all very "hands-on" and confirmed for me what I already knew- that, indeed, I had some good mechanical aptitude. They were wonderful summers when we, this small motley collection of mostly young men had the world by the tail (or so we thought, anyway.) We would often tease each other as we passed one another driving through the refinery in their work-trucks, through that maze of storage tanks, towers and miles of piping that more than a few hours were spent doing nothing, sitting around waiting with, as we used to say, 'Our finger up our bum! We even had an icon for it –just a small circle with a dot in the centre.. With Whiteout for paint, we would soon all have it displayed proudly on our hardhats.

"Les Lumberjacks, Bah!"

Grade nine would prove to be quite an eventful year in a number of ways. One of those was how I was somehow selected to participate in a French- Exchange through my high school, with my solid C/C- average!, an exchange that would first send me to Montreal for two weeks of immersion to stay with a family and then bring "Mon comrade" back to Sarnia for two weeks, later in the year. What an absolute blast it was! My host-family was 'magnifique! And the father would often sit with me at their kitchen table, have me try to say something, correct me and then have me repeat it several more times! It was like having your own private tutor as he sat and 'salted' his beer-foam; I'd highly recommend it, for sure, for sure – the tutor, that is, not salt in your beer!

One day, mind you, found my exchange partner and I attending an Expos baseball game in the then wonderful old, open-air Jerry Park. 'Le Lanceur' is all the French I learned that day, for "pitcher", I believe- but I did learn something else entirely: how to do shots of tequila with salt and lemon wedges! As it turned out, four burly, unshaven lumberjacks planted themselves directly behind us, in town for a couple of weeks after two in the bush. They had the tequila, one even had lemon wedges(in a baggy in his coat..) and still another had the salt-shaker from some poor diner-stop along the way. Oooh la-la! No, not surprisingly, I don't remember who won the game!?

"Tanks for the Memories!"

There were balls and cocks everywhere! I'm serious! I'd never seen so many balls and cocks (not even in a dressing-change room! No, it wasn't from a naughty porno-flick although I suppose it could have been. Instead, it was from my time at one of the largest bathroom fixture/appliance makers in Canada, if not the world. We made bathtubs, urinals, bidets and, of course, everybody's favourite, toilets! Boy, oh, boy, did we make toilets! I worked on a line that received the bowls and the tanks fresh from the kilns, but before the tanks could be finally boxed and palletized for shipping, the 'ball and cock' assembly(that's what It's called!) had to be pieced together and fastened securely to the inside of the tanks. That was my job for a spell; it was piece-meal: we were paid for every tank assembly we completed; I could do 3-5 per minute by the time I finished. It worked out to about thirty-seven cents each, not a 'get-rich-quick scheme' by any stretch....

" Ah, Piece-Meal...!"

You live and learn, right, or at least that's what we're told when we're younger? It took me a while to realize that a guy shouldn't do piece-meal work and that it's certainly not a good retirement strategy!. If you do enough pieces, then you might have earned enough to buy yourself a cheap lunch or dinner-thus the 'meal' part?! Go ahead, Google 'ball and cock ' and see what pops up(so to speak), or you could just take a moment one day and lift the lid off the top of your toilet tank – and see the vertical plastic tube-pipe you see there is called the "cock" while the big balloon-float resembling a ball is strangely enough called the "ball". Another one of those piece-meal jobs I did in my youth was as a casual labourer outside of Dawson Creek in B.C's Northeast(Peace River) region where we were moving twenty-five kilogram bags of artificial, chemical gel (used as lubricant in the drilling operations of the big oil rigs) and cement from inside a railway boxcar, to outside, and then down a ramp onto a flatbed truck where we then re- stacked them on pallets; you see, for whatever reason, the railway bridge leading North was out- unusable- but the drilling rigs operating in the area still needed the stuff. My workmate for the morning was a Hell's Angel, looking for some fast-cash/gas-money; he was a very nice, big burly fellow, as I recall. Most of them are just that or at least in my experience-contrary to their much-hyped media'bad-guy' image He would take two of these bags on every other trip (You can do the math). I tried that but once- before my back moaned out, "No, you don't! You STUPID idiot!" By break time, we had earned enough for a coffee or a pop, at seventeen cents per piece/bag moved! Geez! This job would prove, unequivocally, to be my last piece-meal effort! Whew!

"Bad Wings in Wawa"

Not to damage the tiny town's "tourism industry" at all, if such a thing even exists, but on my wonderful drive-touring trek across this great land of ours from Vancouver to Toronto way back in 2001in the summer before 9- 11, and a few years before I went abroad.., I did have a layover, an overnight in this humble, tiny northern Ontario community. I found a diner-restaurant, maybe attached to a hotel, I can't remember, really. I ordered and ate my way through most of the worst chicken wings I have ever experienced(or ever will..) Several were underdone but all came "floating" in a tomato- sauce which I can confidently assume was a can of Campbell's Tomato Soup! It was just horrible. Oddly enough, I quite like the soup by itself in a bowl with a few crackers; here, it was too difficult fishing out the under-cooked wings!

"On the Façade of Things."

Back to the 'red-dragon' of communist China for a moment, now; the Chinese are very big on and very good at.. ceremony – 'the pomp and circumstance.' -they do so like dressing things up! But that does come with a cousin called 'making mountains out of molehills.' They could even give the Brits a run for their money! New restaurant? Time for speeches, a few local politicians maybe and bring in the dancing girls and costumed-lion, and fireworks for a small parade! They love it, so at every opportunity they will dress-up an event- regardless how small, insignificant or mundane. In fact, at least by my measure, they're often overboard with it. Every morning before classes began at the not-very-international- international school where I worked, they would have us all line up in rows, students and teachers alike in military fashion. We men were all expected to wear ties, even if we all tore them off while walking up the stairs into the school, upon dismissal. For this daily "assembly", there was a one- step stage, podium and microphone. Standing at attention in our rows, we would first get the national anthem(It reminded me some of those old 'God Save the Queen' days back in grade four in Canada Then there was one or two speeches from the puppet-administration/management team, and usually one or two more minor speeches from grade-level representatives, the janitors and so on.... Most all of them, too, were of the 'rah-rah-sis-boom-bah'- variety, of how good our school was and the latest, however minor or miscellaneous, achievements or awards there may have been; it all so reminded me, too, of Orwell's <u>1984</u> where the government propaganda-machine would loudly boast of how they had again raised certain food rations for the population when. ,in fact in truth, they had reallydecreased them!' And today, we are proud to inform you all that our janitorial staff was voted second-best for competency and fewest sick-days recorded in the district-the best ranking since 1994! Nonetheless, we would all stand stupidly in that military style, like drones, for these 'ceremonies', these thirty to forty minutes every day because that's what was expected and then ,only when dismissed, break off to head into the school for classes for the day-that after determining which of us was able to rip off his tie the fastest!. The word "regimented" often comes to mind when I think back on those days and on China itself, generally. Perhaps it is an integral component-that continually reinforced discipline- in any

Communist State.. to the point of numbness.. Who knows? Keeping the masses in check? As I've already mentioned, I often saw 'platoons' of restaurant workers standing, nearly at attention, out on the wide boulevards in front of their restaurants- all this, as a manager/drill-sergeant talked at them and occasionally inspected the uniforms for tears or stains.

Once, we teachers were all bussed the one or one- and- a-half hours to be present at the opening ceremony of a new branch of our school. Great! More speeches! Then, there was the time we were all ushered down to the nearby beach in a big hullabaluh for a big, "invitational" swim- meet with flags and balloons, pretty girls and banners aplenty! Judging from the turnout, however, most places had not accepted their "invita-tions"- a couple of Russians did somehow manage to appear. Whatever it is, you can be sure the Chinese will always find a way to dress it up in ceremonial mystique. and grandeur… to glue on the gorgeous tile work over the decrepit brick… It is only ever tourist-eye deep,but makes for really "nice" photo-graphs and pleasant, colourful memories of an otherwise im-poverished, struggling dusty-grey nation.

" Happipotamus"

Once, back while I was still in high school, my long-time girlfriend and I had a mandatory outing to the PNE and, of course- Play land. You know the place; that's where the boy, always trying to impress his new love still, is sup-posed to win a big, stuffed animal for the girl, I believe. Of course, that's not quite how it played out. We did my fa-vourite 'bumper cars', had some cotton candy and then she promptly won me a medium-sized, polka-dot, pink

Hippopotamus which I immediately named, "Happy" be-cause of the state I was in. I had "Happy" in my bedroom for the next ten years! "Bliss" might have been even more appropriate, as just the sight of him could transport me back to those carefree, wonderful high school days!

"The Pets."

Our names for the family pets I knew as children were hardly creative, I feel. I mean, the rabbit was named, "Hoppy." The beautiful white Persian cat was called, "Puffy." The mice, of course, were different, with no clear defining or distinguishing characteristic (and would assume politician names-Trudcau &Stanfield), but it was the crocodile definitely that shined the most in this menagerie. We called him, "Cronky", after a favouriteT.V. news man, Walter ' And that's the way it was for this Tuesday, January 16ᵗʰ Cronkite. The one guiding principle for our pet-names, it seemed, was they all had to end with "y".Age and stage, I guess…

   (ADDENBUM)

"Back to the Bottom!"

Not of the glass, mind you-but of the woman's backside/ behind. You've got your "confident bums" who, in their magnificent roundness and/or taughtness just exude a certain charm, a certain' je ne sais pas quoi'. Not true. I know exactly what it is… an A.F. , 'Arousal Factor,' Let's Face facts- They tend to put some male glands into a higher gear. These new, soft jeans that are so very sheer and stretchy do these bums wonderful justice, like a too-snug glove pulled down hard over the twin orbs yet still honouring the clear dividing line between them. Hmm….Sexist-pig! Hm Mm.

   (ADDENBUM plus)

"Bum-Talk"

You know, there's an entire silent language out there that centers on the butt. For example, when a young woman walks by a guy she knows is checking out her C.P.' s (remember? 'Convergence Points'), most have several choices in response. One common one is the look-back, or angled shoulder-glance where they are simply confirming what they already knew – the fellow was leering at their behind! The second includes the 'look-back', but also adds a subtle hand gesture where she almost rubs or smoothes one bum cheek-as if to acknowledge the stare that she knows is following her. In essence, the gesture is saying, 'I know you're looking right here The third response is the much more traditional, now almost prudish stern, fast rebuke-glance: how dare you look after me with only lust in your eyes and heart. This, of course, is the least- favoured among many men. for obvious reasons....

"The Triple Toot!"

As a kid, I will always remember Dad's every arrival home because he would always gently 'TOOT' the car horn three times quickly in succession just as he turned into our drive-way. Unforgettable.

(Addenbum) "Tacky Lard Ass!"

To be fair, with all my talk on the derrière, I should spend a moment or two on my own bum. It's not a small bubble-butt by any stretch, but neither is it a huge flip-floppy chilli thing! I do, however, have some padding down that way for sure. It was enough to insulate me from feeling a tack I sat on while teaching one day early- on, when a couple of" fun" grade eight boys set it on my chair when I was distracted and away from the desk. It was twenty minutes later before I discovered it and pulled it out and then only after a guilt-ridden female witness told me about it on her way out the door.

I like to think I still have a lot to bring to the world-stroke or no stroke- (pretty modest, huh?) Canada, or at least Vancouver, is very friendly and open in attitude (one of the best), and quite physically accessible for most of us(i.e. curb-cuts, ramps, automatic doors at entrances, public transit..) China(one of the worst), on the other hand, is simply not that open or friendly, to the disabled, maimed or deformed and certainly does not make much of an effort at all in its built-environment and infrastructure to accommodate those of us with mobility issues unless, of course, the rest of the world is visiting say,... for the' Olympic

&Para- Games'! Then on the 'façade' of things', things look not too bad-but the world leaves, and then you see it's only China left-the real, everyday China,. Then they just might tidy up and rush costly adaptations in construction to make everything 'look good' and it does, temporarily-but scratch the surface and....voila, the glossy multi-coloured tiles begin to chip and fall away because things are often far from what they appear: façade...everywhere really; looks great on the surface, but no real substance underneath. Maybe, I'm just a bitter whistle-blower, huh?TWEEE.T!! Maybe. Smoke and 'Mirror-tiles'.

"The '41 Desoto!"

It belonged to my maternal grandparents and was still parked in their garage in Sarnia when I came along as a young boy. I loved that car-tank! Sometimes, if ever I could get into the garage, I would just climb into the backseat, as dusty and musty as it was(there was no head-in-a-jar,) and sit and dream about what it had seen and done in its hay-days. Nowadays when I think on it, I'm reminded of that scene in "Silence of the Lambs" when Clarice (Jody Foster) breaks into the storage unit and climbs into the huge old car to discover the flutist's head in a big jar in the backseat! No, I never found any heads-in jars! My father-engineer that he was- had the old beast up- and- running at one point when I was still a kid (maybe 5 or 6?). When he would occasionally drive it home back to our place, we had a routine whereby after he turned off the main road and onto our side street, he would then stop, let me get out so I could run around to the driver's side, climb up on the huge winglike running-board (so favoured by early gangster bank-robbers!) and hold on. He, of course, with 'safety always first,' in mind would reach out the open window with his free left arm and wrap it around me lest I fall off. It was so much fun, and we probably only ever reached 10 mph.! Another, grander 'deSoto tale was related to me much later by my Mom who explained how she almost 'lost' me one day as a youngster when she was driving home from downtown in the Desoto. I was in the back, playing 'trampoline' on that sofa-sized backseat, a favorite pasttime. I was all of five or six, maybe. Did I mention yet how in this car, the big metal door handles opened when you pushed them down?? They did. It was a safety feature that has long since been addressed in the auto industry. Mom said she felt a cool draft on the back of her neck which was odd, she thought, as she drove us by the golf course on Christina Street toward home. It was a cool wind, most definitely, not her imagination, she calmly related. She turned around some in the driver's seat to check on her 'Number One Son' and saw that the rear door was wide open and I was on the outside, hanging on to the handle for dear-life and being dragged along on my stomach and knees on the gravel-topped , hard-packed shoulder of the road! One of my downward bounces on the backseat had obviously opened the door and sent me tumbling out....

Fortunately, I suppose, this all happened in the days before Christina Street was even paved, so-yes- I would have several small pebbles imbedded in my skin, but had it been asphalt, I might not have had any skin at all! Good 'ole Sarnia! This is where we had settled, after returning to North America, from our Iranian sojourn and a brief stint in Edmonton.

"L.R. B.S."

"Little Red Bone Shakers." These were China's version of Thailand's 'tuk-tuks'; they were the converted three-wheeled motorcycle-taxis seen everywhere that have a homemade plywood box-compartment on the back to carry passengers., most painted either red or blue..

Inside of this Spartan box, there would be little benches on either side, enough for as many as six adult passengers in all. I remember in Thailand, most of them were very "rude" vehicles, belching and farting down the roads and leaving thick clouds of stinky blue or black smoke in their wake. The Chinese versions were nowhere near as bad, generally, much cleaner and eco-friendly, but like most, there was little or no suspension under their homemade passenger compartments, so those inside would feel every burp, crack and pebble on the pavement; this is why I formally dubbed them 'Little Red Bone-Shakers!' (L.R. B.S.)- but their drivers were always friendly and the fares incredibly cheap(like most everything else)! In Canada, the meter would have clicked over to five dollars within the first few hundred metres. On China's mainland, you could do a ten kilometre round-trip for the same price.

"Something for the Resume"

I have mentioned earlier that I was unapologetically, a bit of a ' Mommy's Boy' and that she might have been at times rather indulgent toward me. On the cusp, as an early teen (14-15), some of our would-be championship hockey team often congregated at the "Orange House" for a night of beer-swilling, smoking and loud rock'n 'roll. Once, I asked my mother if she would help furnish me with a twelve-pack of beer for a party. She did. Coincidently, I'm sure, my Dad was out of town at the time….

I was actually heading down the front hall and out the door to 'freedom', friends waiting in the car in the driveway, with the beer under my arm at the very same instant my father happened to enter the house with his suitcase, having just at that very moment, returned from a six-week business stay in Montreal, The two of us met rather awkwardly in the hallway you might say. Although there was no escape, I vainly tried to soldier- on. "And.. just where do you think you're going with that?" I explained my plans for the evening. There was no discussion, no hesitation, no doubt in him at all.

"Oh, no you don't," he said, taking the case away from me in one easy swoop of his arm .That was that. I would still be allowed to go to the party but empty-handed and embarrassed. Meanwhile, the two of us would have a man-beer conversation the following day, after a much shorter one, I'm sure, that night with his wife. "And just how many beer do you think you can drink, young man?" he started in the next day. The naïveté and bravado of youth won over the moment and I honestly, stupidly replied, "Well, I've had eight before." "The hell you say," he said with almost a laugh. He simply refused or chose not to believe my answer. Thing was, however, it was true. I had already established a fledgling reputation as someone who could hold his liquor and drink any takers under the table. Now, there's something for the resume, huh? Yet in all this time, never once has a job- interviewer ever asked me how much beer I could drink at one sitting! Who's buying..?

"The Vermillion Border."

Once more now, to step back in time to those bachelor, Toronto bygone hay-days, I went out one evening with a good childhood buddy to join him for a game in the recreation hockey-league he was a part of. It was strange for me. Perhaps him, too, because in all those years we had known each other, growing up like con-joined twins some might have said, we had never really played any formal ice-hockey together in an arena setting. Sure, there had been entire, twelve-hour days playing pond-hockey, but this was now the real thing for the first time. I had toiled for years in minor house league whereas he, doubtless because he was a much better skater, had always played a few rungs higher on the ladder at the "rep" or all-star level. I had struggled from a young age with learning how to turn both ways on my blades.. to the point where I had actually modified my game and style so that I could always turn comfortably-hard and fast- to my left side. Let me tell you… it does take away from your game and leave the N.H.L. scouts unimpressed; still, however, I was big and strong, liked the clean "hit" whenever it was there, and was a reasonably smart player with good puck-sense. So, there we were, finally, on the ice together, paired and playing as a defensive unit; things were fine for the first few shifts and, then, I did what I'd seen Serge Savard do on the 'Habs' for years when a fast-rushing forward streaked down the wing toward him, ready to unload a big slap shot on his/my net:I put my stick out to meet the opponent's and the puck, looking to deflect it harmlessly over the glass. It didn't work for me quite that way and, instead, the puck was deflected right up straight into my face, hitting me in the lower mouth. This was in an era- remember- before we stupid 'dinosaurs' had relented and started wearing face-cages and mouth-guards! Whew! So the puck met nothing but teeth and lip! And it's a good thing I have such a big, protective lower lip!. It split wide- open that lower lip, pouring blood down onto my chin and neck and jersey but saves my teeth. I put a hand up and realized instantly things were not good in my mouth region. I got myself back to the bench for a break, some water, and further consideration of my predicament. Watching my friend's eyes grow wide in horror as he looked at me on the bench confirmed what I suspected: a ride to hospital was in order. Once there and in the emergency ward waiting area, I let another young man who had badly burned his lips while " hot-knifing" hash(his mouth looked like fresh calf's liver)… I let him go first. When it was my turn, the young intern assigned to stitch me up, said something quite curious as I lay down on the bed, "Well, we'll want to line up the vermillion- border, here," As I later learned, it is the seam-line where lip meets chin face, rather vital if you were to avoid a \Frankenstein "zig-zag". I agreed, "Please."

"Just Another Brick in the Wall"

I can very happily say that I've been atop the 'Great Wall of China' five times now! Let me tell you,this structure is impressive! To see the majestic landscape that this massive thing snakes through-mostly on the ridges of mountains, to feel the cool wind blowing in your face while you gaze down at one of the many quaint, ancient villages that carefully follow its undulations, each responsible for helping to stock the local garrison/guard-tower with food and water and sometimes, men! Wow! It was easy for me to imagine being a soldier-sentry stationed on the wall, spying out and seeing the hordes of the enemy's army making their way closer and closer. Genghis Khan, maybe? He was, after all, one of the main reasons for its construction to begin with. What I couldn't readily grasp was how-after it was completed and manned with soldiers aplenty- it was continually overrun by foreign armies? I remember my first Chinese guide explained it to me in a rather off-handed way; it was 'bribery, plain and simple- corruption!' Some of the invaders could stand at the base of the wall, look up and just converse with some of the sentries on duty. They would offer most anything and everything (from goats to girls..), and the strategy worked again and again. Just one or two vulnerable, weak-minded guards could help with a grappling hook or ladder and, once the onslaught began, would probably be ruthlessly killed. It was not unusual, apparently, for a family member of one of the sentries from the nearby village to be held, and tortured, by invading troops at the base of the wall, that so the related soldier on top of the wall could see and hear everything being done until he relented and offered to help.

"That Sort of Thing!"

I've already discussed some the rear-ender (MVA) the family was involved in one day in Port Huron, Michigan, a crash that sent the two motorcyclists directly behind us at the intersection, flying through the air over our Volkswagen Bug to smack down hard on the pavement in front of us. Fortunately, both drivers were wearing helmets and survived, but there was still some serious damage inflicted. When I think back to that moment, to the horrible screeching of tires before our car was sent lurching forward on impact, before I turned in my seat just in time to see the four young black men jump from the doubtlessly-stolen car and fan out to run away down the sidewalks. I am reminded of the larger-than-life lesson in it all that my father really taught me. He would take it upon himself to travel back to that Port Huron hospital several times over the next two months to visit the two badly injured bikers and see how their recovery was progressing. He was just doing the right thing, the compassionate thing. That sort of thing! That sort of thing, thinking and action was quite characteristic, quite typical of my Dad. I learned more from him in those moments than in all our math-tutoring sessions combined.

" The Raperbahn"

Hamburg. One of Northern Europe's largest ports and a large U-boat base apparently, in wartime which was one of the reasons, I think, it was so heavily targeted by allied bombing- runs near the end of the war. Here we are again, on my stupendous back-packing, picture-less tour of Europe-obviously the German leg. My good German friend from college days toured me down near the port itself, after I had taken a harbour tour on my own. We went to a special, walled-in section referred to as the'Raperbahn' which he explained to me meant' rope-making place' It was an area of the port laden with bars and brothels , now- many of which had a 'showroom' for the girls to ply a little of their inviting-wares in the windows to curious passersby. It was a bit intimidating on entering because you had to zigzag your way through one of those ugly, forbidding plywood barrier-walls so common in wartime which were plastered with signs shouting "Verboten! No one under eighteen permitted!"

"Orange Water!"

Once, while staying at a highly recommended, cheaper, Colonial-style hotel in Bangkok, I discovered to my delight that there was an outdoor pool, so after doing my bad/sad-writer- 'Hemingway- impersonation' by sitting a while in their lounge and throwing back a couple of highballs, I made my way outside for a swim! Drinking and swimming again! It was just me there on this warm, beautifully clear night and, as it so happened that night, there was a fireworks celebration going on somewhere in the city. I splashed around some and then relaxed, with arms outstretched on the side of the pool. I was entertained by explosions in the night sky over me in the distance with their accompanying, wonderful pinks, yellows, oranges, blues and greens. I'll always remember how, at one point, the surface of the pool all around me was a glowing, vivid orange!

"The Stupid Marble Game."

When on my own again in Chang Mai(North western Thailand)-before I hooked up with some fellow teachers at a nice little hostel-hovel-hotel-I stayed in a small nice hotel on my own. It was a nice place and all but the access to my room was a bit unusual; there was a small, ankle-deep pool of water in the middle of the sidewalk-corridor that I had to navigate around when going to my room. To skirt it, you had to alternately place your feet very wide apart on either side and do this weird 'quick dance' to get to the other side. Can you see where this might be leading? Sure, of course, I went out for a bachelor night-on-the-town, starting at the "night-market"-a must-see for any traveller/visitor and always fun! It's just a narrow, bustling open- air strip full of small booths and their pushy vendors hawking everything from shirts to drink-coasters, statuettes, cheap jewelry and other easy-to-pack tourist-trinkets. These places are always shoulder-to-shoulder people, so prepare to be jostled, but it's worth it. After a couple of hours of declining shop-owners and dickering with a few, I decided it was time for a break and a libation. I found another section nearby that was devoted entirely to those semi-circular, straw-thatched cabana-bars, all bedecked with miniature Christmas lights, as is their way, trying to please and entice we 'western' visitors. It would have been late December by then ,I suppose, although the lights are there all year round. I chose one of the many available, plunked myself down on a stool, and ordered a beer. As is also their way, a gorgeous, young Thai woman had joined me within minutes, no doubt from her lookout- perch in the abundant shadows fringing the area… spotting a big, rich, single foreign man. Then, something happened for the first time that would happen to me twice more: she inched her way out on her stool until she was on the edge nearly, spread her legs some , hiked up her skirt to reveal private areas, and then promptly encouraged me to look, as if to prove she was no 'she-he' that looked like a "she" from the waist up but was a man from the waist down! Some introduction, alright. They don't all have pronounced Adam's apples, you know- hell, I don't even have one of those; I honestly just wanted to relax some, drink my beer and perhaps jot down a few ideas in the afforded dim light; she, however, had other plans for me and my Western-sized wallet, of course. She, and all her nearby working cohorts had this really stupid little 'marble- in- a- wooden maze' game which, I suppose, is an "ice-breaker" and offers those with little English skills a chance to engage a prospective customer. I wanted no part in her ruse, or such a ridiculously stupid game. Staring down at the ground, for me, would have been more interesting! So, I did. Noting my obvious disinterest in both her and her stupid game, while all the while glancing around nervously, she started into the whole gamut of personal-service- sales ploys, starting right off the bat with the least appealing one, "Guilt."

"You don't think I'm pretty?" I would mumble back that I didn't say anything, and she would just keep hammering away. I could stand only so much, quaffed a few beer and said my 'Good Night's'. I made it back to my hotel, slurred a "good night" to the desk clerk and soon would re-discover that quirky, little wading pool on the 'tipsy,' thankfully short walk back to my room. In fact, I misjudged my foot-plants so badly that I fell in and ended up squarely in the middle of the shallow pond on my ass; it took me nearly half an hour to right myself, get out soaking wet and make it the last twenty feet to my room. Whew! And, yes, alcohol was a factor, but of course…

"Beast-Woman."

One of the first-ever big trips-away-from-home for me happened in the spring of my grade nine year when a pal and I hatched a scheme whereby we would catch the train by ourselves to Toronto, hang around at the C.N.E. for a few hours in the morning and then be on an afternoon return- trip back home to Sarnia. It was a terrific trip, memorable for several reasons- exciting to be away from home with no parents around, and no mowing the lawn or other household duties to fulfill! Once there at the fair-exhibition grounds, we toured through the sideshows; ; obviously,this was in a day long before many of them were banned/abolished on grounds of discrimination or abuse... One favourite for both of us was where a young, pretty woman sitting alone on stage, in a one-piece kinda fur bathing suit, grew much longer hair before your eyes until she had transformed into some sort of ferocious beast, a cross between a gorilla and a were-wolf. Then she leapt out of her chair and lunged at the front rows of the audience, scaring all of us outside from under the tent! At one booth in the midway, I got a fake newspaper whose headline boldly shouted that I had lost my pants in the Ladies' Washroom!(Why, I'm not sure?) Do you remember my anecdote about being stranded in the Detroit airport and me getting the names and addresses from a group of unknown, senior female students? It sort of happened again, on board the train enroute home. There was a small group of girls(6-7) by themselves, giggling nearby us in our car. After a spell, I approached them, too, chatted awhile, concocted another tale why I needed contact information from complete strangers and before long was watching as they took turns writing down their names and addresses In hindsight, I can only hope they survived adolescence unharmed and did not meet up with any charming serial killers. Which is not at all to suggest I'm charming. I was at the very least, persuasive! I had overcome the lisp... and that only leaves serial-killer...?

" The Hot Ice-Slide!"

One winter, I'm guessing in my grade seven or eight year, we had this fifty yard long ice-slide on a section of the field-/playground of the school in the winter. Thing was, there was a very select group of girls who, while exploring the bounds of their popularity and confidence, would take turns sliding down it on their bums. We boys lined up on either side like vultures watching, waiting, anticipating… and, when the girl reached the last quarter or so of the slide, we would all 'pile-on' from both sides, until it became a big ball of writhing bodies and groping hands. A bit retroactively ashamed, I did emerge from the pile once with what was clearly a pubic hair caught under a fingernail! My Pulpit Master is still chiding me over that one!

(Addenbum) "Bummed Out!"

To a bum-man, being "bummed-out" can be a very good thing because it has an entirely different connotation; it's reaching a 'saturation-point' of sorts where almost every-where you set your gaze, there's another stellar bum waiting to be brought into focus! Whew! I've been in places like that.

(Funny Bits?) "Locking the Door Behind You!"

You know, there have been and doubtless will continue to be those days when I've consumed perhaps too much java and urgently need to relieve myself. It usually takes some time and effort to find a reasonably accessible place or wash-room. So, I find one. I'm inside, standing at the ready or maybe already midstream when the door opens wide behind me and suddenly there are one or two strangers behind me staring in, and starting to apologize while I stand peeing! In my urgency, I forgot to lock the doorHmm.Too late- the horses have left the barn! A moment like that can really put you off your stream!

The Timeline?

Knowing the time, almost continuously, for me is very important. Maybe that's the teacher in me…always mind-ful of the clock, but personally even I like to regularly monitor/check on my productivity (assembly-line mental-ity?) whether I'm cooking or writing! Sounds a bit twisted, perhaps, but I find it somehow comforting to know how much I've accomplished in that 20 minutes, or two hours…

 ## "Throw-Away Lines!"

I call them that because they are intended to be fleeting, disposable remarks- non recyclable, non refundable, one-time- use 'flippancies', like the old, wooden matches! They are those quippy or snide remarks I might make or mumble, some under my breath, often during the course of any given day. It started way back early for me, sitting near the back of the classroom, and whispering some smartass remark on the heels of whatever the teacher was talking about:quippy, snide, most certainly flippant. It would often land me out in the hot-water reception area of the Principal's office waiting for the strap, but, apparently, I thought it was all worth it!

"The Blob!"

As much fun as my ole' hometown provided me and my peer-group, it did have its darker, shadowy side. I've actually kept a few of the old, leather postcards –no kidding!- that show the maze of pipelines , storage tanks and towers characteristic of the major oil refineries which all had huge operations there or just down river, I should say. That whole area down- river was, collectively in fact, referred to as "Chemical Valley" and it was promoted like a regional tourist attraction! This is where my father went to work every day instead of the railway yards! For years, Sarnia shared some infamy by being second only to Nanaimo, B.C. for having the highest number of bars-per-capita in the land. Also, it was discovered, after we had moved away, that it had the highest infant cancer-mortality rates of the continent, or at least in the country. Hmm…? A few years after that, it was discovered that a huge jelly-like 'blob' lay at the bottom of the adjacent St. Clair River, where some effluent discharge pipes emerged from those same oil refineries, and the hydro-electric generating station… Coincidence, you ask? I think not, and the ensuing investigation didn't think so either

The surface and the rest of the river were quite another thing altogether, mind you. It was where I learned to water-ski, and to fish early in the mornings off the ferry dock for perch. Fresh perch, fried eggs, toast and jam- you simply 'gotta' try it! What a way to start a summer's day!

The other day, however, I had joined some former colleagues in a nearby pub to quaff a few cold ones, and you know what? They were still talking and whining about the same stuff we did almost ten years earlier when I first left the staff and moved overseas. Geez! The subway goes in the same direction; I just got off and on, I suppose.

" The DVD Lockdown!"

Now again, back to my first year teaching in China, at the not-very-international 'international school', Dalian(about 6 million then..) was the largest metropolis to us in our tiny fishing village(Manjitan/Jinshitan) where the school was located and only about 45-50 minutes by their version of 'sky train'. Some of us would make the trip regularly every week, or so, for some shopping and a meal at a recognizable western fast-food joint, or other restaurant and,oh,yes, some pirated-DVD browsing-always. Now, unless you've been living under a rockslide or a porch, most people are aware of how China is infamous for its plentiful piracy (the 'knock-off capital' in fact) that goes on there(from clothing to electronics. DVD movies which would otherwise cost the average Canadian twenty to twenty-five dollars back home, are selling in China for the equivalent of one to three dollars (a piece, that's right!). Mind you, the old adage of 'you get what you pay for' is very much in play because the quality of the copy you would buy is always questionable- and once-this is true, I found myself sitting in the comfort of my own living room watching a movie one night and shouting out loud for the idiots in front to "Sit down!" Doubtlessly taped secretly with a handheld device in some dark theatre, some people, obviously, stood for a moment, so that their heads were all caught on camera along with the movie! Idiots everywhere you go in the world! Now, let's get back to the real story, shall we? The shop owners had quite a police-alarm and lookout- system established. There were 'lookouts' posted at all the entrance and exit-ways who would then signal to people inside the building when any cops were approaching(though the cops probably had alerted them themselves..), at which point, all of us prospective customers would be herded deeper inside the shop-booths away from the doors which were then quickly shut and locked! This weird awkwardness would last fifteen or twenty minutes before the all-clear signal was given and things returned to normal.

We were" trapped" inside the shops, as the police came in usually shouting and literally rattling a few doors. There were always those initial few moments of panic, some police shouting and then a weird, dead-calm before the all-clear signal was given and the shops could resume their normal operations! This would happen quite regularly on weekends, so we became accustomed to it before long. The façade-story for international media, however, would only ever show uniformed policemen getting ready to burn a huge pile of confiscated, pirated DVD's on the sidewalk somewhere to show how they were "cracking down" and being "tough" on movie-theft and black marketeering! Sure. Never showing the warehouses full of the stuff meant for distribution!

 "Mr. 'Shitty Shorts"

He's the neighbourhood spider-conspiracist and is always waxing on(as spiders tend to) about government's wasteful spending of our monies with its buying used nuclear sub-marines or something. I see him every now and again, usually hovering close to coffee shop entrance ways, sitting in his 'web' and waiting for conversation-prey, so he can prattle on about his latest theories, after the unwitting prey-people have triggered his web-sense, 'with as little as a 'hello'. He has wild and woolly grey-white hair. Unfortunately, I saw him one day in the 'Golden Arches', when I stepped in for a quick lunch. He was at a front window stool with two others and the three of them were carrying on like American Idol judges, observing and critiquing each passerby going past on the sidewalk just in front of them. Trouble was, he would occasionally stand from his stool and lean over the counter toward the window for a better look; and when he did, one couldn't help but notice that his cheap, baggy, polyester shorts were very clearly, heavily shit-stained on the back-not a nice image at any time, let alone when you're trying to eat a burger. 'Skidmarks' does not come close to identifying this disaster; it was more like the wreckage of a burnt out car!

"Fear of Blackness"

Once on a family outing across the river to Michigan, we sat in traffic at a red light in Port Huron, with my sister and me in the backseat of our '67 Volkswagen beetle. All of a sudden, there was a terrible screeching of tires behind us where two men sat on their motorcycles directly off our bumper. A big, tan four-door sedan ploughed into them, sending their bikes crashing hard into us, and sending the men sailing over us in the 'bug' where they smacked down on the pavement and lay motionless in front of us. I tried to twist some in my seat and crane my neck to look out the rear window. My father reached back from the driver's seat and tried to push us down lower into the foot space between the seats for safety, I guess; all I did see was four young, black men run from the culprit-car, and then fan out in all directions and run off down the sidewalks.

There was that incident and then there were the Detroit mini-riots of '67. We almost got caught up in the preliminary waves one night, after leaving Tiger Stadium and me having sat in the stands, behind one of my all-time favourite players, Willie Horton, out in left field! While leaving the crowded parking lot and merging into a local, residential street, several young black men assaulted our vehicle. They banged their fists on the windows, a couple of them pressing their faces up hard against the glass and peering in to see who or what was inside. Again, my sister and I were in the backseat with our father reaching over and behind in an effort to push us down away from the windows. For much of my adult life, I've carried that fear and prejudice of young black men with me! I've also long-recognized that not all young black men are like that- but it is the potential behaviours that I've already seen that scare me and make me reluctant to trust them.

(Addenbum) "It's everywhere, Really."

Really, come on, look around you! It's everywhere out there in nature and our day-to-day lives: we've got your busy pollinating bumblebees, a representative from the fruit and vegetable garden with the bumble berry, and then Burl Ives immortalized it as narrator in the animated Rudolph television classic when our lovable group of misfits had to confront the terrible "BUMBLE – beast, until Herbie the dentist-wannabe/ elf removed all of the monster's teeth! Over the years, some have tried smearing the good part-name with "bum-rap" and "bummer", but it's a survivor, that two- cheeked wonder. Anyway, there should only ever be one "bum-wrap" and that is simply a tight-fitting skirt(ha-ha- so bad)....

"Ode to Fanny-May"

Fanny, may I gently squeeze your little bum,
Right here, that's right, between my index and my
    thumb?
You sit all day, compress those perfect mounds,
And rarely, rarely do you make rude sounds.
An admirable state, yours, to be so adored,
And still the catcalls, the whistles.. of which you are
    bored,
But Jeepers, love-a – duck, you do so entice
When you move back and forth
With that famous wiggle, so nice!

Fanny, fanny, two cheeks more,
And in-between, a sliding door…
And there, again, that wiggle- we men so adore;
Oh Fanny oh, fanny, can I see some more?
You there, bright cheeks, with your dividing line. a
    song…
Do you wear 'granny-panties', girl?
We're bettin' it's a thong!
Black or red, I imagine,
Like a slash ofyellow neon, perhaps bright pink there
And there, again,that perfect fine-line
Dividing that lovely pair!
You bring with you the "cat's nose",
When things come together in the end,
A place I could snuggle with for sure And learn to call
    best friend!

"The Driveway Toot."

For maybe three years when I was back in elementary school, I took piano lessons. I would come home every day to a Scandinavian 'housekeeper who would have soup or a sandwich ready for me. My father would make the thirty minute drive home from work and, as he pulled up into our driveway, he would always toot the horn three times in quick succession.

"Bully for You!" (aka Me &My Chair)

Where my wife and I were residing in South Vancouver, like most everywhere else in this healthy, anal city (did I say that?) there's no smoking anywhere in the buildings, or, for that matter, even close to them outside!

I take the elevator down to the lobby and go outside to the boulevard where I'll sit and do my thing peacefully, unobtrusively, on the sidewalk in front of our building. One evening, as I sat on the sidewalk, satisfying my craving, I was approached by a stocky, younger Indo-Canadian man who, I thought, was going to chat to me-as so many people do daily as they go by me in the neighbourhood. However, he had much more on his mind than a friendly chit-chat and before long had launched into a tirade about me sitting in the middle of the sidewalk which he informed me was public property(!) funded by taxpayers. Most of the time, I will move for pedestrians and always for movers or Moms with strollers (I figure they have right-of way)" Just because you're in a wheelchair-you think that gives you special rights!?" he said scornfully, standing beside my chair and staring down at me. "Yes, actually, I do" I answered (Oh, how presumptuous, huh?). He would have to sidestep me and my chair for one, maybe two steps- I didn't think it was such an awful inconvenience, or imposition; he, however, clearly disagreed. He challenged me; he swore at me repeatedly, and finished off with a clear threat, "Next time pal, I'll push you outta you're (bleepin!') chair. Hmm Mmm.I've been out of my chair several times on the ground-it's not a pretty sight: "Whale on the beach! "It's to be avoided at all costs. Like any self-respecting, stupid, rutting male musk ox would do, I returned some of his foul-mouthed rant! He was clearly a thug, a classic "bully", angry at the world and ready to pounce on anyone who got in his way.As I've allluded I have zero-tolerance for such people and offer up that intolerance of mine, unapologetically. If that makes me a bully of bullies, fine. So, we took turns telling each other to "F-off! And other pleasantries, "Go F-yourself! He had tweaked my testosterone- pump by then, so I tried finishing off, myself, with what I thought was a good, if not inflammatory remark to him; I told him to leave me alone and, "Why don't you go home and beat your wife?" He finally left me; maybe that 's exactly what he did do for all I know? I could feel my heart pounding in my chest and the bile rising in my throat as I imagined headlines in the local press the next day of our "skirmish," had it materialized. Happily, I can report we went our separate ways. His parting shot for me that night was, "I know where you live, pal-!" Mine was, "and you have a good night , too, a-hole!" Nice. Fun, little chat.

"Estranged?"

I'm not sure what it is? I don't know why? I have a sneaking suspicion, mind you, as friends and family both seem to slink away from me to the point where several appear to be quite intentionally avoiding me; there are moments I'll even allow myself to feel like I have the hideous plague, or some other terrible contagion. However, I realize that because I am the common denominator in these recurring patterns and that in itself troubles me, stresses and depresses me. When I think I want to be closer, others almost want to distance themselves from me..?I could (and may) move away, move continents again, under the angry, reactive guise of Well,' I don't care anymore either!' However, the trouble with that is, I know it's not true; I still and will always want to connect, but some of me vibrates with the fear of the alternate reaction-if I let my spoiled, little inner-child have his way. 'Fine!' he would shout, 'If you're going to be that way, then so am I!' That'll teach 'em. Tit for tat.(It's tough being so mature…)You don't want to spend time with me? Fine! Then I will happily reciprocate the sentiment,,asshole! I can neglect and ignore you, too!.

What did I do or say to you to so alienate you? Or do you even know? Maybe it's just your "stuff?" Wow! I hope and will try everything in my will and soul to never be a copycat who takes the tragic-easy way out of the game- by quitting entirely. The thought does occasionally cross my mind, but I don't ever want to be another 'fridge in the hall!' Still too much for me to accomplish, too many sunrises to enjoy yet… and turkey dinners and a wonderful wife! Not to mention the fact that I rather enjoy what we've got going on here even as we slide into the climactic apocalypse.

" Down in the Dumps!"

Way, way, way back to when I was a kid (how redundant can a guy be?), just a young boy, several friends and I would regularly visit and scrounge around in the city dump which was only a couple minute bike ride away. It was a great place to spend a summer's morning or afternoon- and, the stuff you could find? Real treasures!

For some reason, Mom was never too keen on my 'dump adventures', and when she did relent with her approval it always came with a non-negotiable order to wear thick-soled shoes or boots and long-sleeved shirts!' Safety first, always..!My newly-found" treasures" would often be out in our trash the following day....

"At least One Word."

I think, among the multitude of extraneous thoughts my mind continually produces is one that says everyone out there has at least one word whose spelling trips them up every time they try to use it. Mine? "Rhythm." I always try to get two "y's in there which brings me to my next topic, sort of: other peoples' rhythyms(sic) and thoughts and feelings. For as long as I can remember, those, things have always weighed heavily on my mind, made me nervous and no doubt contrib-uted to/exacerbated my hypertension!

Sea-Fleas, Lookout!

I did already mention, I believe, (where's my editor? Sorry, I dozed off))the old 3- Horsepower Johnson outboard(pre-war, that's 2!) motor we had in storage for years in the fruit cellar with the pickles, peaches and dead crocodile; all I needed, now, was a boat to put it on!. Providence stepped in one Spring. As it turned out, the next door neighbour's son, maybe ten years older than me, had outgrown his 'sea-flea'-you know, a miniature (8 foot), wooden model of those high speed hydroplanes. It was just so cool! I inherited the neigh-bour's old sea-flea, free of charge and, Dad- wouldn't you know it, had that outboard up and running within a week! Using the old homemade plywood- trailer he had originally built for them in Edmonton, we were able to transport both boat and motor to our yacht club where it would sit idle again for several more months in the long grass by a fence. There was a little, sheltered basin in the inner harbour of the club that was used regularly by our sailing club. I had taken my sailing lessons there years before, too, so I knew the basics and the 'rules of the water.' As the son of a sailor, ex- Navy man and by- then ' Fleet Captain' of the club, it was requisite, so I knew which end was up and which end should point forward, alright? Of course, the pointy-end should always point first, huh?If north is straight ahead, then east is to your right, right..?North grows on mossy side of the tree?

"Paddy's"

Once, way back, again, on a grade nine school 'field trip' to the royal Ontario Museum in Toronto, a few of us, having already been underage drinking since grade eight, took it upon ourselves to sneak away from our tour group, get outside, scale the big pointy, black-iron fence and wind up downtown on the Yonge Street strip –in the real world with all its accompanying sights, sounds and smells! Well, before too long, we had found our way to 'Paddy's Irish Pub', a tiny, narrow and dark hole-in-the-wall drinking- establishment. Very unsure of ourselves but feeling a bit like escaped convicts, we went in, made our way to a dark corner table near the back, sat down and consumed several small glasses of draft beer each over the next hour or so before wending our way back to the museum parking lot and our 'Bluebird' charterschool bus for the appointed "rendezvous time". When pressed by our harried teacher-chaperone 'What happened to us.?! We stuck to our predetermined "lost in the building story" which he didn't seem to buy for a moment….

 ### "Oh, no you don't!"

Having a couple of friends in elementary school, as kids, who would later go on to become local drug dealers at high school did have its limited benefits, for sure, but also a few drawbacks… One of them had this habit of calling his parents by their first names when he sat around the kitchen table helping them to bag-up the one-ounce baggies of pot. So, a couple of us figured why not? After all, maybe that was really the 'norm'?

I, at least, soon discovered that it was most definitely NOT the norm in our house, when I inquired about it one night after dinner . Parents and children do not belong in the same peer group, apparently. Nope, that's "Mom and Dad, to you." Oh.

"You Go-Go Girls"

I am frequently asked , now, what I miss most about China. The prices of most everything come quickly to mind, from celery to shirts to DVD's(even if there are a few heads sticking up during the movie!)smoking still in many restaurants... And, being the shallow-minded sexist I am then there's the always-pretty "beer-girls", usually found in most restaurants where they are easy to spot with their Nancy Sinatra-white plastic mini-skirts and knee-high boots; their sole responsibility was to watch like hawks and ensure that your beer was continuously looked after-take a sip.., the glass would be topped up within a minute or two. It struck me a little like how it must have been in some medieval taverns with their bosomy, ever-watchful serving wenches displaying ample cleavage to their patrons with every round served, except here the bosoms were not so "ample". It definitely smacked of an older man's, old world 'charm' where the testosterone-crowd was catered to unabashedly; the women's movement had taken a wrong turn somewhere and never reached these shores.

A Bully's Bully.

There was one fellow during childhood whose family moved into our neighbourhood one year.

It was clear from the get- go, after he had had three after-school fights in the first six weeks that he was there, plain and simply, a bully. I don't know why exactly (a higher directive, perhaps..?), but I wrote a 'ditty' about him and read it to him one day at recess; it would cause him to immediately challenge me and "call me out" to a fight. I thought my 'poem' limerick not half-bad, myself, but clearly he did not like it one bit. It went something like this (with thanks/apologies to James Taylor..):

'There once was a boy named, Paul
Who God had given no brains at all!
So, he sat on his ass, at the back of the class,
Through winter, spring, summer and fall.' (Thanks to J. T.)

 ## "Wet Mornings"

When our family first relocated to Vancouver from Sarnia, just in time for me to start my grade twelve year at high school, that first fall, I knew where the student cafeteria was located, but I was much too afraid/shy to ever go there on my own. Instead, I would walk twenty minutes or so to a local convenience store, buy a coke, a copy of the National Enquirer(sadly enough) and then dart around the corner, plant myself in the shade of a big tree in the tiny, nearby park there and do 'my thing'. What was my "thing?" Possibly 'contemplation,' with the nicotine habit. We call those sort of people loners, and later in life, homeless. I would read all the 'poetry- wanted' ads and dream of the day-but I knew they were all bogus, so never sent anything in to them.

Catch &Release'

Many of us are blissfully ignorant of the fact of how our human sexual relations and attitudes are closely analogous to hunting and even more so to 'fishing'. Once men kill something/catch one, it's always a "girl" did you ever notice? What a beauty! "She's a beaut!" It could be a four hundred pound male black bear or an eight hundred pound bull-moose, doesn't matter. "Fly-fishing" is just too easy to play with in this regard-if it's tied just right, the fish will bite or take the mock-bait! "Casting, the rod, the hook, etc..etc…" Yep, just too damn- easy. From Sport-fishermen to trawlers to my kind which I can say apologetically was more of a gill-netter/Forrest Gump variety(you never know quite what you're gonna net…). When I did put more time and effort into the game, I did try to be environmentally –friendly by at least catching and releasing- and thank the stars that most men do the same. Right in there with the "frog-kissers." Where would most of us men be without them!?

 ## " The Ole Hometown!"

There's nothing quite like it, is there-for any of us..? Nothing can possibly come close to the place where we were raised , to the place we had so many of the "firsts" of our young lives: riding a bicycle, steps, to first solid poops, warm beer, kisses, fights and joints -nope, nothing can compare!

 ## "The Post-Game Hot Chocolate." ## (The 'Après-game cocoa')

The minor hockey-league games I played as a youngster were always on Saturday mornings and I will forever fondly remember how, when we got home, we would make hot chocolate for me-the' warrior' and how my Dad and I would sit at the kitchen table for a couple of hours of post-game de-brief and analysis, usually consisting of what I had done well, what I did poorly and, of course, how I might improve my game for the following week! These were wonderful, special father-son bonding moments! No, really….

 ## "The Boy who cried Facetious Once Too Much!"

I still haven't been able to quite identify the 'sheep' in this particular metaphor for me, so it clearly needs some more refining-but there is something there that works nonetheless. When I was younger, smaller, somewhere, somehow along the road, I learned to be quippy and sarcastic. That was all fine-at least back then; sarcasm can be funny. The further along I progressed on that path, the more I began to realize how what for me had started out as sarcasm was evolving into something more, the much more complex and thoughtful 'facetiousness'. The big downside, however, was that more and more people would be checking and double-checking with me to see if I was 'being serious or not' with a lot of what I said. For better or worse, it is still very much a part of me, like a protective shield, I suppose: it serves a twofold purpose from my perspective-it is always hedging my bet- not a big gambler: if understood as intended and seen as funny, then I'm a funny guy; if not, however, then I can simply disown it and say, "Oh that, I was kidding!" You didn't think I was being serious, did you? Of course not! It was a 'throwaway.' If my original intent is misread or mis-understood, I can always withdraw sheepishly(I found it!), revise, or recant completely whatever it was that may have caused some discomfort or offense. I've had more than one person (friends and relatives) over the years comment, "I thought you were being sarcastic! , Another is, "Are you be-ing serious..? Really?" It gives me enough time to determine if they were truly hurt by what I said, or actually thought it was funny... Pretty sneaky, eh? O.K., you're right: The am-bush tactics of a coward. That way, my 'desperado' can be a fence-sitter until the last possible minute! If it's good enough for Switzerland. The indecisive one who doesn't want to of-fend or risk at all so plays both black and red at the roulette table...which,to no surprize, I have occasionally done, my-self-and it does rather miss the point.

 ## " Elmira, Elvira!"

One, of course was the rather bosomy late-night vampire hostess of a movie channel while the other one, a small town in Ontario, holds this fabulous maple syrup and-sugar festival every winter with hay-rides and stuff! Do it, if you can!!

"Blueberry Pancakes and Dune-Buggies!"

One trip our family did when I was a young boy was to Petoskey or some other nearby place in Michigan, on the American shores of Lake Huron, where they served us huge, fresh blueberry pancakes at picnic tables on the beach nearly and gave us these wild rides on very wide, fast dune buggies. I'll always remember that as one of my best childhood memories!

"Get the Puck!" (Sad, but true…)

A not-nearly so fond memory happened maybe when I was ten or twelve. I was with a stupid, bigoted childhood acquaintance(there were a couple, if you were wondering..?), playing shinny on the local frozen lake. There came that dreadful moment when I could hear the ice cracking and 'singing' beneath me, see a few lines starting to form and then actually feel the immediate area around me bowing downward some before it gave way and sent me plunging into the frigid water! My so-called "friend" (and I use the term very loosely) was safe and dry on the nearby shore, about one hundred feet away. Honestly,(I wish it were a lie!)he shouted to me several times, "Get the puck!" "Get the puck!" and shouting this, while I was on the brink of drowning in freezing water up to my neck.. I was able to use my hockey stick to help extricate myself after a few doubtful moments and ran the entire 3 minutes back to my home freezing and sopping wet for a hot shower and change! Whew! It could all have ended so very differently, so abruptly…that day.

" L.D.B. Syndrome"

I feel like I should explain a bit about a personal syndrome I suffer from that I've experienced most of my life and have dubbed, 'Little Drummer-Boy Syndrome'. I've been writing, it seems, forever and a lot of that has come out in the form of poetry, quite naturally for me. For as long as I can remember, I've always had a fascination and love for rhyme… from Dr.

Seuss' "Cat in the Hat" and "Grinch," to Ludwig Bemmel-man's Madeleine series. Then, of course, came The Carpen-ters, Cat Stevens, Bob Dylan and Joni Mitchell and before long the world was graced with the likes of the Beatles, El-ton John and Bernie Taupin, then Elton and Tim Rice, Rice and Lloyd Webber etc. They all seemed to like rhyme, why shouldn't I?. If it was good enough for them…?.

Throw in Robert Service, too, with his McGee's and Mc-Grew's! You know, I am still very much drawn to good or clever rhyme and will often choose rhyming verse to express myself- whether it be in a lyric for a friend, retiring colleague or perhaps a poem for my wife, if I'm feeling a bit lovey-dovey. It's not an entirely "lost" art form, or extinct yet, but it could be described, I feel, as at least being on the endangered species list! Onwards, now.(redux) There have been numer-ous times in life when I've crafted a simple poem-ditty to help mark and celebrate a milestone of some sort for some-one, attended a party in their honour- and arrived not bear-ing any visible, traditional gifts; no, I just brought my words to the celebration which are on a sheet of paper neatly folded up and tucked away in a pocket out of sight until needed. So often, I would find myself standing like a lone-sheep(again, the sheep!) to the side of the manger, waiting to be called upon to bleat or 'bang my drum'-when it's all I have! I'm left feeling like how I imagine that little drummer-boy must have felt humming to himself beside a stinky donkey that day so long ago! "Perum pah, pah, pum…!" to bang on his drum. I always felt that I was not bringing enough to the party yet still a lot of me… and would then leave the affair with icing on my chin and some guilt in my heart; consequently I suf-fer from what I personally like to call 'Little Drummer-Boy' Syndrome, or" LD.B.S." Others, like Freud, might just call it-so tediously- inadequacy…

"Ribbet-Thanks to the Frog-Kissers"

Honestly, where would so many of us men be(the island of misfit boys?) if it were not for the silly fairy tales, their stereotypes and the princesses who continue to uncross their legs in the mindless hope, this could be the one, the prince to carry them off into the sunset of never-never land Shortly thereafter, they wake to discover, he is not a prince at all but just another horny toad, an imposter to the throne, but by then it's too late and they've bestowed their ultimate womanly charms already which can never be taken back. On those murky, swampy edges of life's pond, they find plenty of horny toads, some voracious bull-frogs and even a few snapping turtles along the way. Find your own metaphor, I guess.

 ## "Pulling Corn Beards."

My first job ever was when I was maybe thirteen or fourteen years old. My mother found it for me, of course, through Employment Canada, I believe; she didn't want to have me "loafing" around that summer... I was one of many 'youngsters to be bussed out to a farmer's field every morning where we would then spend the next five or six hours walking the rows between corn stalks, pulling the 'beards off the ears of corn, prior to harvest(and you thought ear-hair could be bad) It was actually called "de-tasselling" because the beard-like threads were called, you guessed it, "tassels" and they had to be removed first or else they could foul-up the combines collecting the corn. Yep! De-tasseling corn for an astounding $1.75/hr. I was Rich! When your weekly allowance was three dollars, this would surely afford a comfortable retirement! I didn't even faint once in the hot sun in the week I did it, unlike some of my compatriots.

 ## "God Save the Queen- Oh, no!"

As young children in elementary school, we would start every day off with a less-than rousing rendition of 'God Save the Queen' where many of us were left mouthing the words, winking, mumbling and snickering at each other; this would be followed by the military-styled ten to fifteen 'touch-your- toes exercises. Those, I must admit, could be a little daunting, especially when the girl ahead of you in the row was wearing a short skirt and clearly consuming too much ruffage in her diet. To glance up, even briefly, was to risk seeing brown-stained panties- enough to put a young boy off his game for the rest of the day if not a few weeks! And then there was the picture of the always stern-looking queen staring down at you-surveying her realm-, and having witnessed the whole thing! To make matters worse for me at least, I always thought my mother had a more-than passing resemblance to 'her royal highness in those days. leading to the 'omnipresent Mom'.

"Important Lifeskills!"

Day-Camp in the spring and summer, which was held just outside at our elementary school, was always a lot of fun! This is when we learned those all-important life skills, like weaving lace bracelets AND necklaces, playing checkers using pop bottle caps, playing "Capture the Flag!" in the adjacent woods, and continuing to glance down girls' tops or between their legs- for any hint of what Hefner had already made famous with his air-brushed non-biological toy-women

"Dib, dib, dib, dob, dob, dob!" (Akela!)

Cubs- a place perhaps to learn early social skills, but certainly not to go for language skills. Some secret language that! I was both a cub and later a boy scout-and have good memories from both eras. Those organizations(along with a brief stint much more recently in the 'Toastmasters' organization were about as close to 'military' and discipline as I could ever venture, or would want to… I guess the first two really do provide a foundation for socialization outside of the family sphere, where young boys can learn about leadership and teamwork, an entirely good thing for young men already geared to a 'pack mentality' and driven by sports and testosterone!" Hey! There's a deer-let's go kill and eat it!" (what wolves growl to each other..?)

As cubs – and I, honestly, still have my sash proudly displaying(in a drawer somewhere) all those badges that my Mom worked so hard for (I helped some!). We once held a huge science fair/bake sale-I guess as a fundraiser? My mother had, forgive the pun, planted the seed in my head about doing a terrarium, so 'we' began early nurturing a couple of plants from seeds in wet paper-towels. Quite by accident, as it turned out, I would learn lots about values and ethics, a word which I used to confuse quite often with ethnic-and all because of that silly 'n' letter) because I shared and showed my project to a friend, fellow-cub and neighbour from up the street. Well, he took it upon himself to do likewise, except that for his ultimate, winning version what he did was to simply transplant two or three healthy one foot high apple seedlings into his bowl… No question, his was much more impressive to look at. My mother, by way of consoling me, explained how some people were liars and cheats and it was my fault for even sharing my secret project with him to begin with. One of the days of the fair found another friend and I squatting at the end of my driveway behind our Chevy Impala madly trying to consume one of the two raisin pies of his that hadn't sold at the fair before going home for dinner. Live and Learn, huh?

Fire Escape!

I was 'babysitting' three younger kids (I was fourteen, probably) who lived just down the street from us one spring night, when near-catastrophe- disguised as popcorn- came licking at the door. We were all in the living room watching 'Steve Austin' and his beeping' eye do his thing on the The Six Million Dollar Man when one of the kids suggested we make some popcorn. Good idea, I thought. At that point I was quite accustomed to our own idiot-proof 'Jiffy –Pop version, myself, but not these guys. No, of course not; they had to do it the old-fashioned way by putting some oil in an open pot on the stove, heating it up and then adding the kernels. Maybe there was too much oil, maybe I should have been paying better attention to the whole operation? All water under that proverbial old bridge, now. I mean, I had been shooed away from the kitchen earlier that evening and told they had done it lots before and were old enough to do it themselves! Nope! One of the kids, a few moments later came running into the living room to find me, all the while shouting ," FIRE!" And, I knew instinctually that was not a good sign. I could only assume that 'Steve Austin' managed to get the bad guys again on the Six Million Dollar Man, like he did every week-because I would never see the end of that night's episode. I scooted out to the kitchen, only to confirm the worst of the shouting. The oil in the pot had caught fire and the now rather sizeable flames were lapping at the bottom of the wood cupboards above the stove. It seemed every time I turned around, the flames were somewhere new… So now you ask why I kept turning around at all?

Without thinking too much, and ,again, being all of maybe fourteen myself, I grabbed the handle of the now flaming pot, badly burning my hand in the process, spun around with it and quickly deposited it in the sink where I immediately turned on the cold water, thinking to douse the flames. WRONG! Oil and water. The kids had all gathered by now at one end of the kitchen to watch the commotion, so I shouted for the eldest to take his siblings upstairs quickly and out of harm's way. Meanwhile, as soon as the water hit the boiling, flaming oil in the pot, it sent globules of flaming, lava-like oil spitting outward to land on and burn holes in the linoleum kitchen floor. By now, too , the flames when in the sink had reached up to ignite one side of the little curtains hanging above the sink! So, with all the kids safely upstairs, I grabbed the flaming curtain, rod and all and made a wild dash for it, through the French doors in the Living Room to outside, to throw the burning mess on the lawn and stomp it all out. Then there would be the dreaded… phone call to the mother and father at their cocktail soiree. Whew!

Toilet Humour?(sorry)

Being this close to the ground so much of the day in my wheelchair, I rub shoulders(ankles..?), not surprisingly, with a lot of what might be termed 'lower life', other disabled folk like myself, street people who are sitting or laying in parking lots, alleyways or on boulevards, as I pass by. As I've come to discover all-too-well about this barely –above-ground 'network' or community is that most of them will be able to tell you exactly where all the best handicapped washrooms are located in the vicinity. Some of them spend a lot of their waking time there, hovering close by. A few of them, of course, take care of all of their hygiene needs(if they do at all..?). They can scrub up reasonably well with the free soap and then have a limitless supply of paper towels to dry off with. Yep. Unfortunately, there's always some of this same crowd who are less-than-hygienic, who may have trouble even getting up or transferring from their scooter or wheelchair to sit on the john and, then, still others who manage to spread their fecal deposits from the floor to the seat, to the neighbouring walls-leaving me wondering, 'How the hell did they even do that??!(a poop scatter-gun..?) The golden arches is definitely a favourite for many. Which immediately makes me reluctant to go visit happy-faced 'Ronald.'.

Once while I was there, I found the washroom in such revolting shape upon entering I struggled with those involuntary oesophageal writhing bursts that usually precede vomit. I had to ask and then wait thirty minutes for an employee-attendant to clean up the mess enough before I could use it. I almost peed my pants just waiting! That's the thing for me, or at least one of them. When I'm out and about, I have beverages and, like everyone else, will soon have to pee-but, ideally, I need a good wheelchair-accessible washroom and there's not always one handy and as I explained earlier the random, vertical posturing is not so much an option any more. Some coffee-shops I've been in, I can't even get my chair through the door. Now, there's a weird moment. I don't know whether to laugh or cry!. I'm in the doorway, within ten feet of a useable bowl but can't access it; sometimes, urgency demands that I brake my chair, stand and walk in, using the door as guide/helper until I can reach the sink counter or towel rack close to the toilet just to tinkle! Several times in those less-than four-star eating establishments, I can barely wheel my chair down the always dimly-lit and crowded back hallway/corridor which is being used as overflow storage space for extra inventory. In many of the fast-food joints out there, that is my principal competition, so although I know those fast-food places will, by policy, have usually big, spic'n'span restrooms, it is those others in the area who tend to use them most I'm aware of who will always make me a bit 'leery.'

The Man in the Corner Booth!

It's me, of course! I've got a favourite restaurant/coffee-shop in the area where I like to go where I can sit undisturbed, undistracted for a few hours, have some coffee and do some writing. I feel comfortable, what can I say..? Furthermore, because I have just the one functional arm and hand, it is difficult for me to open sugar packets and creamer for each cup. Consequently, all of the serving staff have been 'trained up' and are very accommodating to me with mixing my perfect coffee- formula. I feel content there and can even pop outside occasionally to indulge my 'nasty habit and leave my pens and notebooks on the table with no fear of removal or theft!

"The Stupid Gene"

I think I mentioned earlier how one of my wife's favourite 'terms of endearment' for me (and one which, ironically, I created myself..) was and remains, "Big, Strong, Stupid and Ugly!" It was how I once described to her a new living room coffee table I had delivered one day from IKEA in Beijing ;it was, in my thinking, just that…very male, very functional-utilitarian: No style, no taste. She had astutely replied with a grin, "Ah, you mean like you…?" Yes. I could only smile and nod my head. Men have it, women don't– the 'stupid gene', I mean. Few people seem to know that scientists discovered this gene way back in 1962 in a California campus laboratory, first in chimpanzees, then homo sapiens, but a massive government-academic cover-up followed to prevent the findings from ever being made public and causing a furor and possibly upsetting the delicate patriarchal balance the world-over!

Where Have All the Virgins Gone..?

Judging by the sheer numbers of women wearing white gowns at their weddings, the world must be full of them? Personally, I think they're all sequestered on a separate, isolated island somewhere maybe close to Jurassic Park..(?), just waiting for the terrorist souls to show up and claim their prize.

Lard Ass!

To be fair, I guess I should spend a moment or two talking about my own bum. It's neither a small, 'bubble-butt' by any stretch but nor is it a huge flip-floppy chilli-bum. I do have some padding down there to be sure. Once, early on in my teaching career, I had a couple of smart-alecky grade eight boys who took it upon themselves to put a tack on my chair when I was away from my desk, stalking the rows for a homework check. I didn't notice it immediately when I first sat down- and could not understand the wave of snickering that followed. In fact, I didn't really discover it fully until twenty minutes or an half hour later after I had dismissed the class and a conscientious girl straggled behind and told me what had happened; only then did I even check for it to find this one solitary tack buried to the hilt in my downstairs cheeks!

"In Your Face!"

You don't see too many trash-talking Asians ever in the sports world-or anywhere for that matter. Nope. Dignity, one of many things I think our culture could probably re-learn from theirs-no, they just simply go out there and consistently out-perform their competition: ping-pong, platform diving volleyball, badminton, gymnastics, figure-skating. They just let their actions speak for them, no braggadocio, no finger-pointing, no sly comments. No thank you, I'm just here to win. And do what my coaches trained me to do, and wht my countrymen expect. That's all. Me? Somewhere between the two, I suppose: I've always found rubbing shoulders, a gentle smile and a whispered one-liner at that pre-game skate or pre-play snap-of-the-ball- instant was equally effective and required much less energy. What's more, if your target-audience did not clearly hear your initial comment, then you are actually given an opportunity to repeat the whispered slur or quip -still accompanied with sardonic smile, of course! The Chinese and their Asian cousins just never go there. Modesty pervades the culture and does not allow for such crassness(crassity?), rudeness. And anyways, understatement and that' quiet(smouldering..?) delivery' can often be more devastating for any opponent because the door for angry outbursts has not been opened for them to walk through and retaliate in like kind; no, they have no choice but to turn and simply walk away as 'losers'.

(Addenbum) "Booty-what?"

'My body's too 'booty-licious' for you…!' Wasn't me! If I have my facts straight, it was the older(eighties, I mean), all-black women's' group, Destiny's Child crawling around in their bikinis on a wet shoreline-and what shoreline, isn't wet? That song, almost single-handedly, I feel, helped to create an entire subset within the culture- all centered on the 'booty', the rear-end, the caboose…paving the way(so to speak) for the "booty-shake" and the laughable 'video-ho' bum cheek applause! Quite a moniker for my favourite part of the female anatomy, the "gluteus maximus" Maybe it should be renamed the "glutey-call". Since then and even more so, recently, more and more women and admiring men have been revelling in celebration of the double-cheeked 'boo-tay.'There it was, women openly acknowledging the fact that they knew just how appealing their backsides are. I felt somewhat vindicated because I had been a huge admirer of the female bum for many years and the rest of the world was just catching up to me! The derriere was no longer mine and mine alone; I was losing my exclusivity on the women's behind. And, like any of the body parts integral in the male-female sexual attraction and coupling puzzle, the 'caboose' came in all shapes and sizes, to please every taste –or dis-taste out there." Some like the athletic variety, some like tiny, some big, some even favour the large chilli-bum' (like a big pot of chilli..), and still others, like myself, prefer the firm, rounder "balloon-bum" so commonly found in Asian women(most especially in my wife, of course..). Its unfor-tunate slide in today's vernacular has really almost equated the "booty-call" with what the old Newlywed show used to innocently enough refer to as "whoopee", or Ursula Andress in Dr. No sang as "bulooloo" Hello..? Hello? Knock, knock, is anybody home? Can vulva come out and play? Now, of course, the 'booty-call' is an oh-so thinly veiled metaphor for intercourse. You want a booty-call? Then, quite natu-rally, you will have to see the girl's naked rump as she un-dresses and then as things progress, you will need to squeeze it some for good measure, all of which takes us right back to what I've always argued: the bum offers the true "love handles" in this world, not those extraneous hangover 'muf-fin tops' on the hips. Let's move along , shall we?

The Downside of BIG...

Humour is a funny thing alright, isn't? It's got me into the occasional fight, out of a few others, helped me persuade some women to share their 'wiles' and groin dimples with me, chafed both family and friends for years. I have what I might personally describe as a reasonably sharp wit coupled with a sometimes acid tongue. When you join that to an old 'Tyson' philosophy of 'when someone 'hits you, you strike back-always- but twice as hard…, then it becomes a formi-dable combination, whether it's on the scrimmage line of a football game, in the pregame hockey warm-up skate, or in a nightclub hunting princesses and dancing to Donna Summer.

" Teeth marks, No Blood!"

(Not sure..? Go back and re-read 'The Astronaut knows') O.K.O.K., it was probably me, alright? Happy? If you haven't yet been able to piece the puzzle bits together; it was, in all likelihood, me who did the mostly harmless gentle biting of the girl's bum those many years ago between the houses! I own up, I confess to probability. The good news is that I've been rehabilitated since then and have put that issue mostly 'behind me', so to speak-sorry, I couldn't resist. That's not to say, I still don't get the occasional urge to grab hold of a nice-looking rump and sink my teeth into a cheek! Fortunately, most of my inhibitors are in good working-order!

It was especially amusing for me so many years later while a student at U.B. C. and staying in residence to find that the floor above me called themselves 'The Bum-biters!'

" N.Y. N.Y., Bus-Boy"

After a brief two day hiatus in Toronto where I stayed with a cousin and his wife, I connected to my next bus to finish my trip to New York and take a little bite out of the Big Apple where I would catch my "standby" flight to London, England and embark on my year-long backpacking trek! I wanted to see the Empire State Building, of course, so I plotted my route out the night before by subway and walking on a tourist map I had picked up. Presto, suddenly there I was, just an elevator ride away from the observation deck, or so I thought! I thought I was that close to King Kong-dom with just the push of a button when a security guard approached me and politely asked, "Excuse me, sir. Where are you going? Like doh! Where do you think, idiot?(Too much Simpsons..) My mind was saying A Forrest Gump moment!. My mouth, instead, managed," Oh, just up to the observation deck for some pictures…" The guard, to his credit, politely and patiently explained that there was no 'observation deck' here. This was not the Empire State Building at all! Instead, I had found my way into the Chrysler Building which was all private business offices/floors. Good navigator, Kim! I could only hope this was not an omen for my backpacking adventures across the European continent! Yikes! (Does anyone even use 'Yikes!' any more..?)

" Football Heroes."

Pretty easy , that one for me. Offensively speaking, it was none other than pantyhose-wearing 'Broadway Joe' Namath who so confidently(arrogantly, some might interject..) led his upstart AFC Jets to early Superbowl history by defeating the 'old guard' NFC Baltimore Colts (what? 16-7? I'm not sure now, without checking..?)

Under Johnny 'U' and Earl Morrall. Defensively, it's equally easy, too. It was all about the 'Black and Blue' central division of the NFC .You know: Detroit(back in the day!), Green Bay, Chicago, and Minnesota's Purple-people eaters. And of them all, there reigned supreme Mr. #51, Dick Butkus of the Bears! I saw them both, these two men, larger than life in their two huge posters that helped adorn my walls through childhood, my 'tweens' and into high school. They shared the space with a prehistoric Raquel Welch and 'Meanest Son of a Bitch' poster!

(Addenbum) Rump Roast and Raisin Pie (aka It's a "B"!)

Even the Little Drummer Boy, a favourite of mine, if you listen really closely to the always -mumbled lyrics, was a 'bum-man' (in the making, then..): "Pe-rump-ump-ump-BUM!' Even he, though he may have been standing beside the donkey was, unbeknownst to most, was thinking even then that the shepherd's daughter had a cute behind. Enjoyed a good "rump" roast, lately? Go ahead, eat a bum! (I won't say a thing!)

The Woman in Me.

I do miss some of the swagger that comes from the man's ability to pee almost anywhere from an upright position. Oh, I still do it occasionally, don't get me wrong, but as of late,

I've taken to some sitting down behaviour because it almost eliminates the likelihood of an uncomfortable, sopping-wet front. Occasionally before, I could stand at the ready, double and triple-check all systems were a "Go!", and let go with a steady stream, finally-only to find that the horse had not really cleared the barn doors, and the front of my nice dry, clean pants had given way to an ever-widening urine stain! It would leave me murmuring "idiot!" to myself and having to change plans immediately-as I now had to go back in and change my pants for the second time that morning! Lovely, just lovely! It was just so much easier to sit down, tinkle and reflect for a moment or two on why there was no 'vagina-envy'?

 ## "Where's Your Report Card?"

In many of the large clinics and rehabilitation centres administering to the brain-injured and paralyzed among us, you'll sometimes see flyers posted on their bulletin boards advertising some of the 'education' courses offered to the patient-residents. Recently, I was in such a place and could not miss the clear, bold signs here and there promoting various classes and workshops for the live-in resident population, such as 'anger management (a biggy..). However, also, in the mix was 'bowel control and management class', one I feel, at least, should be mandatory for all. And what parent is not proud of their child bringing home a report card in which they were given A or A+ for 'bowel management' class. But…, how would you like to be seated next to the kid who failed that class!? Yikes!(I can easily picture a poem by the same name being recited by Henry Gibson on the old "Laugh In" television show!

Ho, Ho, Ho- Ho?

Once, for a staff party, I accepted the request for me to play 'Santa' and to help hand out surprise gifts to everyone. I might not have been so willing to say" yes" had I known the kind of anxiety that would bubble up in the fuss-bucket, well-intentioned coordinators of the short role-play. It was

Reporting Period 1 September–December

Teacher's Comments: Kim is making satisfactory progress at this time. He seems to take his work seriously and sets good standards for himself. He tries to do his work neatly. Kim is well-liked by everyone.

Reporting Period 2 December–March

Teacher's Comments: Kim has shown improvement in Social Studies and Mathematics. Language and Science are somewhat lower since Christmas. Lately, Kim has experienced some difficulty completing his work. If he can overcome this tendency, he should have a successful year.

Reporting Period 3 March to June

Teacher's Comments: Kim has successfully completed the work of Grade 5. Kim raised his marks since March and has been able to complete his work better. Keep up the good work, Kim, and you'll have a good year in Grade 6.

all mapped out and choreographed for me-when exactly I would enter the room, when I would start my Santa laughter and ho's, how many to say (four is too many, three only please!), and at what volume! Worse, too, was the fact that they were adamant about me sticking to their plan; I could only see the goat tethered to that same old silly tree As soon as I picked up on that I started plotting my fourth 'ho', haha!I was equally adamant to introduce a slight variation to things… Yes, that's me, alright, often trying to move people away from their comfort-place or 'policy-box'- mentality. Outside the Lines! Move the goat away from the tree! Remember, 'King of the Hill' on a big pile of snow?

"Lol-eata?"

Now we are hopping back for a moment back to that first year of mine living on my own in that Beijing suburb. It took me a while to fully understand and then perfect the routines expected of all customers in the local grocery stores there where you had to go to a special counter upon entering and check your backpack until you came back out and had paid, and then there are the female store attendants standing here and there yelling out time-limited sales to you as you pass by. One day, in my local store, I was standing at the counter getting ready to hand in my bag, when a young, beautiful girl(I hesitate to say lady-I thought at most she was probably 19 or 20..) sidled up to me and quickly became very chatty to this foreigner. I must admit that visions of sugarplums and 'Lolita's' did dance in my mind for a few seconds; after all, she was quite striking from the tip of her nose down to her toes! It's easy to tell here when so many of the younger women here in China will often wear those ankle length form-fitting silk dresses,or other figure-revealing fashions! Well, my 'Lolita-fantasy' evaporated fairly quickly and was reduced to a meeting the next afternoon for some Frisbee in the local park!!

 The Stallion Shuffle!

Like any good Canadian lad I love hockey, as I've said, and weirdly enough one of the things I enjoy about an NHL pro game on the tube is the pre-game warm-ups and the singing of the anthems when the cameras pan down the players lined up on their respective blue lines; several can be seen doing what I've nicknamed 'the stallion shuffle' when these elite athletes-vibrating with pre-game jitters- much like the thoroughbreds do in the gates prior to a race at the track- will shuffle from foot to foot trying to release some of that pent up nervous energy prior to the opening whistle. Yep. Like the moment the pilot releases the brakes of the jet to begin a thunderous take-off.

" First Grouse Run!"

I'm not a downhill skier at all, but back in high school, one of the first acquaintances I made out here on the West Coast in my new high school most definitely was; in fact, he was a bit of a "hot-dogger" and could do those wide splits over big moguls and stuff. He took me up to our local 'Grouse Mountain' for an evening once. Me? I would try to avoid all moguls entirely and happily snowplough my way down the bunny slope – for my first-time ever downhill skiing! It was a blast! Then, we went into 'the Nest' and, both under-age, ordered and drank a couple of pints. It was memorable, alright. My father I could tell instantly, did not like this new boy at all from the very first time he came to pick me up; he had that sort of a faux-cocky swagger and that weird-arro-gant energy that causes him and others like him to bounce-vibrate from one foot to the other, almost as if they can't stand still for more than a moment at a time. The stallion-shuffle,alright, even if he was more of a donkey….ADHD.? Tape him to his desk.

 ## " The Sheep and the Rivers".

Of course, during my many European back-packing adven-tures, there were so many precious, memorable moments. One of them that will always stand out for me was the time I spent in Koblenz in Northern Germany on my way to Hamburg to see an old friend. It is one of the world's prettier cities in my view. It was for me, at least, for a few nights. I stayed in a hostel located in the ruins of an old castle on a hill whose pan-oramic views looked down on the twinkling city lights right at the juncture of the Rhine and Mozelle rivers!

The couple of joints I shared with a fellow hosteller might have contributed to my appreciation of the magnificence of the moment, sure-; I ended up at night, perched on the remains of an ancient stone wall while beneath me several tiers on a slope was a small flock of gently bleating sheep. Aaghh…yes.(Not a Jamaican crab in sight.)

"In Malcolm"

Since the song first came out or I first heard it- I've always liked it, but I've also misheard the lyrics. "I Believe in Miracles…, you Sexy Thing!" What the heck? I always thought they were singing I believe in' Malcolm' –and had convinced myself there was probably a reasonable explanation for such unusual lyrics.

" The Geese and Ducks Under the Sink!"

In my childhood home back in Sarnia, we always kept a big, plastic bag under the kitchen sink(no, not full of dog-poop, don't be silly!) where we would collect all the old, hard, stale or burnt bread/toast from the week. It was a 'funny bag' I always thought, but when it was nearly full, we would all take it over and make a family adventure of it at the local 'animal farm' and spend a few hours together feeding the ducks and geese population on the little lake there.

" Drugstore Poet"

Back in high school, one of the things I did do was preside over our 'creative writing club' and a second was to be 'head-over heels' crazy for my then girlfriend, 'K'. I was feeling the love every day; I was happy, I was inspired and would regularly write several love poems each week. Often, I would sit up later in the evenings in our recreation room downstairs in front of the crackling fake- fire(Presto logs!), pretending I was a 'Romantic' poet somewhere up in a cold, damp cottage in the Lake District before the hearth and penning my thoughts in my lap. One of them, I suppose my homage to the Beatles "Lucy in the Sky of Diamonds" and N. Young's 'Sugar Mountain' was called "Peanut Butter

Fog" and found its way into the school's annual, or literary supplement that year. Well, many years later, in fact after I had, myself, been teaching for almost a decade, I met up with a younger woman in my local drug store who stopped me, after recognizing me, introduced herself and explained that she had always loved that poem of mine and even had a copy of it tacked up at her work-station in her cubicle because it would make her smile every day. Wow!! I was blown away. So moved!-Finger-licking permitted

 ## "Peanut Butter Fog"

Slowly is spread the peanut butter fog
With chocolate fingers and rich egg nog
On our raspberry land with its blueberry skies
Skyscraper buildings from golden French fries;
 And standing all around are our gumdrop trees
 Branches bent slightly by the peppermint breeze
 Chocolate animals all over, run to and fro'
 Leaving melting prints in the golden honey snow;
 Brown sugar soil helps the cherry trees grow old,
 When coconut people sprinkle them with orange-gold.
 Though sweet-toothed monsters devour our honey bees,
 And even eat our spearmint gumdrop trees,
 They may lick the chocolate fingers and drink our special nog…,
 But in dreams they will all die soon.. in our peanut butter fog!
(Dec 22, 1975)

 ## "Wheelchair Bully!"

It's awful to see anywhere, at any time-Bullying, I mean- and how, now I'll admit, I have a zero- tolerance. Not long ago I witnessed something I found especially disturbing: a bully in a wheelchair no less who was picking on another man in

a wheelchair. The 'victim', a much smaller, native man was happily listening to loud music on his headphones. Anyone nearby could hear an accordion which led me to believe it was polka- style. The bully heard it, too and had his opening..." Don't know how you listen to that shit," he started in. "Do you wear a dress, too?" To his credit, The smaller First Nations' man just ignored it, but I couldn't be that close and let it pass, so I wheeled my chair over and parked between them, as a buffer. He was a younger man, with a couple of tattoos on his neck he obviously thought made him look 'tough'; something about neck tattoos just squeezes my testosterone pump, I guess. I smiled enough to get his attention and then volleyed in with, "You always been a bully, or just since you've been in your chair?" He gave me his best intimidating look, I think, but like his tattoos to me they all came up short; it just reflected his trying too hard- as far as I was concerned. So, after some stares and a brief, spicy exchange, he finally continued on his way… Ah, me!

 ### "Don't be that Way!"

I don't actually remember the exact circumstances and it really doesn't matter, but there was a moment somewhere in that distant past of mine when I was angry at a family-member or friend and remained in that state for a few days. When he learned of it, my father offered one of those cogent life-gems which has only shone brighter in the years since then, and his death, because of my increased understanding of it. All he said was quite simply, "Don't be that way, Kim." A simple sentence, like a Mike Tyson right cross! Not a week goes by now when I don't think of that all-encompassing simple sentence; it has become almost a mantra for me. We all have a choice every day with how we want to greet the awaiting world beyond our bedrooms and kitchen, and all the other bipeds who will cross our paths. 'Nuff said on that.

"Always Wear Clean Underwear, Right?"

Once, years ago, a former colleague, a rather bosomy creature at that, came along to a staff party where we all went
out for a short harbour-cruise on a nice yacht, after we had
'warmed up' some first at a gastown pub. For me, having
practically grown-up on our family sailboat back East, I had
learned early on the importance of good flat-soled 'deck
shoes' and of balance while out on a boat; she seemed to have
no sense at all of being on the water or, more than likely, her
vanity had over-ridden any shred of common sense she may
have had, so she showed up in a mini-skirt (albeit a cute one)
and, worse, high heels! Excuse me, You're going on a boat!
It was a recipe for disaster or, at the very least an underwear
-flash. Sure enough, at one point she climbed down a ladder leading from one deck to another to join the bulk of our
cocktailing crowd. Well, credit to her for getting down even
two-thirds the way on the ladder before a heel got caught
in the grating step and sent her tumbling down the rest of
the way to land in a rather less-than graceful and somewhat
undignified position on her rear-end, legs splayed outward to
the sides which hiked the skirt high up on her thighs to reveal her underwear Another drink, anyone? No Marmaduke,
no Scooby-Do, not even Winnie the Pooh! Not even butter-
flies!

 ## "The New 'G-Spot"

Anal Retentives (A. R.' s beware! Go ahead, and silently,
smugly correct all the grammatical errors you find and laugh
inwardly/outwardly at how the writer doesn't "grammar
good!" Are you out there? I see you, Ohh, yeah! Your Google-
Veil is see-through, you know..? Yep, I just love that element
in today's e-tech-driven world. People can go home after hearing something at the office, at school or on the bus and, then,

magically-within under a minute-they Google –it and become "instant experts" on whatever the issue is. Sorry, but that does and forever will foment resentment in me-it chafes me; it simply adds more pretence to our already virtual-enough world, our increasingly artificial, unreal environment. I am one of those who still stupidly, stubbornly remains mired down in the real tar pits of evolution with my other, few dinosaur-friends who believe that only years of study and life-experience and a good dictionary truly brings that elusive wisdom-thing, not a keystroke to Google.. The teacher says one thing in- passing in the course of one class only to have two or three kids return the next day, now, to correct him when he said," blah,blah,blah…" It's a dangerous, self-righteous path that one, I think- where more and more people(and not just students!) then presume to know something or everything(!) because they've read two or three sentences about it in their Blackberry. If it's not in the computer, or on my Blackberry, then it can't exist….. Yowsa! Burgeoning collective arrogance, a veneer over a foundation of ignorance- that's what the world needs, for sure. And I keep hearing the incestuous cousin, television shamelessly and idiotically promoting it with the likes of "Never before in our history have we been so connected! Sure-but connected to WHAT?! Gimme a break!Hollywood gossip? A downtown sports' riot, a rave-rape?. Silly me and I thought what the world needed was a solution to homelessness, starvation and addiction!? Or are these just the new "penny-universities'? where anyone who can go to the coffee shop-or buy an e-tech device can access the world's cultures, histories and disciplines without attending classes, paying outrageous tuition fees, or even meeting any minimum entrance requirements etc… Everyone's the same, after all, right? Wait! There's a name for that, isn't there? There are no losers any more; we can all be chiefs, supervisors, now, and give ourselves grandiose-sounding titles. Wonderful! No winners or losers? Then all forms of sport can become obsolete. Then, a lot of people do not get exorbitant monies for staging or participating in the spectacles!

"Prayer Negotiations."

Sometimes I get those thoughts, you know, many still steeped in ugly judgment-coming from the darker side of my otherwise good "Pulpit Master" (otherwise known as the 'Bench-Voice!') thoughts which frown upon those who when praying presume in their ignorant, altogether shallow ways, to 'barter' with the Lord.. They're everywhere, believe me. There is no room for negotiation there in those moments. For those who do, it's as if they're in the open-air produce market and haggling over the price of potatoes or celery! "If.." some of them begin," ...You, God, do just this one thing for me, to help me catch the winning-touchdown pass in the championship game, or overcome this disease, or-a favourite- win the lottery, then..." they continue," I will not only do the laundry and cut the lawns, but I promise on Monday I will start volunteering my time at the orphanage or nursing home and sign my organ-donor card!" Deep, real deep and somehow, I suspect, not fully engaged in the spiritual journey-quest.

"Snail's Pace, Thank you."

Whoops! Here we are back in Beijing, me living a pretty comfortable existence on my own in a suburb about 30-40 minutes by light rail to downtown. After first moving down to their capital and having settled into my new "digs", it was probably 2-3 weeks before I gathered up enough courage to venture out past the local grocery store which was located almost directly across the street from my apartment compound(a large area that contained at least six, possibly eight big, individual apt.buildings. Yep, everything was slow for me which, in hindsight, I can most-assuredly say does reflect a good portion of my personality:CAUTIOUS. Some days, it was almost like I had to fight the urge to drop breadcrumbs behind me when I did venture out! I would find a little plaza about a twenty minute walk away, with a bank, pharmacy and dry-cleaners. As it turned out, the plaza, itself, was just across the street from the gym-pool where I had a membership and went three or four times each week, as part of my deal in moving to Beijing. I was getting to know my area, meter by meter, step by step. And, crumb by crumb, I always managed to find my way home again!

 ## "Kiss 'n' Tell-All"

It would be one of the last real birthday parties of my youth, then in grade nine when my mother and sister chaperoned me and 5/6 friends to the high school's spring 'Mardis Gras' fund-raising carnival.

It was like.., a dollar a visit/kiss. You 'paid the man,' then walked in through a simple ramp-maze hastily constructed for festival purposes from plywood and 2X4's… Eventually, it opened up into one large, unlit room where a blindfolded, grade eleven girl sat alone in the middle. She was a brunette with long, slightly curly locks and, I thought, reasonably attractive. Enough for me to pay her a visit six or seven times and even to try and convince a few of my friends to do likewise. Nope, I was the only taker! It was a short kiss to be sure, but full-on, full-lipped and for this fourteen year old, "exquisite!" I was doing THAT while my less adventurous, long-time friends were a few booths over in the gym playing darts or 'whack the rodent!' games for toys. Ha! No, stuffed bear for me, on this trip!

 ## "The Goober Primaries."

Only in America, you say? Probably. I just couldn't help myself but snicker some during the2012 presidential campaign coverage . Where do they come up with these names anyway? 1960's television? I was reminded of years ago at the Oscars when M.C. Billy Crystal had some fun introducing Oprah Winfrey to Uma Thurman:

OPrah-Uma, Uma-Oprah;I mean, think about it, we have Mitt, Newt, Potsie,Squiggy Goober and Festus and of course, that gold-hearted, thick-as-a brick marine, Gomer! And, ladies and gentlemen …introducing the President of the United States, your 'Commander-in-Chief', Festus Carbuncle!..., and his vice-president 'Hoss' Flatulence! Now, 'Gomer and Goober' would make a good running- pair, don't you think?

 ## "Personally, I Don't Get It."

I have a friend (honestly, it's not me!) and he has a way of denegrating most everything in life with his quippy, often cliché or two-dimensional stereotype zingers and one-liners; I guess that's just part of his managing- life strategy, trying to package the most complex issues of this crazy life into neat, little,' individualized cereal boxes' which are easier for him to deliver and store, I guess. And I've been guilty of that myself; too, on occasion He's been everywhere (!), done most things, so there's no shine left on anything in this world any more. I suppose it's a lifelong cynicism that has simply become'jadedness.' It's too bad, but I can't be around that sort of poisonous air for more than a few minutes at a time before I erupt in some way or simply have to move on. For me, life just doesn't lend itself to that kind of absurd over-simplification. Happy in your marriage..? Give it time and like all those before you, it'll fail and end in divorce-they all do, anyways. With him, whether it's someone, a mutual friend dying of cancer, to a crumbling relationship or pending divorce, you often get his generic and dismissive wave of the hand with a," Yeah, yeah, yeah-been there done that"-like it's nothing, meaningless and doesn't deserve any more time or attention in conversation because he went through it twenty or twenty-five years earlier. Wow. I only hope I never get to that place, but maybe we all do and I know it will take a conscious effort to avoid that ditch. Perhaps it's inevitable for us all? Nah! He has long ago forgotten the awe, the wonderment of seeing a rainbow, of being in love, or of sharing with another in that ultimate earthly relationship. And see-ing that…, makes me a little sad for him. There's no spark, no "joie de vie." Hell, I don't even detect any warm embers in the ashes of his fires any more.

Do I pity him? No, though I do feel badly to see how he has lost all that childhood naiveté-sparkle we are all gifted with as kids. I will always get excited as the pilot first releases the brakes and revs the engines and the 70 ton jet- plane lurches forward to start its thunderous path down the runway toward takeoff! It's an amazing thing! Who couldn't possibly get ex-cited about it? It brings to mind for me another moment in time in my early teaching days when I asked an English teacher-col-league if he got sad, too, when he watched Zefferelli's Romeo and Juliet because I was in the process once more of showing it to a class and I always cry. 'Ah my, no, Goodness, I've seen it so often by now it no longer has that effect.'

I wanted to chide him for not respecting one of my all-time favorites enough! How can you not be moved? I ball my eyes out every time. During the final death-scene in the Capulet crypt I'm one of those who is sorely tempted to stand up in the theatre and shout warnings to them both. "She's NOT dead! Wait. Wait!!Don't do it, Romeo, Stop !When Things are fun, exciting and new and, for me at least-every time they happen, again and again. All-consuming first-love; an ancient grudge reconciled in death-the fairest rose, the fair-est maid. Life! I was still crying on the drive home later that same afternoon! Oh-Grow-Up!-why don't you..?

 ## "Lazy and Manipulative?"

It seems only too clear to me how there are a lot of people out there who have never worked in a job that was piece-meal. They are used to working by the clock, often fall victim to 'clock-watchers disease' (C.L.OW.-D.) by the hour- where many can and do stretch out the simplest, shortest task sim-ply to get more money. Fine, most all of us would like more money for what we do, but it's that accompanying mentality that's a bit alarming and more than a little annoying to me.

For me, having done plenty of both jobs, it's easy and hell-ishly frustrating to sit back and watch one of those types who is more concerned with billable hours than in complet-ing tasks to the best of their ability.

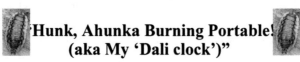

"Hunk, Ahunka Burning Portable! (aka My 'Dali clock')"

I taught at my high school for almost a dozen years in one of two or three outdoor portables nestled in beside the school's small gymnasium or bordering the ball diamond. The area right there beside the school was a favourite locale for some underage teens to party-down on weekends, protected some from winds, passing headlights and prying eyes. So, perhaps, I was lucky to go as far as I did without incident, but the call eventually came one Saturday evening to meet with our prin-cipal the following day at my portable at the school: there had been a fire overnight and my classroom was pretty much destroyed. I did manage to salvage a few smoky file boxes from a storage closet, and I also found the school-issue plain black, plastic clock which had melted in the heat into some sort of 'Dali dream'-I took it home as memorabilia- having spent a good ten years in that classroom! A keepsake?

"I Know How that Oedipus fellow Felt."

There was a brief spell during my childhood and maybe for all boys if the psycho-analysts are right, when I had a crush on my own mother, it's true-what can I say? She was a beau-tiful woman, after all. In the neighbourhood-Mom-Circle that I was at least familiar with, she stood out. Even as a pre-tweenie at 8, 9, 10, by which time I had already seen Elizabeth Taylor play that Egyptian hussy, Cleopatra in the de Mille classic. That's who my mother reminded me of any-way-and 'Liz' was a 'looker', alright.

'Ohh, Canada!'

Only in Canada, you say? Probably. We are ,without doubt, one of the global leaders of the Politically Correct Movement (not an auspicious honour in my book by any means..), Canada has started banning/outlawing smoking in even open-air spaces in some major cities. Just a bitter nicotine-addict, O.K.? Wait, it gets better! Now, I think we're on the verge(it's actually started in some places..) of banning physical contact in some "contact –sports" such as hockey and football. Soon, strippers will no longer remove their clothes, cab-drivers will all have to be clean-shaven, and regular weapons in our army will be replaced by paint-ball guns(that one's ok..)! What's scary to me is the fact that there are real people, sad to say, acting on councils and boards throughout the province and across the land who are raising their hands in vote to support such absurd notions. Soon-enough, User-fees for air, water- and how about 'views' (remember those old view-finders at Niagara Falls?)? Someone in the Canadian publishing industry took it upon himself to edit the lyrics to 'Twas the Night Before Christmas' by omitting the reference to Santa's corncob pipe! (Both he and 'Frosty' indulged, O.K.?)Probably didn't want him finishing his second glass of scotch or last line of coke either before boarding the sled… Why not, instead, just have ole Mr. Kringle go on a speaking tour of schools in which he addresses the evils of smoking, and addictive behavior? Let's remove it altogether -and pretend it was never there to begin with O.K.? After all, he is a role-model, right? So, he should not be smoking! Furthermore, he should be put on a new healthy regime of good diet and exercise to lose a few pounds! Santa at yoga class, maybe?

"Leave Well Enough and Pipes, Alone!" (on censorship, really..)

Oh, what to do with you…?
With you, and your censoring type:
He HAD BEADY eyes,
Loved small children,
And he SMOKED A CORNCOB PIPE!
Truth to tell, no one really knows,
So, just leave it and walk away-
His ruddy complexion, red cheeks and red nose

Came easy with three rum and nogs per day.,
Yes, even the famed ho-ho-ho's!

In the back- forty, way out there by the shed
Were his great team of reindeer, well-slept and, yes,
    well-fed.
Yet Donner and Blitzen, not pleased at all those two with
    their names
Knew well Kris' night-prowls
And OH Dear! A few special X-reindeer games
This, too, was close to the little ones,
Always toiling, those pointy-eared elves
Of course they had their stories, too
And knew of 'pre-dawn' raids, themselves!

Even he though never smoked, while out back there, near
    the barn,
Never wanting his "deer", ever, to come to any -harm!
Himself a rep, card-carrying member of Reindeer-Keep-
    ers Four-Twelve.
Though he wouldn't abide talk or union himself, for
    those little elves…

Little-known was that most came from Africa, India, and
    such faraway places,
Pointy ears, yes, big white smiles in dark faces;
Oh, yes, to a one, at Santa's beck and call
Happy in their straw beds, no benefits-those Immigrants,
    all!

You, there, with your whiteout like some stupid magic-
    wand
You like life-its good parts- of those-oh , yes!- you're
    fond.
But the rest, in those shadows, the not so-happy-fare
Those, you try to conceal lest the children might be
    scared
So, life is all sunrise, there's no setting sun…

But darkness comes to us all, my friend:
That, you simply can't outrun.

So you there, with your whiteout, go paint your nails and
    then your knees!
Just stop trying to change our history; stop changing fact
    there, if you please
(On hearing that one independent female Canadian pub-
    lisher edited/revised the favourite traditional Christ-
    mas lyric, 'Twas the Night Before Christmas' to omit
    Santa's nicotine addiction/filthy smoking habit!! Come
    on! Get another cat; Fall, 2012, Beijing!)

Napkin Swordfish?"

It was in Portugal where it happened, on that great, glorious
European backpacking adventure all those years ago. I was
travelling at the time with those four Canadian girls and one
American fellow after we had all hooked up in the Barcelona
train station. We eventually found our way to Portugal's gorgeous Algarve region. On this one night, we were all dining together in a nice, cozy restaurant. Trouble was none of
us knew any Portuguese, so we had a frustrating, wonderful
giggly time with our reasonably patient waiter. I wanted the
shrimp ("gamba"? I think..?) and drew my version of shrimp
on a napkin to help him understand my order; my rendering
probably looked more like pubic hair which I did not find
any of in the dish, thankfully.. In time, he would return to
our table and finally set down in front of me a thick slab of
grilled, greyish-brown meat. Sure didn't look like shrimp or
anything close to what I had drawn on the napkin for him. It
turned out to be a grilled swordfish steak-and it was one of
the best meals I've ever eaten!!

"And Nobody Ever Fell In!"

Let's return briefly back now to those early teenage years
of mine. Whew. I spent innumerable nights with a buddy
or two at the yacht club, sleeping on our sailboat for the

The family sailboat, "Panique" at dock in Vancouver, 1998)

night. Of course, there was always a mini-party during such sleepovers, and because our boat did not have a working 'head,' we were all forced to either get off and walk the two minutes over to the spanking-new washroom /showers building- or else, pee off the stern while holding on to the stern-stay for balance. In all those stupid times filled with lukewarm beer et al, we never lost a man overboard!. Fate and luck, I guess, intertwined like spaghetti noodles.

"Giving Voice"

The 'crazies' among us. Honestly, the more I reflect on the great or best writers of our time and even those earlier in history, I'm left feeling strongly that many of them, male and female alike, were or are probably bipolar, if not full-blown schizophrenics Who isn't bipolar, these days?! Like that "A.D-.H.D.-thing" in schools where a child is eventually diagnosed as having Attention-Deficit/Hyperactivity-Disorder, and then over-prescribed Ritalin to help keep it in check Now, they're saying we pretty much all suffer from it-it used to be called 'childhood.' Patience. Then the pendulum will swing to the other side. Getting back to those writer-types again, We know some writers have struggled with the bottle, some with prescription meds. Wait and watch for it... When they've heard those inner voices, they've simply written them down to indulge and perhaps offer themselves a certain therapeutic release or escape. Most are not wandering outside on the boulevards, pushing shopping carts about and talking loudly to the clouds with smarties in their hand, nor are they snarling at bushes or conversing with crows; no, they're at home hunched over their desks or computer-screens wrestling with self-talk of a different sort... over the length of a sentence, diction, syntax and punctuation! Would the character actually SAY that in such a moment? You have to get into his head to really know!

"Are We There Yet? Are We There Yet??"

Not quite, but it's in sight. Most, really, don't care that much and, in fact, become rather like impatient children in the backseat on those long family drives: "Are We There Yet? Are We There Yet? Slight pause... 150 meters. When the creative turns to the commercial, things change. Are We There Yet? I speak now of the arrival of copies of my first book which many people(bless'em) had ordered on-line almost a year earlier. Now that they've received them, it's my turn to turn the tables about them actually reading it!!" You done yet..? Done yet? Well? Now, Are you done?" It's not that I care so much one way or the other, but I want them to experience the same, tedious buzzing of a nuisance –mosquito as they gave me for a year or more awaiting its arrival!Nice, huh?

A Chaplain-What?!

It was the summer that a former partner of mine and I had planned and undertaken a long-awaited holiday- trip to Europe, principally to visit her elderly grandmother in northern Scotland, visit the Roman baths and then, in, theory, have some quiet couple- time on the French Riviera. On our return flight to Vancouver, just a half hour or so before scheduled touchdown, I was suddenly being paged over the cabin intercom of the plane. I waved my hand until acknowledged by a hostess and confirmed who I was for her. The hostess explained that my mother and sister would be waiting for me in the "chaplaincy." I didn't hear this rarely-used word clearly and was left somewhat confused. Sure enough when we did rendezvous, we went straight to that little, somber room for a collective-cry-my father had died during my absence.

How presumptuous..? But so be it; I don't know for sure, but I strongly suspect that if I were to achieve even the slightest attention, any public acclaim/notoriety in some media circles in regard to my first novel; it would be enough for some acquaintances to come forward, claiming to be friends –and I would be there to tell them how wrong, how mistaken they are. And even some former friends to still lay claim to that title when, again, they would be mistaken , for having not been in touch with me for two or more years , and having allowed it to lapse….That type of person, quite frankly, does nothing for me, except perhaps to cause a resentment rash because I know we do not have a genuine or close friendship at all. They would apparently have an attraction and curiosity to the limelight shining on my new and minuscule celebrity, instead. Honestly, I despise that kind of shallowness and insincerity and won't subject myself to it, period. Cut 'em loose-more space in the address book.

"Idiot-Proof Childhood"

Let me explain a bit. My mother (Bless her heart!) was a bundle of contradictions: she was somewhat of a hoarder, reluctant to let go of many things yet, at the same time she was an extreme organizer: so everyone one of us had his/her schedules from appointments to baseball games and piano lessons penned in clearly on the calendar which hung prominently beside the phone as constant reminders…Between the material world and the emotional one was a great divide.

***"Fuss-Buckets!" ***

Can't stand 'em! No apologies-not even the meaningless Canadian version of "Sorry." Nope, they're right up there with E.P.' s (Elevator People, remember?) in the SPC-Stupid People's Category. You see, and their defenders will rush to point this out in defense, they are full of good intentions (much like I've heard the road to hell is paved!) They may mean well, sure, but they cannot grasp how they trample other people's ideas and egos every time they put forth an idea they think is better about even fairly insignificant things, too; they will never get an invite to the H.S. P.(Highly- Sensitive- Peoples) Club.

"Too Many Mind-Too Much Comma!

Half borrowed from Last Samurai-half very much mine. My first year English professor at college was a cute sweetie-pie with a fashion penchant for wearing these Medieval ankle-length dresses who, with just enough faint praise would encourage me in her gentle way to keep up the writing. And this, even as she commented once in regard to a just-returned essay: "What do you do, Kim? I'm curious; do you finish writing the paper, then go back over it with a handful of commas and sprinkle them in here and there, willy-nilly? Pretty much, I was thinking- how did she know?

(an excerpt from one of those early comments goes like this: 'What you have written is good and reads easily. If you can keep up your confident use of language, your future efforts should be good.' -J.P.) –and another: 'It seems important for you to take a strong line when discussing any subject.' Damn-right! None of this wishy-washy stuff for me, thanks!

I do readily admit the comma is a favourite mark of mine and that I do tend to overuse it(I can see you nodding your heads..)-so, there was little to no vindication for me in Truss' wonderful 'Panda' book…But, again, for me it was akin to dead catfish all over the road…I've always found that the world keeps spinning and mostly ignores sentence fragments and comma splices. I'm hopin' so.

Thank you for stopping by and sharing your time; it is the most precious thing we have! (Watch for more AKimbo coming your way In Verse!)

Toodle-Oooh. -K. P.

Hey, Why Sow-Bug?

Why not? It is my story, after all! I've always been intrigued by the little fellows…Accurate biology aside, they were somewhere between turtles and tiny, tail-less armidillos;You know the ones I mean: they will roll up into little balls inside those grey-brown exoskeletons of theirs and roll away sometimes when threatened. Many legs, so I'm guessing they belong to the same family as centipedes and millipedes..? Sure, maybe I do have "leg-envy", considering I do have just the one functional one for the moment; they have so many, they probably don't even notice if one is broken or even missing, unlike some of us! Since my stroke, in the first few years of recovery and rehabilitation when I was writing these memoirs, I've met and befriended people who-for various reasons, have lost one, even both of their legs and are re-learning how to stand and walk on artificial limbs. You want to talk about determination, spirit, and perseverance? The skittery(probably hypertense!) sow-bug merrily plods along until it finds an obstacle of some sort in its path and then it will simply and deftly divert or detour around whatever it is. Keep moving. Move forward, step after step, one leg at a time. The weird little animals are also one of the best indicators, predictors of increasing humidity and the likelihood of rain-showers because they will always navigate to higher and drier, protected ground just prior to much rain. Yep, they just Keep Goin!' In fact, that could be a mantra for many of them (If they wore running shoes, they would have to be Nike!). And I feel I share at least that much with them, minus the shoes! What are the choices? Keep going with the familiar or else what? Give up? Stop taking in oxygen? Roll up into a tiny ball (impossible for me, anyways.to be tiny anything...) and disintegrate back into the earth? Sure, they may be plodders, but they keep moving forward; I suppose in that way at least, they're a bit like sharks(bear with me)- depending on forward locomotion to remain alive, and nary a coffee break....

Snakes? I don't writhe, generally, unless I'm in the company of a stupid person which is why I try to avoid that contact as much as possible. Even then, it's probably more of an uncomfortable squirm (my A..D-H.D?) than it is a beautifully controlled locomotive action. Of course, snakes and sharks both, move too fast to be accurate metaphors for me in my existence. Sow-bugs, on the other hand, have this grim determination and drive I like – a bit like tanks and all-terrain vehicles-they're going to get there, regardless! To be always that slow, suggests to me they must have an abundant supply of patience, at least with themselves, if not for the other bugs around them. Slugs? Too ugly (Ha!). Turtle? It's become too cliché for many disabled folk like me (there's even a newsletter..)and, furthermore, personally, I find them too slow and too stupid; they are what those politically-correct among us might describe as 'unique and live life at their own pace. Ha!

The Sow-bug, I feel, is probably a fairly bright (?), tiny creature. Underneath that crusty, little exterior, I'm sure, is an intelligence and wit that only those closest to it can fully appreciate. They do look down an awful lot, but never at others around them simply because their physiology precludes that sort of thing... And, in actual fact, though you might at first think they appear to be rather solitary creatures, they are actually very social, especially just prior to rain when you can find them seeking shelter under an old piece of wood, or occasionally you'll often find several dozen congregating in one place on higher cardboard, or under a flap of tarpaulin. For a long time now; if I had to guess, since I was eight or nine, I've known that words were powerful things, precious things that were charged with meaning and emotion and how they could have tremendous effect on people for better or worse. They were not to be used mindlessly because they, essentially, reflected the soul and intentions of those who used them. 'Say what you mean; Mean what you say!' A wonderful sentence and sentiment, but, unfortunately, just an empty platitude today understood by a small segment of the population, and heeded by even fewer.

"Last Call!" *

For critics and the watchful readers, you would have picked up by now that there seems to have been a lot of alcohol involved in the story. It's true-but in no way, shape or form do I condone its use, especially in the underage crowd! I was lucky to have survived through it all and though I may have included it here-that is not to suggest I'm proud of it; I'm not. But it is what it is, whether consumed alone or socially.

Watch for more 'Akimbo' coming your way…in the near-future! Verse, that is!

Cheers, everybody! K. P.

Early days in Iran-Hard to get a moment alone. When ya gotta go, ya gotta go! I gotta go! Thanks for stoppin' by!-K.P.

Review Requested: If you liked this book, would you please provide a review at Amazon.com?